StartUp

Ken Beatty, Series Consultant

7

Linda L. Lane
Paul MacIntyre
Nancy Blodgett Matsunaga
Jenni Currie Santamaria
Geneva Tesh

StartUp 7

Pearson, 221 River Street, Hoboken, NJ 07030

Staff credits: The people who made up the StartUp team representing editorial, production, and design are Gregory Bartz, Peter Benson, Magdalena Berkowska, Stephanie Callahan, Jennifer Castro, Tracey Munz Cataldo, Dave Dickey, Gina DiLillo, Irene Frankel, Christopher Leonowicz, Bridget McLaughlin, Kamila Michalak, Laurie Neaman, Katherine Sullivan, Claire Van Poperin, Joseph Vella, Peter West, and Autumn Westphal.

Cover credit: Front cover: Javier Osores/EyeEm/Getty Images. Back cover: Klaus Vedfelt/Getty Images (Level 1); Alexandre Moreau/Getty Images (Level 2); Matteo Colombo/Getty Images (Level 3); Javier Osores/EyeEm/Getty Images (Level 4); Liyao Xie/Getty Images (Level 5); Ezra Bailey/Getty Images (Level 6); guvendemir/Getty Images (Level 7); Yusuke Shimazu/EyeEm/Getty Images (Level 8); tovovan/Shutterstock (icons)

Text composition: emc design ltd

Library of Congress cataloging-in-publication data on file.

Photo and illustration credits: See pages 167–168

Printed in the United States of America

ISBN-10: 0-13-468421-4

ISBN-13: 978-0-13-468421-5

ISBN-10: 0-13-517840-1 (with app and Online Practice)

ISBN-13: 978-0-13-517840-9 (with app and Online Practice)

1 2019

ACKNOWLEDGMENTS

We would like to thank the following people for their insightful and helpful comments and suggestions.

Maria Alam, Extension Program-Escuela Americana, San Salvador, El Salvador; **Milton Ascencio**, Universidad Don Bosco, Soyapango, El Salvador; **Raul Avalos**, CALUSAC, Guatemala City, Guatemala; **Adrian Barnes**, Instituto Chileno Norteericano, Santiago, Chile; **Laura Bello**, Centro de Idiomas Xalapa, Universidad Veracruzana, Xalapa, México; **Jeisson Alonso Rodriguez Bonces**, Fort Dorchester High School, Bogotá, Colombia; **Juan Pablo Calderón Bravo**, Manpower English, Santiago, Chile; **Ellen J. Campbell**, RMIT, Ho Chi Minh City, Vietnam; **Vinicio Cancinos**, CALUSAC, Guatemala City, Guatemala; **Viviana Castilla**, Centro de Enseñanza de Lenguas Extranjeras UN, México; **Carlos Celis**, Cel.Lep Idiomas S.A., São Paulo, Brazil; **Bernal Cespedes**, ULACIT, Tournón, Costa Rica; **Carlos Eduardo Aguilar Cortes**, Universidad de los Andes, Bogotá, Colombia; **Solange Lopes Vinagre Costa**, Senac-SP, São Paulo, Brazil; **Isabel Cubilla**, Panama Bilingüe, Panama City, Panama; **Victoria Dieste**, Alianza Cultural Uruguay-Estados Unidos, Montevideo, Uruguay; **Francisco Domerque**, Georgal Idiomas, México City, México; **Vern Eaton**, St. Giles International, Vancouver, Canada; **Maria Fajardo**, Extension Program-Escuela Americana, San Salvador, El Salvador; **Diana Elizabeth Leal Ffrench**, Let's Speak English, Cancún, México; **Rosario Giraldez**, Alianza Cultural Uruguay-Estados Unidos, Montevideo, Uruguay; **Lourdes Patricia Rodríguez Gómez**, Instituto Tecnológico de Chihuahua, Chihuahua, México; **Elva Elizabeth Martínez de González**, Extension Program-Escuela Americana, San Salvador, El Salvador; **Gabriela Guel**, Centro de Idiomas de la Normal Superior, Monterrey, México; **Ana Raquel Fiorani Horta**, SENAC, Ribeirão Preto, Brazil; **Carol Hutchinson**, Heartland International English School, Winnipeg, Canada; **Deyanira Solís Juárez**, Centro de Idiomas de la Normal Superior, Monterrey, México; **Miriam de Käppel**, Colegio Bilingüe El Prado, Guatemala City, Guatemala; **Ikuko Kashiwabara**, Osaka Electro-Communication University, Neyagawa, Japan; **Steve Kirk**, Nippon Medical School, Tokyo, Japan; **Jill Landry**, GEOS Languages Plus, Ottawa, Canada; **Tiffany MacDonald**, East Coast School of Languages, Halifax, Canada; **Angélica Chávez Escobar Martínez**, Universidad de León, León, Guanajuato, México; **Renata Martinez**, CALUSAC, Guatemala City, Guatemala; **Maria Alejandra Mora**, Keiser International Language Institute, San Marcos, Carazo, Nicaragua; **Alexander Chapetón Morales**, Abraham Lincoln School, Bogotá, Colombia; **José Luis Castro Moreno**, Universidad de León, León, Guanajuato, México; **Yukari Naganuma**, Eikyojuku for English Teachers, Tokyo, Japan; **Erina Ogawa**, Daito Bunka University, Tokyo, Japan; **Carolina Zepeda Ortega**, Let's Speak English, Cancún, México; **Lynn Passmore**, Vancouver International College, Vancouver, Canada; **Noelle Peach**, EC English, Vancouver, Canada; **Ana-Marija Petrunic**, George Brown College, Toronto, Canada; **Romina Planas**, Centro Cultural Paraguayo Americano, Asunción, Paraguay; **Sara Elizabeth Portela**, Centro Cultural Paraguayo Americano, Asunción, Paraguay; **Ana Carolina González Ramírez**, Universidad de Costa Rica, San José, Costa Rica; **Luz Rey**, Centro Colombo Americano, Bogotá, Colombia; **Octavio Garduno Ruiz**, AIPT Service S.C., Coyoacán, México; **Amado Sacalxot**, Colegio Lehnsen Americas, Guatemala City, Guatemala; **Deyvis Sanchez**, Instituto Cultural Dominico-Americano, Santo Domingo, Dominican Republic; **Lucy Slon**, JFK Adult Centre, Montreal, Canada; **Scott Stulberg**, University of Regina, Regina, Canada; **Maria Teresa Suarez**, Colegios APCE, San Salvador, El Salvador; **Daniel Valderrama**, Centro Colombo Americano, Bogotá, Colombia; **Kris Vicca**, Feng Chia University, Taichung, Taiwan; **Sairy Matos Villanueva**, Centro de Actualización del Magisterio, Chetumal, Q.R., México; **Edith Espino Villarreal**, Universidad Tecnológica de Panama, El Dorado, Panama; **Isabela Villas Boas**, Casa Thomas Jefferson, Brasília, Brazil

LEARNING OBJECTIVES

WELCOME UNIT

page 2 In the classroom | Learn about your book | Learn about your app

Unit	Vocabulary	Language Choices	Conversation / Speaking	Listening
1 What's over there? **page 5**	• Words related to travel planning	• Present perfect vs. simple past • Indefinite pronouns • Types of adverbs	• Talk about travel plans • Talk about space exploration • Discuss urban exploration **Conversation Skill** Share your ideas informally	• Listen to a podcast about space exploration **Listening Skill** Listen for stressed words
2 What's your superpower? **page 17**	• Superpowers	• Present and future unreal conditional • Future real conditional • Present real conditional	• Talk about superpowers • Talk about how to excel • Discuss why we love superheroes **Conversation Skill** Accept an opinion before offering a conflicting one	• Listen to a podcast about how to excel **Listening Skill** Listen for sequence
3 How'd you come up with that? **page 29**	• Words related to accomplishments	• Verb + gerund vs. infinitive • Gerund usage • Verb + object + infinitive	• Talk about what a genius is • Talk about fictional worlds • Talk about different senses **Conversation Skill** Defend arguments informally	• Listen to a podcast about fictional worlds **Listening Skill** Listen for definitions signaled by pauses
4 Are you an animal person? **page 41**	• Words to describe unusual things	• Articles for general and specific nouns • Quantifiers with singular vs. plural verbs • Articles for known and unknown information	• Talk about animal videos • Discuss animal personalities • Discuss animal behavior **Conversation Skill** Use circumlocution when you don't know a word	• Listen to a podcast about animal personalities **Listening Skill** Summarize
5 Is this going to work? **page 53**	• Words related to starting a business	• Reported speech patterns • Changes in reported speech • Common reporting verbs	• Talk about starting a small business • Talk about inventions • Talk about a success story **Conversation Skill** Show interest in a conversation	• Listen to a podcast about inventions **Listening Skill** Selective attention

Pronunciation	Video Talk / Discussion	Reading	Writing	Problem Solving
• Rhythm and stress patterns	• Listen to or watch a talk about abandoned places **Note-taking Skill** Make lists **Discussion Skill** Invite others to participate	• Read about deep-sea exploration **Reading Skill** Identify metaphor	• Write a descriptive essay **Writing Skill** Use active verbs	• Consider how to reduce vandalism at famous sites around the world
• Pausing and intonation in transitional phrases	• Listen to or watch a talk about why we love superheroes **Note-taking Skill** Note examples clearly **Discussion Skill** Return a discussion back to the main point	• Read about technological superpowers **Reading Skill** Use a KWL chart	• Write a definition essay **Writing Skill** Use rhetorical questions	• Consider how to reduce cheating among athletes
• Pronouncing *to* in infinitives	• Listen to or watch a talk about synesthesia **Note-taking Skill** Note unfamiliar names and words **Discussion Skill** Summarize ideas to focus the conversation	• Read about creativity-boosting ideas **Reading Skill** Annotate the text	• Write an opinion essay **Writing Skill** Refer to outside sources	• Consider whether reading escapist literature leads to problems in society
• Reductions in quantifier phrases	• Listen to or watch a talk about animal behavior **Note-taking Skill** Identify a speaker's key examples **Discussion Skill** Tell an anecdote	• Read about animals that use language **Reading Skill** Recognize definitions	• Write a persuasive essay **Writing Skill** Use strong, emotional language	• Consider how to avoid the spread of invasive species
• Sentence stress in conversations	• Listen to or watch a talk about a success story **Note-taking Skill** Use Cornell Notes **Discussion Skill** Build on what others have said	• Read about alternative foods **Reading Skill** Paraphrase	• Write an online review **Writing Skill** Use titles and subtitles	• Consider how entrepreneurs could get new ideas to market faster

Unit	Vocabulary	Language Choices	Conversation / Speaking	Listening
6 Can I have a raise? page 65	• Words related to work and compensation	• Subject-verb agreement: Review and expand • Probability and certainty in the future • Expressing future time	• Talk about compensation • Talk about the gender pay gap • Discuss wealth inequality **Conversation Skill** Add comments to soften an opinion	• Listen to a podcast about the gender pay gap **Listening Skill** Infer goals
7 What are you going to do about it? page 77	• Words related to social advocacy	• Passive voice: Form and use • Passive voice: Reporting structures • Passive infinitives and causatives	• Talk about making a difference • Talk about citizen journalism • Discuss the impact of social media **Conversation Skill** Identify gaps between thought groups	• Listen to a podcast about citizen journalism **Listening Skill** Tone of voice
8 What's our story? page 89	• Marketing words	• Modifying relative clauses • Participle clauses • Infinitive clauses	• Talk about a solution to a problem • Talk about promotion strategies • Talk about corporate origin stories **Conversation Skill** Speculate about the future	• Listen to a podcast about promotional strategies **Listening Skill** Anticipate words
9 Do you follow any sports? page 101	• Athletic abilities	• Modals for speculation and expectation • Expressing necessity and obligation • Permission, strong advice, and prohibition	• Talk about athletic competition • Talk about esports • Talk about what a sport is **Conversation Skill** Build empathy with active listening	• Listen to a podcast about esports **Listening Skill** Infer the target audience
10 Remember when? page 113	• Phrasal verbs for talking about life events	• Future in the past • Past perfect and past perfect continuous • Expressing the past: Review	• Talk about a life-changing decision • Talk about a memoir • Discuss life in the past **Conversation Skill** Maintain interest with question tags	• Listen to a podcast about memoirs **Listening Skill** Comparisons

Pronunciation	Video Talk / Discussion	Reading	Writing	Problem Solving
• Stress in compounds	• Listen to or watch a talk about wealth inequality **Note-taking Skill** Use a KWL chart **Discussion Skill** Acknowledge others' contributions	• Read about a job market trend **Reading Skill** Recognize hedging	• Write a compare and contrast essay **Writing Skill** Use parallel structure	• Consider the pros and cons of getting additional education
• Pronunciation of *-ate* endings	• Listen to or watch a talk about the impact of social media **Note-taking Skill** Include key definitions and examples **Discussion Skill** Interrupt politely	• Read about environmental solutions **Reading Skill** Create a process flow chart	• Write a petition **Writing Skill** Consider your audience	• Consider how to get more reliable, accurate news
• Phrasal prepositional verbs	• Listen to or watch a talk about corporate origin stories **Note-taking Skill** Listen for restatement **Discussion Skill** Ask follow-up questions	• Read about deceptive marketing **Reading Skill** Skim	• Write a personal essay **Writing Skill** Use redundancy	• Consider the consequences of products not lasting as long as they used to
• Expressions of necessity	• Listen to or watch a talk about what a sport is **Note-taking Skill** List a series of arguments **Discussion Skill** Express strong opinions	• Read about sports fans **Reading Skill** Understand referential cohesion	• Write a set of instructions **Writing Skill** Write like a reader	• Consider how to limit the injuries sports can cause
• Auxiliary *had* and stress in past perfect	• Listen to or watch a talk about life in the past **Note-taking Skill** Listen for reasons **Discussion Skill** Ask rhetorical questions	• Read about memories **Reading Skill** Use a cause-and-effect T-chart	• Write a report **Writing Skill** Omit unnecessary information	• Consider how to prevent the world's languages from disappearing

TO THE TEACHER

Welcome to *StartUp*

StartUp is an innovative eight-level, general American English course for adults and young adults who want to make their way in the world and need English to do it. The course takes students from CEFR A1 to C1 and enables teachers and students to track their progress in detail against the Global Scale of English (GSE) Learning Objectives.

StartUp Level	GSE Range	CEFR	Description
1	22-33	A1	Beginner
2	30-37	A2	High beginner
3	34-43	A2+	Low intermediate
4	41-51	B1	Intermediate
5	49-58	B1+	High intermediate
6	56-66	B2	Upper intermediate
7	64-75	B2+	Low advanced
8	73-84	C1	Advanced

English for 21st century learners

StartUp helps your students develop the spoken and written language they need to communicate in their personal, academic, and work lives. In each lesson, you help students build the collaborative and critical thinking skills so essential for success in the 21st century. *StartUp* allows students to learn the language in ways that work for them: anytime, anywhere. The Pearson Practice English App allows students to access their English practice on the go. Additionally, students have all the audio and video files at their fingertips in the app and on the Pearson English Portal.

Motivating and relevant learning

StartUp creates an immersive learning experience with a rich blend of multimedia videos and interactive activities; podcasts, interviews, and other audio texts for listening practice; humorous, engaging conversations with an international cast of characters for modeling conversation skills; high-interest video talks beginning at Level 5; media project videos in Levels 1–4; presentation skills videos in Levels 5–6; and problem-solving challenges in Levels 7–8 for end-of-unit skills consolidation.

Personalized, flexible teaching

The unit structure and the wealth of support materials give you options to personalize the class to best meet your students' needs. *StartUp* gives you the freedom to focus on different strands and skills; for example, you can spend more class time on listening and speaking. You can choose to teach traditionally or flip the learning. You can teach sections of the lesson in the order you prefer. And you can use the ideas in the Teacher's Edition to help you extend and differentiate instruction, particularly for mixed-ability and for large and small classes.

Access at your fingertips

StartUp provides students with everything they need to extend their learning to their mobile device. The app empowers students to take charge of their learning outside of class, allowing them to practice English whenever and wherever they want, online or offline. The app provides practice of vocabulary, grammar, listening, and conversation. Students can go to any lesson by scanning a QR code on their Student Book page or through the app menu. The app also provides students with access to all the audio and video files from the course.

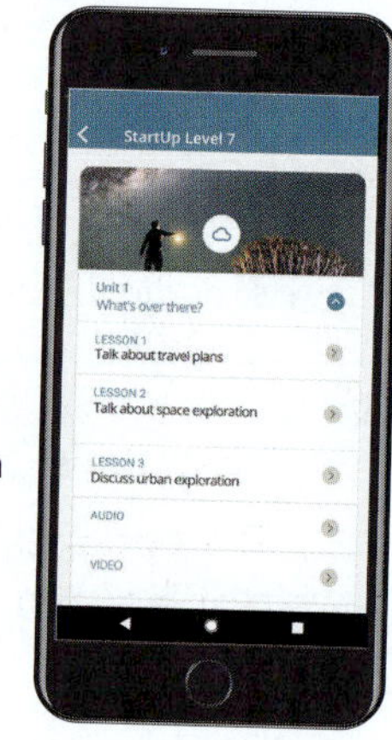

Components

For the Teacher

StartUp provides everything you need to plan, teach, monitor progress, and assess learning.

The ***StartUp* ActiveTeach** front-of-class tool allows you to

- zoom in on the page to focus the class's attention
- use tools, like a highlighter, to emphasize specific text
- play all the audio texts and videos from the page
- pop up interactive activities
- move easily to and from any cross-referenced pages

The interleaved **Teacher's Edition** includes

- an access code to the Pearson Practice English App and all digital resources
- language and culture notes
- teaching tips to help you improve your teaching practice
- *Look for* notes to help assess students' performance
- answer keys to all Student Book exercises
- and more!

Teacher's Digital Resources, all available on the Pearson English Portal, include

- the Teacher Methodology Handbook
- a unit walkthrough
- ActiveTeach front-of-class software
- ExamView assessment software
- teacher's notes for every Student Book page
- rubrics for speaking and writing
- hundreds of reproducible worksheets
- answer keys for all practice
- audio and video scripts
- the GSE Teacher Mapping Booklet
- the GSE Toolkit

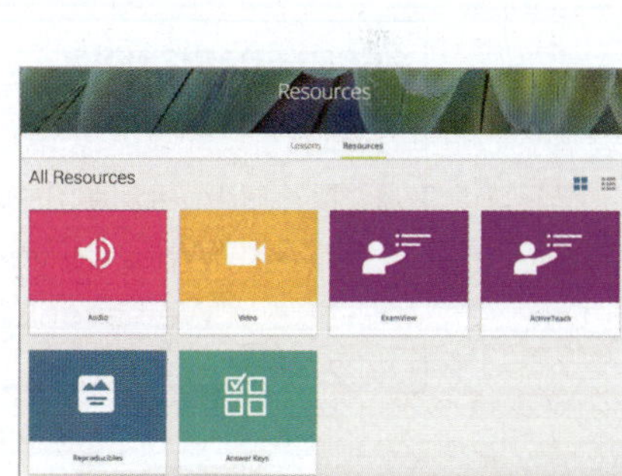

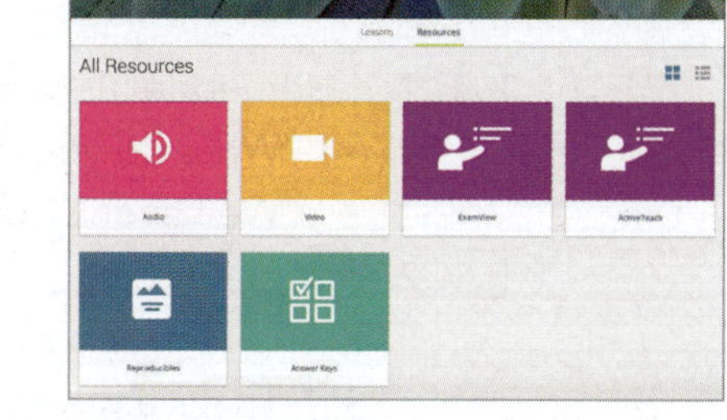

For the Student

StartUp provides students with everything they need to extend their learning.

The optional **MyEnglishLab for *StartUp*** gives students more formal online practice and provides immediate feedback, hints, and tips. It includes

- grammar practice (called Language Choices in *StartUp* 7 & 8 to better reflect the level)
- vocabulary practice
- speaking and pronunciation activities
- listen-and-record practice that lets students record themselves and compare their recordings to models
- auto-graded reading and writing practice that reinforces skills taught in the Student Book
- summative assessments that measure students' mastery of listening, vocabulary, grammar, pronunciation, and reading
- a gradebook, which records scores on practice and assessments, that both students and you can use to help monitor progress and plan further practice

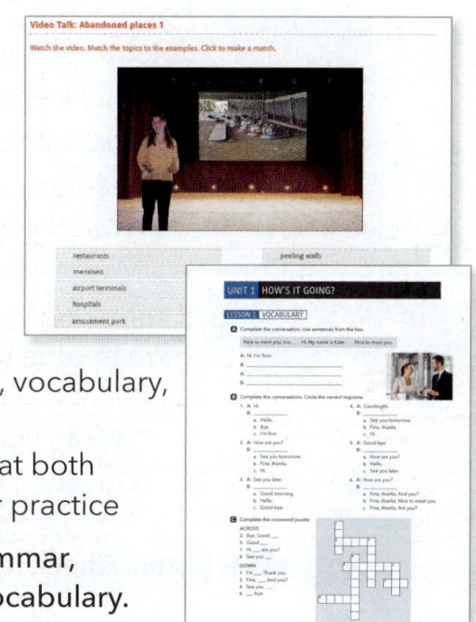

The optional ***StartUp* Workbook** provides practice of vocabulary, grammar, reading, and writing and includes self-assessments of grammar and vocabulary.

1 IN THE CLASSROOM

A Get to know your classmates

Talk to your classmates. Find someone who matches each prompt. Write his or her first name on the line. Then ask follow-up questions.

- loves to read __________
- has ridden a motorcycle __________
- enjoys cooking __________
- can play a musical instrument __________
- has traveled to another country __________
- is very artistic __________

A: Excuse me, do you love to read?
B: Yes, I do! My name is Onur. O-N-U-R.
A: Thanks! What kinds of things do you like to read?

B Strategies for class and business discussions

Here are some examples of strategies that will help you overcome challenges in discussions with classmates or colleagues. Complete the tips with the problems in the box.

~~doesn't participate~~	goes off topic	speaks too softly
speaks too quickly	speaks too much	interrupts others

☐ 1. If someone doesn't participate, invite him or her to join in by saying things like…
- "What do you think, Diego?"
- "We haven't heard from Chiyo yet. What do you think about…?"

☐ 2. If someone __________, get him or her back on track by saying things like…
- "Let's return to what Lanh was saying."
- "That's a good point, but let's get back to the main issue."

☐ 3. If someone is impatient and frequently __________, you can say…
- "Wait your turn, please. You'll have a chance to talk in a moment."
- "Hold on. Let Malik finish what he's saying."

☐ 4. If someone __________ and others don't have the opportunity to speak, you can politely interrupt by saying…
- "Thank you, Noor. Now let's hear what other people have to say."
- "That's an interesting idea. What do you think about that, Jae-jin?"

☐ 5. If someone __________, ask him or her to slow down by saying…
- "Would you mind slowing down?"
- "Could you say that a little more slowly, please?"

☐ 6. If someone __________, and others have trouble understanding what is being said, get him or her to speak up by saying…
- "Would you mind speaking up a little?"
- "I'm afraid we can't hear what you're saying."

C ▶00-01 Listen. Check (✓) the strategies from 1B that you hear.

D DISCUSS In groups, discuss the strategies in 1B. Which ones are the most / least useful? Say why.

2 LEARN ABOUT YOUR BOOK

1. Look at pages iv–vii. What information is on those pages? ______
2. How many units are in the book? ______
3. How many lessons are in each unit? ______
4. Look at page 6, Language Choices. Where is the practice? ______
5. Look at the QR code [QR code]. Find it on page 7. What does it mean? ______
6. Look at the I CAN STATEMENT. Find it on page 11. What does it tell you? ______
7. Look at this icon [search icon]. Find it on page 13. What does it mean? ______

3 LEARN ABOUT YOUR APP

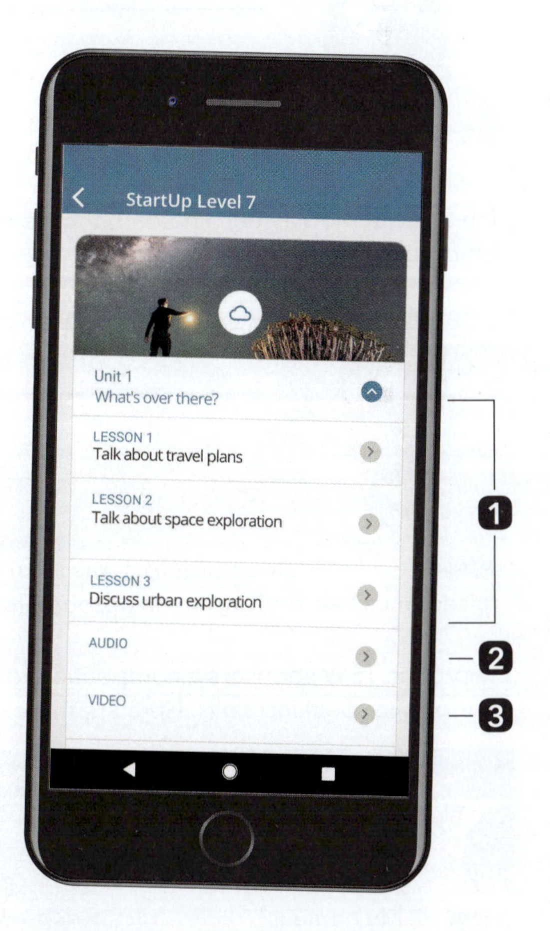

1. Look inside the front cover. Where can you go to download the Pearson Practice English App for *StartUp*? ______
2. Where are the instructions for registering for the app? ______
3. Look at the picture of the app. What do you see? ______
4. Look at the picture again. Fill in the blanks with the numbers 1–3.
   a. Number ______ shows the practice activities.
   b. Number ______ shows the video files.
   c. Number ______ shows the audio files.
5. Look at the picture again. What does [cloud icon] mean? ______
6. Look at the QR code on page 7 again. What happens when you scan the code? ______

TSW MEDIA — MEET THE PEOPLE OF TSW MEDIA

To find out more, listen to the introductions!

TSW Media is a big company with big ideas. It has offices all over the world. It works with international clients to help them market their products and services.

TAE-HO KANG
Videographer

▶00-02 Hello! My name is Tae-ho Kang. I live in Daegu, South Korea, where I work as a videographer.

ESRA KARA
Computer programmer

▶00-05 Hi, everyone. My name is Esra Kara. I live and work in Istanbul, Turkey, as a computer programmer.

CARLA LUGO
Social media coordinator

▶00-03 Hi there! My name is Carla Lugo. I'm a social media coordinator in the New York office.

HIRO MATSUDA
Project manager

▶00-06 Hello! I'm Hiro Matsuda. I'm a project manager. I grew up in Tokyo, but now I live in New Jersey.

MATEO ROMERO
Accountant

▶00-04 Hey! I'm Mateo Romero. I was born and raised in La Paz, Bolivia. I'm an accountant.

KATE SANDS
Market researcher

▶00-07 Hi! I'm Kate Sands. I'm a market researcher in Toronto.

Every year, TSW sponsors a competition for employees to get mentoring and coaching to improve their public speaking skills. Here are three of the winners!

ADRIANA LOPEZ

▶00-08 Hi. My name is Adriana Lopez. I work in the technology department in the Quito office.

KENDRICK SCOTT

▶00-09 Hey! I'm Kendrick Scott, and I'm a designer in the Vancouver office.

DAVID CRUZ

▶00-10 Hi. My name is David Cruz. I'm from Florida, but I've lived and worked in Singapore for the past six years. I'm an advertising manager.

1 WHAT'S OVER THERE?

LEARNING GOALS

In this unit, you

- talk about travel plans
- talk about space exploration
- discuss urban exploration
- read about deep-sea exploration
- write a descriptive essay

GET STARTED

A Read the unit title and learning goals. What does the word *exploration* make you think of?

B Look at the picture. Make a few quick notes to describe it and then compare your ideas with a partner. How are your descriptions similar or different?

C Read Esra's message. What does she mean when she says she has "traveling on the brain"? How does Esra's message relate to the picture?

ESRA KARA

@EsraK

I have traveling on the brain. I love traveling, and I'm really looking forward to my next fantastic adventure!

@EsraK

Going to Thailand this summer. I've got so much planning to do!

1 VOCABULARY Words related to travel planning

A Look at the brochure. Who planned the last vacation you took? How much was planned before you went?

B ▶01-01 Read and listen. Notice the words in bold.

Here at Vista Travel we've got you covered, **high season** or **low season**! Like to **plan ahead**? We can work out a detailed **itinerary** for you—we'll even **plan out** all of your meals and **day trips**!
Prefer to **play it by ear**? We can help you with that, too! We'll keep it organized but **open-ended**, leaving you plenty of room for **impromptu** day trips and **serendipity**!
Take off with us!

>> FOR PRACTICE, PAGE 125 / DEFINITIONS, PAGE 155

2 LANGUAGE CHOICES Present perfect vs. simple past

A Read the example sentences. Then complete the chart with *Present perfect* or *Simple past*.

Present perfect example sentences	Simple past example sentences
I **have traveled** to six countries.	Last month, I **traveled** to six countries.
Rob **has gone** on day trips every weekend.	Rob **went** on day trips every weekend.
Have you ever **done** anything spontaneous?	**Did** you **do** anything spontaneous?
I**'ve** just **finished** planning the trip.	Anna **wanted** to travel to Mexico.
Tourism in Peru **has tripled** in the past fifteen years.	Tourism in Peru **tripled** in the past fifteen years.

Present perfect vs. simple past	
________ is used for	• a single action completed at a definite time in the past. • a habitual / repeated action in the past that no longer continues. • an action or situation that started and ended in the past. • a state in the past that no longer applies.
________ is used for	• a situation that started in the past and continues into the present. • an action that happened at an unspecified time in the past that is still relevant in the present. • an action that started in the past and ended very recently or at the time of speaking.

>> FOR PRACTICE, PAGE 125

B Why does Speaker 1 use the present perfect while Speaker 2 uses the simple past?

Speaker 1: I**'ve researched** a lot of flights, but none of them work for me.
Speaker 2: I **researched** a lot of flights, but none of them worked for me.

3 CONVERSATION SKILL

Share your ideas informally

You can introduce ideas and opinions informally with expressions like these:

I'm telling you,...	*Here's my advice.*
That sounds...to me.	*Take it from me.*
Just so you know,...	*Trust me.*

A ▶01-04 Read the conversation skill. Then listen. Notice the words the speakers use to introduce an opinion. Complete the sentences.

1. ___________________ , we should wait for summer.
2. ___________________ like an awful lot of work ___________ .
3. ___________________ You don't want to go there during high season.

B PAIRS Student A: Make a travel suggestion. Student B: Respond with an expression from the conversation skill box.

4 CONVERSATION

A ▶01-05 Listen. What do Esra and Mateo talk about?

B ▶01-05 Listen again. Answer the questions.

1. Compare Esra's and Mateo's styles of vacation planning.
2. How does Esra feel about Mateo's style of vacation planning?
3. At the end of the conversation, what does Mateo recommend?

C ▶01-06 Listen. Complete the conversation.

Mateo: Well, ___________________ : Just go for a walk and stop somewhere that looks good.

Esra: Yeah, that is *not* my style.

Mateo: Well, that's how I found the best meal I've ever eaten. I just trust that things will work out, and they usually do! Exploring is what makes travel fun!

Esra: Hmm. I guess I'm not much of an explorer. That ______________________________ .

5 TRY IT YOURSELF

A MAKE IT PERSONAL Which parts of a vacation do you plan? What do you prefer to leave open-ended? Think of reasons or examples from your travel experiences. Take notes in the chart.

	Hotels	Tours	Meals	Museums	___________
Plan? (✓ / ✗)					
Reasons / Examples					

B PAIRS Share your ideas. Use expressions from the conversation skill box to introduce your opinions. Explain your reasons and give examples.

ESRA KARA
@EsraK
Listened to a podcast about exploring Mars. It's harder than it seems in the movies!

1 BEFORE YOU LISTEN

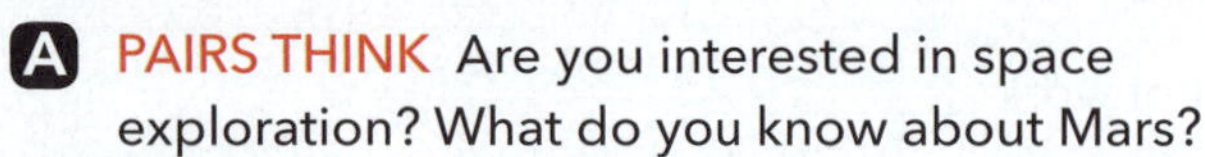

A PAIRS THINK Are you interested in space exploration? What do you know about Mars?

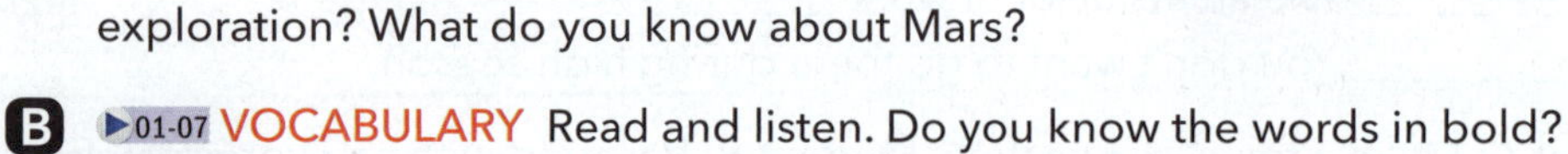

B ▶01-07 VOCABULARY Read and listen. Do you know the words in bold?

MARS: The Red Planet

There are about fourteen **spacecraft** on Mars. Six of them are **rovers**.

Some people hope that we can **terraform** the planet to make it more like Earth and then **colonize** it.

Mars is **inhospitable**.

It gets hit by 200 **asteroids** every year and **bombarded** with **radiation**.

There are **massive dust storms** and **toxic** substances.

>> FOR PRACTICE, PAGE 126 / DEFINITIONS, PAGE 155

2 LANGUAGE CHOICES Indefinite pronouns

A Read the example sentences. Notice the underlined verbs and circled objects. Use the indefinite pronouns in bold to complete the rules in the chart.

Example sentences

1. The technician was asked a lot of questions. **Several** were about the failed take off.
2. Two scientists authored the article. **Both** share (their views) on space travel.
3. **Nobody** knows just how big the universe is, but **many** have guessed.
4. **Neither** of the astronauts wants to discuss (his fears) while traveling in space.
5. **Everyone** is emailing (his or her* questions) to the astronauts in space.
6. **Everything** was perfectly visible through the microscope.

*In speech and informal writing, to avoid *his or her*, the plural *their* is often used with a singular antecedent:
Informal: ***Everyone*** *is emailing (their questions) to the astronauts in space.*

Indefinite pronouns	
Always singular	anyone, someone, everybody, no one, anybody, everything, somebody, each, one, either, ________, ________, ________, ________
Always plural	few, others, ________, ________, ________
Singular and plural (depending on usage)	all, any, more, most, none, some (of space / of the astronauts)

>> FOR PRACTICE, PAGE 126

B Read example sentences 1, 2, and 3. What do you think these indefinite pronouns refer to?

1. *Several* ________ 2. *Both* ________ 3. *many* ________

3 PRONUNCIATION

A ▶01-09 Listen. Read the pronunciation note.

B ▶01-10 Listen. Notice the stressed syllable. Then listen and repeat.

1. colonization, first in the nation, organization, building a station, life could survive there
2. obstacle, most of them, argument, half of it, substances
3. at the end of it, inhospitable, the performances, it's an asteroid, I'm afraid of it

Rhythm and stress patterns

Rhythm is the pattern of stressed and unstressed syllables in phrases or sentences. In a phrase or sentence, one word is usually stressed more heavily than others. Words also have a pattern of stressed and unstressed syllables. Phrases and sentences can have the same syllable-stress pattern as words. For example, the word *toxic* and the sentence *Take it* both have two syllables, with stress on the first syllable.

toxic *Take it.*

C ▶01-11 Listen. Cross out the word or phrase that has a different syllable-stress pattern.

1. civilization, organization, serendipity, evaluation, for the technician
2. it's excellent, I'm resting, it's optimal, in front of it, unfortunate

4 LISTENING

A ▶01-12 Listen. What is the main idea of the podcast?

B ▶01-12 Read the Listening Skill. Listen again. Write the thing that the speaker is talking about with each stressed word.

LISTENING SKILL Listen for stressed words

Speakers often stress words to emphasize an idea.

*It is **EXTREMELY** difficult to guess what will happen in the future.*

*The circumstances were **NOT** what we expected.*

*This project is going to be **DECIDEDLY** more difficult than people realize.*

1. EXPENSIVE ______________
2. EXTREMELY ______________
3. MINUS ______________
4. DECIDEDLY ______________

C ▶01-12 Listen again. Complete the chart with the arguments for and against going to Mars.

For	Against

D PAIRS REACT Were you surprised by any of the information in the podcast? If yes, explain what surprised you and why.

5 TRY IT YOURSELF

A THINK Do you think we should postpone space exploration until we solve problems here on Earth? Why or why not? Give reasons. Take notes about your ideas.

B DISCUSS Make a *For / Against* chart on the board. List the arguments for and against postponing space exploration. Vote on which side has the strongest arguments.

C ANALYZE Take a poll. What percentage of the class thinks we should go to Mars?

☐ I CAN TALK ABOUT SPACE EXPLORATION.

ESRA KARA
@EsraK
Have you heard of urban exploration? It's something I definitely have to try!

1 BEFORE YOU LISTEN

A PAIRS THINK Have you ever seen an abandoned building or site? Describe it.

B ▶01-13 VOCABULARY Listen. Do you know these words?

rust	crumble	moss-covered
abandon	peel	rot
damage	dilapidated	collapse

>> FOR PRACTICE, PAGE 127 / DEFINITIONS, PAGE 155

2 LANGUAGE CHOICES Types of adverbs

A Read the example sentences. Then complete the chart with the adverbs in bold.

Example sentences

1. We could **barely** see the ceiling.
2. **Even** the rotted trees looked beautiful.
3. **Curiously**, the house hasn't collapsed yet.
4. **Apparently**, the renovation was affordable.
5. There are **seldom** any floods in this area.
6. The houses here are **mostly** abandoned.

Type of adverbs and use	Examples	Usual sentence position
Sentence adverbs describe the speaker's opinion of the sentence	*honestly, frankly, obviously, regrettably, strangely, clearly,* ___, ___	at the beginning
Focus adverbs focus the listener's attention on a particular part of a sentence	*also, just, mainly, either, neither,* ___, ___	before or after words they modify; meaning can change depending on position
Negative adverbs give negative meaning to a sentence	*hardly, scarcely, rarely, never, little,* ___, ___	the same as *not*: before main verb; after first auxiliary verb; after forms of *be*

>> FOR PRACTICE, PAGE 127

B Notice how the focus adverb moves in each sentence. How does the meaning change?

Only employees may photograph the building.
Employees may **only** photograph the building.
Employees may photograph the building **only**.

3 VIDEO TALK

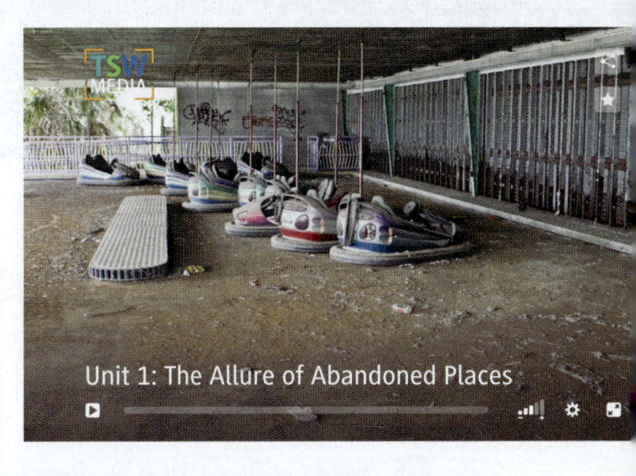

A ▶01-15 Listen or watch. What is the main idea of the talk?

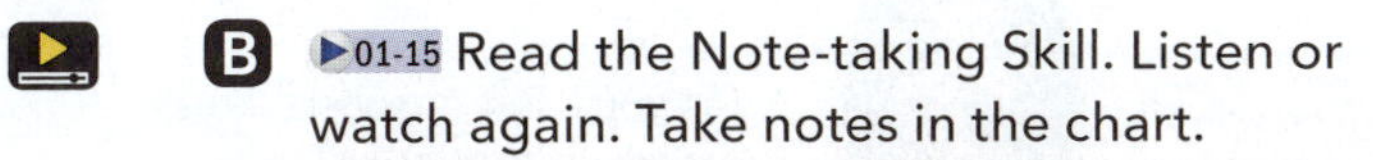

B ▶01-15 Read the Note-taking Skill. Listen or watch again. Take notes in the chart.

NOTE-TAKING SKILL Make lists

As you listen, try to identify categories of information. Keep lists of those categorical items under appropriate headings. Arrange the items vertically under the heading, putting each one on a separate line so they are easy to see and read when you review your notes.

Kinds of abandoned places	Why urban exploring is dangerous	Why people like abandoned places

C What does the speaker conclude about urban exploration?

D PAIRS REACT Do you think photographs of abandoned places are interesting? What do or don't you like about them?

4 DISCUSSION SKILL

Read the discussion skill. Which of these phrases do you use in your discussions now?

Invite others to participate

Invite others to participate in a discussion with phrases like these:

What do you think about…?

Do you have any thoughts on this?

Do you want to add anything…?

5 TRY IT YOURSELF

A THINK Think about the abandoned places you have seen in this lesson or in real life. Would you like to explore them? Why or why not? Write your ideas.

____

____

B DISCUSS In a small group, discuss your reasons for and against exploring abandoned places. After you speak, invite others to participate in the discussion.

C EVALUATE Decide which arguments are most convincing. If your group thinks urban exploration should be discouraged, explain ways to do that. If your group thinks it's worthwhile, think of new places to explore.

☐ I CAN DISCUSS URBAN EXPLORATION.

LESSON 4 READ ABOUT DEEP-SEA EXPLORATION

ESRA KARA

@EsraK

Did you know the ocean is still mostly unexplored? Check out this interesting article!

1 BEFORE YOU READ

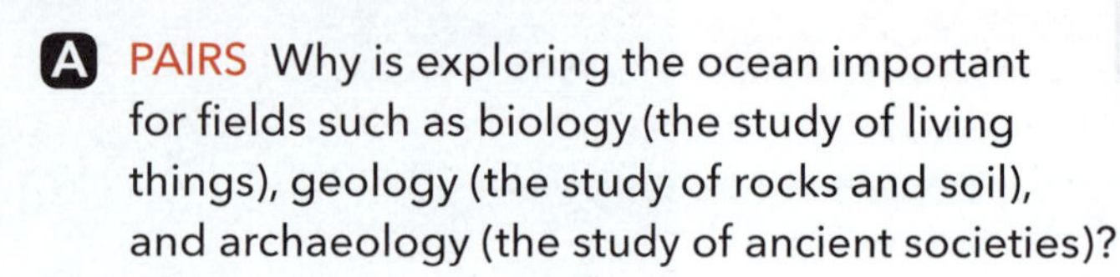

A PAIRS Why is exploring the ocean important for fields such as biology (the study of living things), geology (the study of rocks and soil), and archaeology (the study of ancient societies)?

B ▶01-16 VOCABULARY Read and listen. Do you know these words?

malfunction	nutrients	transmit	a wealth of	bacteria
illuminate	be accustomed to	an artifact	a spire	dissolved

>> FOR DEFINITIONS, PAGE 156

2 READ

A PREVIEW Read the title, look at the picture, and read the caption. What questions do you think the article will answer?

B ▶01-17 Read and listen to the article. Were your predictions correct?

A remotely operated vehicle explores the ocean floor.

UNDERSEA EXPLORATION: DOWN TO THE DEPTHS WITH *HERCULES*

The sea is calm as the 64-meter-long *Exploration Vessel Nautilus* (*EV Nautilus* for short) lowers a robotic submarine named *Hercules* over the side. Its mission is to explore the Cayman Trough, the deepest point in the Caribbean Sea. As *Hercules* descends to 4,000 meters, testing its limits, there is fear on board that the vehicle might
5 malfunction or be crushed. The spotlights illuminate the blackness for its cameras, the eyes of the scientists in the ship above. They confirm the existence of springs of superheated water that are sources of nutrients for marine ecosystems and even discover a new species of shrimp. *Hercules* has passed the test!

Equipped with mechanical arms to collect samples, *Hercules* is one of several remotely operated vehicles
10 that help the *EV Nautilus* force the deep sea to give up its well-guarded secrets. It scans the ocean floor up close with high-definition video cameras and bright lights that frequently startle creatures accustomed to life without sunlight. The stunning images are sent up to the *EV Nautilus* along a fiber-optic cable, transmitted via satellite to a university space center in the U.S., and uploaded to the internet for the world to enjoy.

Since its launch in 2003, *Hercules* has sent up a wealth of images of extraordinary life forms of all colors,
15 shapes, and sizes, from deep-diving whales curious about the light source to jellyfish that are living fireworks displays. Of particular interest are the unlikely ecological systems that form around hydrothermal vents that eject seawater as hot as 450°C, creating prominent and often beautiful formations known as chimneys or spires. There, in total darkness, bacteria come to feed on dissolved metals, gases, and minerals. They, in turn, nourish tube worms and mussels, which themselves provide food for small crabs, shrimp, fish, etc.

20 *Hercules* is also interested in archaeology. Weather, wars, mechanical failures, and human errors have been sending vessels to a watery grave for centuries, leaving many historical artifacts on the sea floor. *EV Nautilus* has inspected not only wooden wrecks of the ancient world but also modern ones of steel and iron, including battleships, submarines, and airplanes. Dr. Robert Ballard, the president of the Ocean Exploration Trust, which owns *EV Nautilus*, is particularly fascinated by shipwrecks—it was he who located the sunken
25 *Titanic* in 1985.

>>

>
The exciting new applications of technology by *EV Nautilus* have even caught the attention of NASA. A remotely operated vehicle similar to *Hercules* would be perfect for investigating the oceans that exist on other planets and moons in our solar system. Scientists could control such a mission from the safety of Earth, examining images transmitted back that might reveal signs of life around hydrothermal vents at the
30 bottom of an ocean on a distant world.

3 CHECK YOUR UNDERSTANDING

A Answer the questions according to the article.

1. Why does the author write "*Hercules* has passed the test!"?
2. How is data collected and shared with scientists?
3. How has *EV Nautilus* enriched the field of archaeology?
4. Why is *EV Nautilus*'s technology particularly suited to exploration in space?

B CLOSE READING Reread the lines. Then circle the correct answers.

1. In lines 18–19, why does the writer use *in turn* in the second sentence?
   a. to introduce a process that is faster than the one in the first sentence
   b. to introduce a process that is the result of the one in the first sentence
   c. to introduce a process that conflicts with the one in the first sentence
2. In lines 21–25, how is the second sentence connected to the first?
   a. It provides a notable example.
   b. It describes the method used.
   c. It presents a solution to a problem.

C Read the Reading Skill. Find the metaphorical language in the article and complete the sentences.

1. In line 6, *Hercules's* ___cameras___ are compared to the scientists' eyes because ___they allow them to see the bottom of the ocean___ .
2. In line 10, the ocean is said to keep ______________ because ____________________________________ .
3. In line 15, jellyfish are called living ______________ because ____________________________________ .
4. In line 21, the bottom of the ocean is compared to a watery ______________ because ____________________________________ .

READING SKILL Identify metaphor

In a metaphor, language is used for dramatic effect, for example: *The internet is a window on the world.* Although the internet isn't an actual window, the word *window* suggests how we use the internet to obtain information about the world.

D PAIRS Summarize the article in 3-5 sentences.

Search online to find out more about the *EV Nautilus* and watch videos posted online of its past expeditions.

4 MAKE IT PERSONAL

A THINK Consider the exploratory work of the *EV Nautilus*. What aspects seem the most important to you? Why? Take notes.

B GROUPS Discuss which aspects of the work of *EV Nautilus* are the most important, in your opinion.

C EVALUATE As a group, decide on the two aspects that you agree are the most important. Then choose one person to present your ideas to the class.

☐ I CAN READ ABOUT DEEP-SEA EXPLORATION.

ESRA KARA

@EsraK

My friend Anita has been to some amazing places, and she writes about them on her blog. Here's a place I really want to visit!

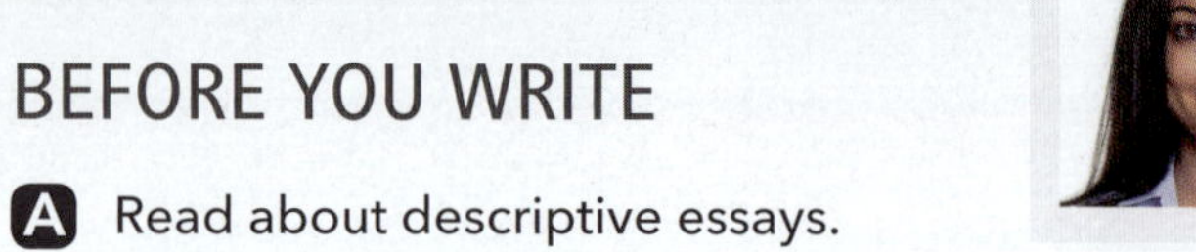

1 BEFORE YOU WRITE

A Read about descriptive essays.

A descriptive essay is usually used to describe a place or a person. It has a formal structure with an introduction, multiple body paragraphs, and a conclusion. But the content of the essay is creative rather than academic. Descriptive essays often engage the readers' senses (sight, sound, smell, touch, taste) to enable them to visualize the place or person being described.

B Read the model. What does the writer describe?

Blog | About | Destinations | Contact   Logout  

About
RSS Feed
Social
Email
Posts
Search

As a child, I lived in the Sonora Desert. This desert, in the northwest of Mexico, is one of the most beautiful places that I have ever seen. You may think of deserts as dry and empty. But the Sonora Desert is abuzz with life and boasts many unusual plants and animals.

If you visit, take a hike through one of the desert parks. The dry, hard earth crunches under your feet, and you can see the most strange-looking plants dotting the landscape. The most famous plant here is the stately saguaro cactus. Its trunk is as thick as a tree, and it stands twice as tall as a person. Ocotillo plants have many spiny branches like tentacles, which reach upwards toward the deep blue sky. These plants bloom with red flowers in the springtime. Creosote plants, more squat and bushy, have bright yellow blossoms and fuzzy white seeds. These bushes release an earthy, herbal scent during rainstorms.

The desert heat is intense, so during the day most animals will not venture out. If you are lucky, you may see a roadrunner. These famous birds have long tails which stretch out behind them when they run. Or you may see a jackrabbit with its long ears, hiding in the shade. But most animals emerge only in the evening. When the sun descends, painting the sky pink and orange, the air becomes much cooler. Then you can hear many birds twittering and crickets singing. But be careful: Venomous animals, like rattlesnakes and gila monsters (giant lizards), are also active in the evening. Watch the ground closely to avoid stepping on these dangerous creatures.

You probably won't find the Sonora Desert on a list of top ten places to travel, but its unique landscape makes it a great place to explore. Anyone who loves wildlife and unusual places will be thrilled by the sights, sounds, and scents that can be found only here.

C PAIRS What senses did the essay appeal to? Give an example of each.

D Read the model again. How did the writer describe the desert? Complete the chart.

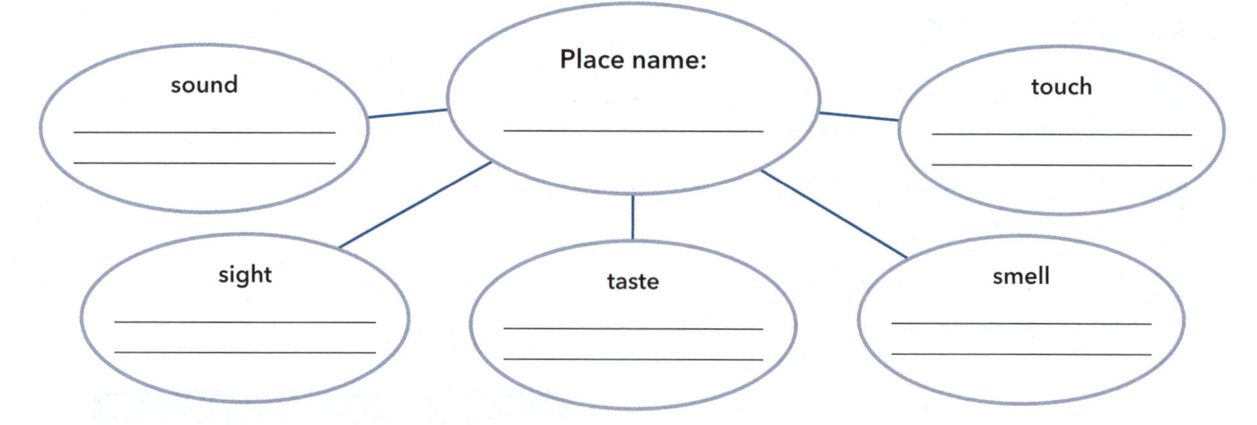

2 FOCUS ON WRITING

Read the Writing Skill. Then reread the descriptive essay. Complete the chart.

WRITING SKILL Use active verbs

We know that using adjectives and other descriptors can make writing more interesting. But your writing can be even more exciting if you use a variety of active verbs.

Paragraph	Verb or verb phrase	Meaning
1		has something great
2		found all across
3		go outside
3		come out
3		goes down
3		singing

3 PLAN YOUR WRITING

A Think of an interesting or unusual place that you know well. What are some of the things you can see, hear, feel, smell, or maybe even taste in that place? Create a chart like the one in 1D.

B PAIRS Discuss your ideas.

I'm going to write about the city Kyoto.

Writing tip

There are many approaches to organizing your ideas for writing. Sometimes you may need a two-step, ("bottom-up" followed by "top-down") approach. First, think about the details you want to describe. Then organize those details into broader categories.

4 WRITE

Write a first draft of a descriptive essay about the place you described in 3A. Remember to give sensory details using strong descriptive adjectives and active verbs. Use the essay in 1B as a model.

5 AFTER YOUR FIRST DRAFT

A PEER REVIEW Read your partner's essay. Answer the questions.

- Do the details help give you a clear picture of this place?
- Does the categorization of the features make sense?
- Does the essay use strong descriptive adjectives and active verbs?
- Are a variety of sensory details included, such as sights, sounds, and smells?
- Does the essay have a clear organization, with an introduction, 2–3 body paragraphs, and a conclusion?
- Does the introduction give the name of the place, explain where the place is, and explain how the writer knows the place?
- Does the conclusion say something new, but still relate to the body of the essay?

B REVISE Write another draft, based on the feedback you got from your partner.

C PROOFREAD Check the spelling, grammar, and punctuation in your essay. Then read it through again for overall sense.

☐ I CAN WRITE A DESCRIPTIVE ESSAY.

PUT IT TOGETHER

1 PROBLEM SOLVING

A CONSIDER THE PROBLEM Tourism may be the biggest business in the world. With more and more people traveling, many famous sites are being vandalized. Review the chart and answer the questions.

World Monuments	Created	Visitors in 2013*	Visitors in 2018*	Most common vandalism
The Great Wall of China	c. 220 BCE	9	10.5	graffiti, littering, theft of stone pieces
The Colosseum, Italy	c. 70 CE	5.11	7.4	graffiti, theft of stone pieces
Machu Picchu	c. 1450	1.2	4.4	graffiti, littering

*in millions

1. Which monument has had the most tourism? ______________________
2. Which monument is likely the most difficult to protect? Why? ______________________
3. What is the most common type of vandalism? ______________________

B THINK CRITICALLY What factors might lead to increases in vandalism? Discuss with a partner.

C FIND A SOLUTION Consider the data, the problem, and possible solutions in small groups.

Step 1 **Brainstorm** How could vandalism of world monuments be reduced?

Step 2 **Evaluate** Choose the best solution. Consider the size of the monument and the type of vandalism.

Step 3 **Present** Explain your best solution to the class. Refer to the data to support your ideas.

2 REFLECT AND PLAN

A Look back through the unit. Check (✓) the things you learned. Highlight the things you need to learn.

Speaking Objectives
- ☐ Talk about travel plans
- ☐ Talk about space exploration
- ☐ Discuss urban exploration

Vocabulary
- ☐ Words related to travel planning

Conversation
- ☐ Share your ideas informally

Pronunciation
- ☐ Rhythm and stress patterns

Listening
- ☐ Listen for stressed words

Note-taking
- ☐ Make lists

Language Choices
- ☐ Present perfect vs. simple past
- ☐ Indefinite pronouns
- ☐ Types of adverbs

Discussion
- ☐ Invite others to participate

Reading
- ☐ Identify metaphor

Writing
- ☐ Use active verbs

B What will you do to learn the things you highlighted?

2 WHAT'S YOUR SUPERPOWER?

LEARNING GOALS

In this unit, you

- talk about superpowers
- talk about how to excel
- discuss why we love superheroes
- read about technological superpowers
- write a definition essay

GET STARTED

A Read the unit title and learning goals. Each of us may have a superpower—a skill that lets us help others or ourselves in a special way. What's your superpower?

B Look at the picture. What do you think it means? Does the woman know she has superpowers? Is it a metaphor?

C Read Tae-ho's message. He defines *superpower* in a humorous way. How would you define it?

TAE-HO KANG

@Tae-hoK

What if we all have secret superpowers? I'd say my superpower is an ability to sleep through anything, like my alarm!

TAE-HO KANG

@Tae-hoK

That feeling when you're sitting in your office just wishing you had superpowers...

1 VOCABULARY Superpowers

A Look at the comic. Which superpower do you think is the most valuable?

B ▶02-01 Read and listen. Notice the words in bold.

>> FOR PRACTICE, PAGE 128 / DEFINITIONS, PAGE 156

2 LANGUAGE CHOICES Present and future unreal conditional

A The present and future unreal conditional is used to talk about an unreal current event situation or about an unlikely future event or situation. Read the example sentences. Then circle the correct answers in the chart.

Example sentences

1. **If** I **were able** to teleport, I **would go** to the conference in Brazil tomorrow.
2. **If** she **could read** minds, she **would know** what we're thinking.
3. We **could finish** this project on time **if** we **had** superpowers.
4. I **would want** to be invisible right now **if** I **were** you.
5. **If** you could teleport, where **would** you **go**?
6. What **would** you **do if** you **had** super strength?

In informal contexts, we often use *was* with subjects *I*, *he*, and *she* in the unreal conditional.

Present and future unreal conditional

- The unreal conditional is **the same / different** for present time and future time.
- Use the **present / past** form of the verb in the *if*-clause.
- When the verb in the *if*-clause is a form of *be*, use the form ***was / were***.
- In the main clause, use ***will / would*** or ***can / could***.
- Separate the *if*-clause and the main clause with a comma when the main clause comes **first / second** in the sentence.

>> FOR PRACTICE, PAGE 128

B Explain the difference between these sentences.

If I were a superhero, I'd use my powers to teleport and avoid traffic.

If I were a superhero, I'd use my powers to teleport and avoid this horrible traffic jam!

3 CONVERSATION SKILL

A ▶02-04 Read the conversation skill. Then listen. Notice the words the speakers use to accept an opinion. Complete the sentences.

1. Well, _________________ , but I'd still want to go on road trips once in a while.
2. _________________ fun. _________________ , they might sit down on you because they don't see you.
3. _________________ , but cleaning the house isn't a very exciting thing to do with a superpower.

Accept an opinion before offering a conflicting one

To accept someone's opinion and then offer a conflicting one, use expressions like these:

That could be… On the other hand…
True. But…
That may be the case, but…
I suppose that's true, but…

B PAIRS Student A: Make a statement about a superpower. Student B: Respond with an expression from the conversation skill box and offer a conflicting opinion.

4 CONVERSATION

A ▶02-05 Listen. What do Tae-ho and Carla talk about?

B ▶02-05 Listen again. Answer the questions.

1. Which superpowers do Tae-ho and Carla discuss?
2. According to Tae-ho, what are the disadvantages of telepathy?
3. According to Carla, what is one disadvantage of teleportation?

C ▶02-06 Listen. Complete the conversation.

Tae-ho: If I just had super hearing, I would know what they're saying.
Carla: That *would* be useful, wouldn't it? _________________ , you would hear what everyone else in the office is saying, too. That could get pretty annoying.
Tae-ho: ____________ . But maybe I could focus it, so I only hear the people I want to hear.
Carla: Hmm, I think telepathy _________________ . Then you could read their minds while they watch your video.

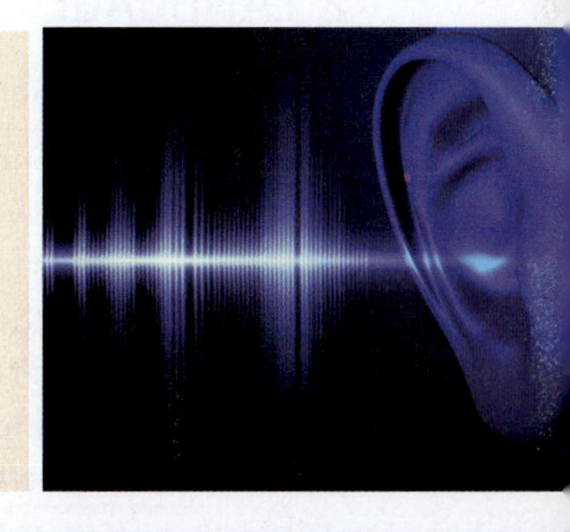

5 TRY IT YOURSELF

A MAKE IT PERSONAL Write down three superpowers. What would their advantages and disadvantages be? How would your life change if you had them?

Superpower	Advantages	Disadvantages	Effect on my life

B GROUPS Decide which superpower would have the most positive effect on a person's life. Use expressions from 3A to accept your classmates' opinions and offer conflicting ones. Report your ideas to the class.

☐ I CAN TALK ABOUT SUPERPOWERS.

TAE-HO KANG
@Tae-hoK
I listened to a podcast about how to excel, and I think I already do some of these things. Go me!

1 BEFORE YOU LISTEN

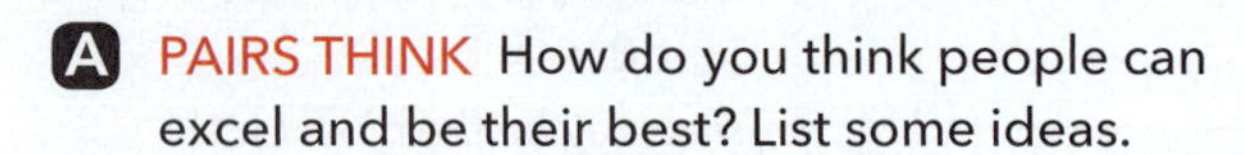

A PAIRS THINK How do you think people can excel and be their best? List some ideas.

B ▶02-07 VOCABULARY Complete the chart with all of the family members: the verb, noun, and adjective forms. Then listen and check your answers.

Verb	Noun	Adjective
excel	*excellence*	*excellent*
optimize		*or*
	reflection	
inspire		
		persistent
	rage	
		promising

>> FOR PRACTICE, PAGE 129 / DEFINITIONS, PAGE 156

2 LANGUAGE CHOICES Future real conditional

A Read the example sentences. Then circle the correct answers in the chart.

Example sentences

1. **If** you **keep working** on a skill, you **will get** better at it.
2. **If** she **wants** to excel, she **must optimize** her efforts.
3. I **can finish** the job on time **if I'm not interrupted**.
4. We **shouldn't be** afraid of small failures **if** we **want** to succeed in the end.
5. You **won't improve unless** you **push** yourself harder.
6. **Unless** we **reflect** on our mistakes, we **won't learn** from them.

Future real conditional

- We use future real conditional for situations that are **possible / impossible**.
- To express the condition, use an *if*-clause and the simple **present / future** form.
- To express the future result, use the simple **present / future** form or **the present continuous / a modal + verb**.
- The main (result) clause is **always at the beginning / at the beginning or end** of the sentence.
- *Unless* means ***if / except if***.

>> FOR PRACTICE, PAGE 129

B What are the differences between these sentences, in meaning and form?

We'll overcome our challenges if we keep trying.
If we keep trying, we'll overcome our challenges.

3 PRONUNCIATION

A ▶02-09 Listen. Read the pronunciation note.

B ▶02-10 Listen. Notice the pauses and changes in intonation.

1. A: As you've probably heard, persistence is key to mastering any skill.
   B: True, but what if I don't get better?
2. A: In my opinion, you can learn anything if you really want.
   B: Yes, but playing an instrument requires a lot of practice.

C ▶02-11 Listen. Add a comma where you hear a pause.

A: First of all many top athletes inspire people to follow their passion.
B: On the other hand you don't always have talent for sports.
A: I suppose that's true but you can excel at anything if you're determined.

Pausing and intonation in transitional phrases

When a transitional phrase like *On the other hand* begins a sentence, there is usually a small fall or rise in intonation, followed by a pause. The pause tells the listener to focus on what comes next. It's often marked with a comma.

On the other hand, / making mistakes helps us learn better.

On the other hand, / making mistakes helps us learn better.

4 LISTENING

A ▶02-12 Listen. What is the main idea of the podcast?

B ▶02-12 Read the Listening Skill. Listen again. Write the main ideas.

LISTENING SKILL Listen for sequence

A speaker may have a number of main ideas followed by details such as explanations or examples. Listen for numbers and sequencers (*next*, *then*, *last*, etc.) to follow along with the main ideas. Use numbers to list the main ideas in your notes. Add details under or next to them.

Key	Main Idea	Details
1.	be persistent	
2.		
3.		
4.		
5.		

C ▶02-12 Listen again. Complete the chart with examples.

D PAIRS REACT Do you think all five of these keys to success are equally important? Are there any you would omit? Can you think of any you would add?

5 TRY IT YOURSELF

A THINK Which of the five keys to success do you use (at least sometimes)? Give examples.

Keys to success I use	Examples

B DISCUSS In small groups, compare and contrast the information in your charts. Identify the keys to success that are most and least common in your group.

C ANALYZE Come to a consensus about why some of the keys are more and less common. Share your conclusions with the class.

☐ I CAN TALK ABOUT HOW TO EXCEL.

1 BEFORE YOU LISTEN

A PAIRS THINK How do you feel about superheroes? Do you watch superhero movies? Why or why not?

B ▶02-13 VOCABULARY Look at the words and listen to the sentences. Do you know these words?

churn out	resemble	trauma
innate	intervene	avenge
self-evident	consistently	thrust

>> FOR PRACTICE, PAGE 130 / DEFINITIONS, PAGE 156

2 LANGUAGE CHOICES Present real conditional

A Read the example sentences. Then read the rules in the chart. Are they true (*T*) or false (*F*)? Correct the false rules.

Example sentences

1. Audiences **feel** more connected to the character **if** they **can relate** to the hero's story.
2. **If** our family or friends **need** assistance, we **should step up** and help.
3. **When** there**'s** a new superhero movie, I usually **watch** it.
4. Superheroes always **intervene when** someone **is suffering**.
5. **If** a superhero **is thrust into** a dangerous situation, he or she almost always **comes out** fine.
6. **If** someone**'s** in trouble, **do** you **react**?

Present real conditional

- Use the present real conditional for situations that are impossible. ______
- Use the present real conditional to describe an event (cause) that is always followed by another event (result). ______
- Use *if* or *when* in the *if*-clause or the result clause. ______
- Use the simple future form of the verb in the result clause. ______
- Use the simple present form of the verb in the result clause. ______
- We can use modals in the *if*-clause or the result clause. ______
- Separate the clauses with a comma when the result clause comes second in the sentence. ______

>> FOR PRACTICE, PAGE 130

B Read the sentences. Which sentence is the more appropriate choice and why?

If someone suffers from trauma, recovery can be difficult.
If someone suffered from trauma, recovery could be difficult.

3 VIDEO TALK

A ▶02-15 Listen or watch. What is the main idea of the talk?

B ▶02-15 Read the Note-taking Skill. Listen or watch again. Take notes in the chart.

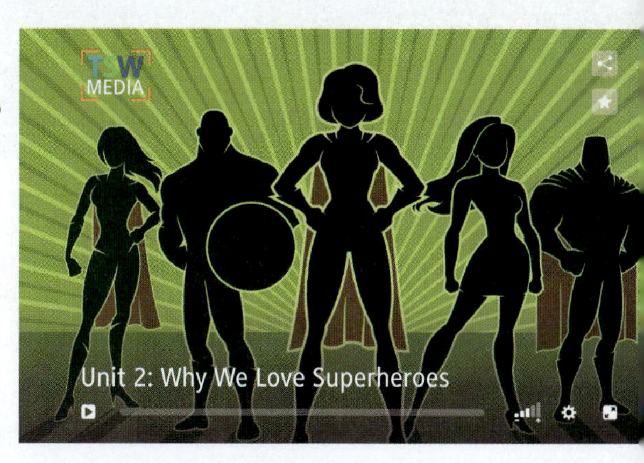

NOTE-TAKING SKILL Note examples clearly

Speakers often give examples to illustrate their main ideas. If you're using a Main ideas / Details chart, write the examples in the Details section of your notes. It's also a good idea to use abbreviations like *e.g.* or *ex.* in front of them so that they stand out.

Main ideas	Details
Attraction to people who protect others ___________ .	
People connect with ___________ .	• •

C What does the speaker conclude about superhero stories?

D PAIRS REACT Do you think it's true that people connect with the kinds of stories the speaker describes? Why or why not?

4 DISCUSSION SKILL

Read the discussion skill. Which of these phrases do you use in your discussions now?

Return a discussion back to the main point

If a discussion gets off track, use polite expressions like these to get it back to the main topic:

Let's get back to…

What we were saying earlier was…

5 TRY IT YOURSELF

A THINK Choose a movie, TV show, or book you like. Think about the talk in 3A. Then answer the questions in the chart. Include an explanation and example.

Does the hero protect others?	Does the hero's origin story follow one of the patterns?

B DISCUSS In small groups, talk about the hero from your chart. Explain how he or she does or doesn't exemplify the speaker's ideas.

C ANALYZE Come to a consensus about which hero is the closest to or furthest from the speaker's ideas. Tell the class your conclusion and explain your reasoning.

☐ I CAN DISCUSS WHY WE LOVE SUPERHEROES.

TAE-HO KANG
@Tae-hoK

Check out this article. Is this really what the future is going to look like? I hope so!

1 BEFORE YOU READ

A Read the Reading Skill. Then create a chart with three columns labeled K, W, and L.

B PAIRS The article below is about technologies that can enhance human abilities. Write at least three things you know about this topic in column K of your chart.

C 02-16 VOCABULARY Read and listen. Do you know these words?

pioneering	adhere	sheer	bulky	render
microscopic	scale	state-of-the-art	limbs	imperative

>> FOR DEFINITIONS, PAGE 157

READING SKILL Use a KWL chart

A KWL chart is a graphic organizer with three columns labeled K (what I **know**), W (what I **want** to know), and L (what I **learned**). It can help you prepare to read a text, engage with it, and organize what you learn.

2 READ

A PREVIEW Read the title and subtitles and look at the pictures. What do you want to know about the topic? Write at least three questions in column W of your chart.

B 02-17 Read and listen. Did the article answer your questions?

SUPERPOWERS | THEY ARE NOT JUST FOR SUPERHEROES ANYMORE

Imagine a universe where people climb steel and glass skyscrapers as naturally as walking along the street. Nobody wears eyeglasses as everyone has vision that is several times more powerful than yours or mine, and they operate machines using thoughts alone. If you think I'm talking about the Marvel cinematic universe, guess again. These superpowers are already available to normal humans, and more are on the 5 way—thanks to some pioneering technologies.

CLIMB LIKE A GECKO

Over 2,000 years ago, the climbing ability of the little gecko amazed the Greek philosopher Aristotle, who wrote that it could "run up and down a tree in any way, even with the head downward." In fact, an adult gecko has a grip that can support up to 130 kilograms (or 286 pounds). In 2002, scientists discovered the gecko's secret: Its feet are covered with thousands 10 of tiny hair-like structures. Then extending from the end of each one of those are approximately 1,000 more microscopic "hairs" that adhere to the bonds between molecules. Researchers have used the same principle to create climbing gloves that allow a person to scale sheer surfaces. Move over, Spiderman!

A gecko's foot is covered in microscopic hair-like structures.

ANYONE CAN BE IRON MAN

Tony Stark, the billionaire genius who becomes Iron Man, has a normal body and a weak heart. It's his high-tech 15 exoskeleton that gives him his superpowers. Similarly, real-world exoskeletons greatly multiply the strength and endurance of the wearer, and there are countless applications. For example, in the shipbuilding and automobile industries, workers wearing exoskeletons effortlessly lift heavy sheets of steel, and in the military, exoskeletons allow soldiers to carry more and heavier equipment than ever before. While those state-of-the-art models are still bulky and ugly, sleek ones like a "second skin" made from lightweight materials are at the conceptual stage.

>>

>

MIND OVER MATTER

20 One of the superpowers of Jean Grey, perhaps the most powerful member of the X-Men team, is telekinesis: the power to manipulate matter in the world around her with her mind. In the real world, technology-aided telekinesis begins with recognizing the electrical signals our brains produce when we think different thoughts, such as *on*, *off*, *go*, *stop*, or the letters of the alphabet. A headset can detect these signals and convert them into commands via computer to operate a device or type words. This technology promises to enable humans 25 to operate, telekinetically, computers and computer-equipped machines, including cars and appliances. It's also great news for physically disabled individuals, who will be able to control not only wheelchairs but also mechanical limbs with their thoughts.

Other technological superpowers in development include uploading information directly to the brain, technology that renders objects invisible, and jetpacks to allow us to fly long distances airplane-free. Critics 30 worry that such superpowers will give unfair advantages to those who have them. They fear this could become a new divide similar to the digital divide that has separated those with access to computers and internet technology and those without. That's why as scientists and researchers create new superpowers, it's imperative that they make them accessible to everyone.

3 CHECK YOUR UNDERSTANDING

A PAIRS Read the article again. In column L of your chart, write at least three things you learned. Then share and discuss them.

B Answer the questions according to the article.

1. How have scientists made use of the gecko's "secret"?
2. What is meant by the heading *Anyone Can Be Iron Man*?
3. How does technology-aided telekinesis work?
4. What does the author compare to the "digital divide"?

C CLOSE READING Reread the lines. Then circle the correct answers.

1. According to the sentence in lines 18–19, ______ .
   a. only bulky exoskeletons are currently in use
   b. exoskeletons that are currently in use are sleek
   c. sleek exoskeletons will be weaker than bulky ones
2. In lines 20–21, it is implied that Jean Grey ______ .
   a. is the most powerful X-Men character
   b. relies primarily on telekinesis
   c. has more than one superpower

D PAIRS Summarize the article in 3–5 sentences.

Search online to find out more about these and other technological superpowers that are currently in development. 

4 MAKE IT PERSONAL

A THINK Think of additional real-world applications for "gecko" climbing gloves, exoskeletons, and technology-aided telekinesis to help improve society.

B GROUPS Present your ideas to the group. Clarify any points they have questions about.

C EVALUATE Discuss the pros and cons of your ideas. Decide on the best one for each of the three technologies and have one person present them to the class.

☐ I CAN READ ABOUT TECHNOLOGICAL SUPERPOWERS.

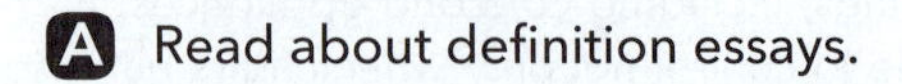

TAE-HO KANG

@Tae-hoK

Not all heroes are in the newspaper or in comic books! 😉 I've been thinking about what makes a hero…

1 BEFORE YOU WRITE

A Read about definition essays.

A definition essay is an essay that seeks to define a term or concept. More than just a simple definition, the essay analyzes all the nuances of that concept. Examples help to explain and clarify the different aspects of the concept being considered.

B Read the model. What three qualities does the writer feel a hero must exhibit?

When you think of a hero, do you think of Superman or Wonder Woman? Or do you think of real-life heroes, like firefighters? Well, there is one more category of hero: the *unsung hero*, someone who does heroic acts in everyday life. For me, one such person was my grandmother. Why? She demonstrated three qualities that I think all heroes must exhibit: bravery, leadership, and wisdom.

My grandmother was an amazing woman. Brave? Yes, indeed, she was incredibly brave. Bravery to me means staying calm in the face of danger and putting other people before yourself. My grandmother showed this quality every single day. She was the principal of my elementary school. At a time when not many women held this job, this by itself was brave! One time, she was called upon to act like a true hero. It was a day when there was a big earthquake in our town. At school, we had not had earthquake drills, and we did not know what to do. But my grandmother stayed calm. She announced that all children should get under their desks. Then she personally came around to help people. Her bravery that day was astonishing.

My grandmother was also a real leader. Leadership, like bravery, requires staying calm. It also requires the ability to make people listen to you. My grandmother did this at school all the time. She was a small woman, and yet somehow we all paid attention to her and did what she asked—even the teachers.

And finally, my grandmother showed great wisdom. This is an important quality in a hero because heroes are people who learn from their experience and help pass on what they have learned to others. I remember a day when I got angry with another boy at school, and I pushed him. The teacher sent me to see the principal—my grandmother. I was scared that she was going to punish me harshly. Instead, she talked to me about strength. "Everyone gets angry sometimes," she told me. "But a strong person knows how to show restraint." She asked me to think about other ways I could have handled the situation. Finally, she called the other boy in and made me apologize to him. I really understood the lesson, so my apology was sincere.

The lessons I learned from my grandmother have stayed with me for my whole life and helped to shape me as a person. She was a true hero, to me and also to my community.

C PAIRS Discuss. Do you agree with the writer's selection of personality traits that make a hero?

D Read the model again. Take notes in the chart.

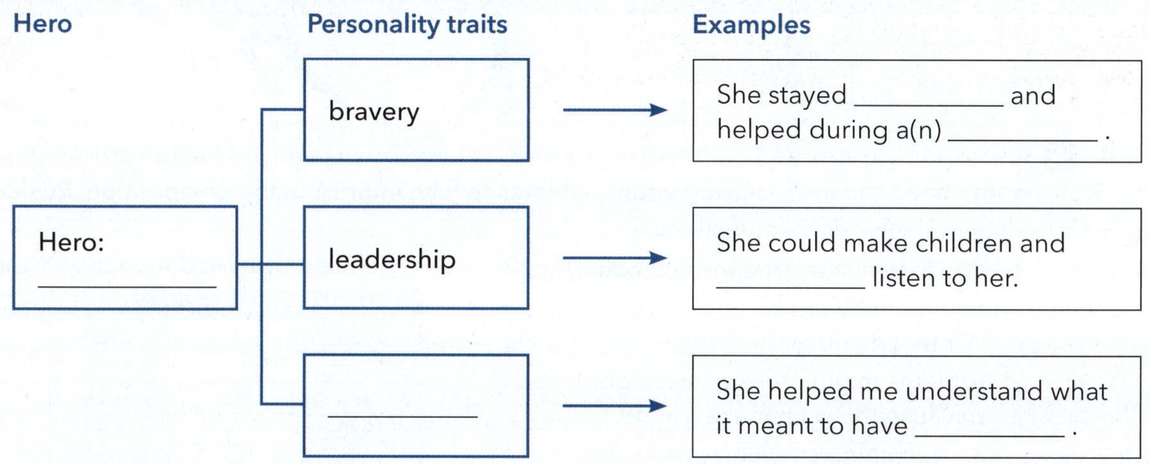

2 FOCUS ON WRITING

Read the Writing Skill. Then reread the model. Underline all of the rhetorical questions.

WRITING SKILL Use rhetorical questions

When you ask *rhetorical* questions, you don't expect or need an answer. Ask rhetorical questions in your writing to make the reader feel engaged with your topic.

3 PLAN YOUR WRITING

A Who is a hero to you? Choose someone from your own life, or choose a fictional or historical person. What personality traits make that person a hero? Create a chart like the one in 1D.

B PAIRS Discuss your ideas.

I think heroes have to be generous, resourceful, and kind. For example,...

4 WRITE

Write a first draft of a definition essay about the personality traits that make someone a hero. Remember to use rhetorical questions. Use the essay in 1B as a model.

Writing tip

Don't worry if you stray from your original plan as you write. Often, the act of writing will make you think of new ideas or better examples. If this happens, stop and update your plan to make sure it will still make sense. Then keep writing.

5 AFTER YOUR FIRST DRAFT

A PEER REVIEW Read your partner's essay. Answer the questions.

- Does the essay stay on topic?
- Are three personality traits stated in the introductory paragraph?
- Do the body paragraphs give examples for each personality trait?
- Does the essay use rhetorical questions?
- Does the conclusion sum up the writer's ideas?

B REVISE Write another draft based on the feedback you got from your partner.

C PROOFREAD Check the spelling, grammar, and punctuation in your essay. Then read it through again for overall sense.

☐ I CAN WRITE A DEFINITION ESSAY.

PUT IT TOGETHER

1 PROBLEM SOLVING

A CONSIDER THE PROBLEM As long as people have been involved in high-stakes sports, some have cheated, causing young athletes to lose interest in the competition. Review the data and answer the questions.

1. Which years had the most cheating?
   Summer Olympics: ____________________
   Winter Olympics: ____________________
2. Athletes might cheat to win a gold medal because they can make a lot of money ___ ?
   a. becoming coaches
   b. endorsing products
   c. selling medals
3. What might explain years with no cases of Olympic athletes cheating?
   a. honest athletes
   b. stricter rules
   c. weaker testing

Athletes **BANNED** from the Olympics

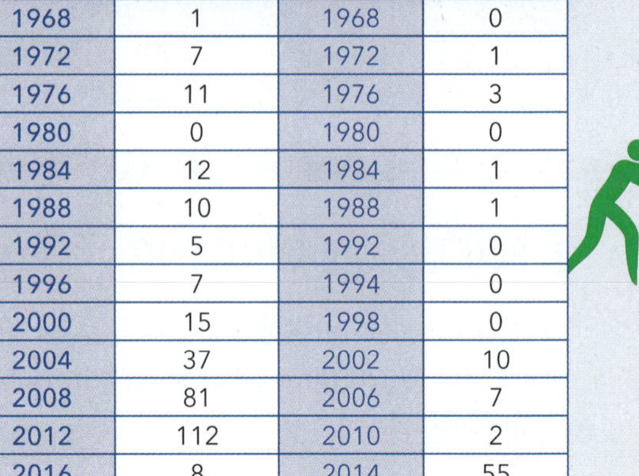

SUMMER GAMES		WINTER GAMES	
1968	1	1968	0
1972	7	1972	1
1976	11	1976	3
1980	0	1980	0
1984	12	1984	1
1988	10	1988	1
1992	5	1992	0
1996	7	1994	0
2000	15	1998	0
2004	37	2002	10
2008	81	2006	7
2012	112	2010	2
2016	8	2014	55

B THINK CRITICALLY Is cheating in sports increasing or decreasing? Discuss with a partner.

C FIND A SOLUTION Consider the data, the problem, and possible solutions in small groups.

Step 1 **Brainstorm** Think of 3–5 ideas to reduce cheating among athletes.

Step 2 **Evaluate** Choose the best solution. Consider costs and efficiency.

Step 3 **Present** Explain the best solution to the class. Refer to the data to support your ideas.

2 REFLECT AND PLAN

A Look back through the unit. Check (✓) the things you learned. Highlight the things you need to learn.

Speaking Objectives
- ☐ Talk about superpowers
- ☐ Talk about how to excel
- ☐ Discuss why we love superheroes

Vocabulary
- ☐ Superpowers

Conversation
- ☐ Accept an opinion before offering a conflicting one

Pronunciation
- ☐ Pausing and intonation in transitional phrases

Listening
- ☐ Listen for sequence

Note-taking
- ☐ Note examples clearly

Language Choices
- ☐ Present and future unreal conditional
- ☐ Future real conditional
- ☐ Present real conditional

Discussion
- ☐ Return a discussion back to the main point

Reading
- ☐ Use a KWL chart

Writing
- ☐ Use rhetorical questions

B What will you do to learn the things you highlighted?

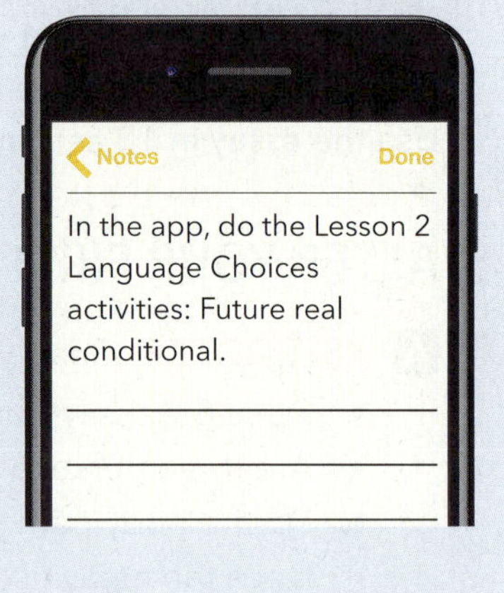

3 HOW'D YOU COME UP WITH THAT?

LEARNING GOALS

In this unit, you

- talk about what a genius is
- talk about fictional worlds
- talk about different senses
- read about creativity-boosting ideas
- write an opinion essay

GET STARTED

A Read the unit title and learning goals. People are inspired in different ways to come up with new ideas. What inspired an interesting idea you had?

B Look at the picture. What might be on the other side of this door?

C Read Kate's message. What does she mean when she says the novel "took me to another world"? Do books or movies sometimes take you to other worlds?

KATE SANDS

@KateS

I just finished a new novel that took me to another world. Who wants to read it next?

@KateS

Feels like a good time to listen to some really great music.

1 VOCABULARY Words related to accomplishments

A Look at the headlines. Would you go to one of these events?

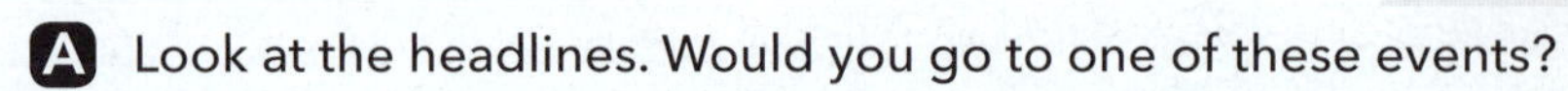

B ▶03-01 Read and listen. Notice the words in bold.

Culture

Review: 6-year-old **Prodigy** Gives Performance at the Pavilion

Mary Lin, whom critics are calling a **virtuoso**, was discovered in the *Star Child* **talent** search, a competition for artistically **gifted** children in... READ MORE

Lectures at City Hall

- **Renowned** local writer Amaya Salas, who is very **knowledgeable** about the history of this area, will talk... READ MORE
- Author Saul Abrams will discuss his **insightful** biography of Isaac Newton, *The* ***Genius*** *of Newton*.
- Sports historian Tina Murray will talk about soccer **legends** Pelé, Valderamma, Hamm... READ MORE

>> FOR PRACTICE, PAGE 131 / DEFINITIONS, PAGE 157

2 LANGUAGE CHOICES Verb + gerund vs. infinitive

A Read the example sentences. Then write the letter of the example that matches the definition in the chart.

Example sentences

1. a. We **forgot to go** to Sophie's piano concert.
   b. I **remember reading** about her concert in the news.
2. a. We **regret to inform** you all of our positions have been filled.
   b. I **regret not applying** for a position sooner.
3. a. Jackie **quit dancing** for the Houston Ballet.
   b. She **quit to return** to medical school.
4. a. I **tried to play** guitar, but I'm not a talented musician.
   b. Have you **tried taking** lessons?

Some verbs change the meaning of the sentence depending on whether they are followed by a gerund or an infinitive. Such verbs include *remember, forget, regret, stop, quit, try, go on,* and *mean*.

Verb + gerund vs. infinitive

- **remember / forget** = to indicate someone performed or didn't perform a task ______
  remember / forget = to recall or not recall an event in the past ______
- **regret** = to wish something hadn't happened in the past ______
  regret = to give bad news ______
- **stop / quit** = to end one activity in order to begin another ______
  stop / quit = to completely quit some activity ______
- **try** = to make an effort ______
  try = to experiment with a new or different approach ______

>> FOR PRACTICE, PAGE 131

B Why do you think the writer uses gerunds in this sentence? Is it possible to replace the gerunds with infinitives? How would that change the meaning of the sentence?

After he quit playing professional basketball, Michael Jordan tried playing baseball.

3 CONVERSATION SKILL

Defend arguments informally

You can use informal expressions like these to defend an argument:

Seriously... *Think about it...*
I'm not kidding... *You've got to admit...*

A ▶03-04 Read the conversation skill. Then listen. Notice the words the speakers use to defend an argument. Complete the sentences.

1. ______________ . He doesn't just have physical skill.
2. No, ______________ , she can name all the elements in the periodic table!
3. But ______________ she has a lot of talent.

B PAIRS Student A: Express an opinion about someone or something being great. Student B: Disagree. Student A: Defend your opinion with an expression from the conversation skill box.

4 CONVERSATION

A ▶03-05 Listen. What do Kate and Mateo talk about?

B ▶03-05 Listen again. Answer the questions.

1. What does Kate say about the Beatles?
2. What reasons does Mateo give for his opinion about the Beatles?
3. At the end of the conversation, what do they conclude about genius?

C ▶03-06 Listen. Complete the conversation.

Kate: He's the ______________ of our time!
Mateo: Really?
Kate: Well, one of them at least! ______________ , he's known as a virtuoso. He even won a Pulitzer Prize!
Mateo: Oh, yeah...I remember hearing something about that. I guess I always think of a "genius" as being someone whose work has, you know, stood the test of time. Like Mozart. Or maybe the Beatles.

5 TRY IT YOURSELF

A THINK Who do you think is (or was) a genius? Write the names of three people and take notes on what makes (or made) them geniuses.

Name	Why do you think this person is / was a genius?

B PAIRS Compare your lists and explain why you think each person is a genius. Defend your opinions. Decide with your partner which person on the list can best be described as a genius.

A: You think J. K. Rowling is a genius?
B: Think about it. She...

KATE SANDS
@KateS
Listened to a podcast about fantasy writers. It's amazing how they can create a whole world and bring us along for the ride.

1 BEFORE YOU LISTEN

A PAIRS THINK What makes a story a fantasy? Brainstorm a list of things you would expect to find in a fantasy story.

B ▶03-07 VOCABULARY Write the noun form of each word. Then listen to check.

to craft / a ______________
to map / a ______________
to approach / an ______________
to detail / a ______________
to focus on / a ______________
to comment / a ______________

>> FOR PRACTICE, PAGE 132 / DEFINITIONS, PAGE 157

2 LANGUAGE CHOICES Gerund usage

A Read the example sentences. Then read the rules in the chart. Are the rules true (*T*) or false (*F*)? Correct the false rules.

Use	Example sentences
Subject	**Creating** fantasy characters requires great imagination.
Object	She enjoys **reading** fantasy and science fiction novels.
Subject complement	One of his biggest accomplishments was **publishing** a fantasy novel.
Object complement	I had a hard time not **binge-watching** the entire series.
Object of a preposition	Tolkien became a legend by **crafting** an imaginary world.
With a possessive	Martin's **writing** is excellent.

Gerund usage

- A gerund can be used to make general statements. ______
- A gerund is a noun that is made by adding *-ing* to the base form of a verb. ______
- A gerund can be a subject or object. ______
- A gerund as a subject is plural. ______
- To make a gerund negative, add *not* after the gerund. ______

>> FOR PRACTICE, PAGE 132

B PAIRS Notice the use of the gerund in the first sentence. Complete the next two sentences with your own ideas. Then share them and discuss the different uses of the gerunds.

His careful **planning** has certainly paid off.
By **planning** carefully, ____ .
Planning carefully____ .

3 PRONUNCIATION

A ▶03-09 Listen. Read the pronunciation note.

B ▶03-10 Listen. Notice how *to* is pronounced. Then listen and repeat.

Pronouncing *to* in infinitives

The preposition *to* is usually unstressed and pronounced /tə/ in infinitives when the following verb begins with a consonant: *to stop* /təstɑp/. When the verb begins with a vowel, *to* can be pronounced /tu/ and links to the vowel with the sound /w/: *to*ʷ*answer* /tuwænsər/.

/tə/ + verb	/tu/ + ʷ + verb
to comment, to focus, to remember, to make music, ________, ________, ________, ________	to answer, to expect, to approach, to attract, ________, ________, ________, ________

C ▶03-11 Listen and repeat the verbs. Then write each verb under one of the columns in 3B.

4 LISTENING

LISTENING SKILL Listen for definitions signaled by pauses

Speakers sometimes define the terms they use. One way they do this is by giving a definition just after they use the term, pausing between the term and its definition. When you hear a specialized term, listen for the definition.

Rowling's characters play Quidditch (term), *[pause] a game that involves flying on broomsticks* (definition).

A ▶03-12 Listen. What is the topic of the podcast?

B ▶03-12 Read the Listening Skill. Listen again. Complete the definition for each term.

1. High Valyrian = one of the ________ spoken in his books
2. Hogwarts = the ________ of magic

C ▶03-12 Listen again. Take notes about the world that each writer created.

D PAIRS REACT Do you like movies or books about fantasy worlds? What do you like about them? What don't you like?

5 TRY IT YOURSELF

A THINK If you were going to create a fantasy world, what elements would you like it to have? Write a short description for each element in the chart.

The place	The character	An aspect of the culture

B GROUPS Share your charts. Choose one of the worlds and add more details to it.

C COMPARE Describe the fantasy world your group created to the class. Which world would you like to live in?

☐ I CAN TALK ABOUT FICTIONAL WORLDS.

KATE SANDS

@KateS

Just watched a talk about a neurological condition called synesthesia. I'm amazed others can experience the world so differently.

1 BEFORE YOU LISTEN

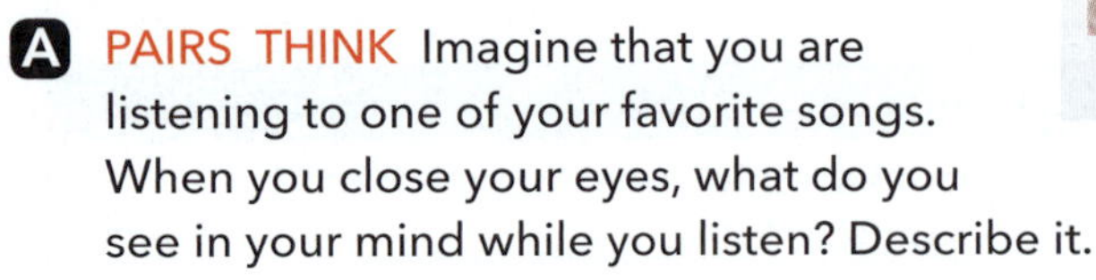

A PAIRS THINK Imagine that you are listening to one of your favorite songs. When you close your eyes, what do you see in your mind while you listen? Describe it.

B ▶03-13 VOCABULARY Complete the chart with the word families. Then listen and check your answers.

Verb	Noun	Adjective
imagine	imagination	*imaginative* or *imaginary*
	perception	
	detection	
	combination	
	vision	
	association	

>> FOR PRACTICE, PAGE 133 / DEFINITIONS, PAGE 157

2 LANGUAGE CHOICES Verb + object + infinitive

A Certain verbs are followed by an object and an infinitive. Read the example sentences. Circle the objects and underline the infinitives. Then circle the correct answer to complete the statements in the chart.

Example sentences

1. I **want you to listen** to this new song.
2. Marisa **invited us to go** to an art exhibit with her this weekend.
3. Please **remind your son not to touch** the artwork.
4. Synesthesia **causes people to perceive** things with several senses.
5. His music **allows him to express** his feelings.
6. Franz Liszt **expected his orchestra to associate** sounds and colors the same way he did.

Verb + object + infinitive

- Verb + object + infinitive shows the sequence of events. In other words, it shows how the action of the **subject / object** includes the **subject / object**.
- The main verb can be followed by a noun or a **subject / object** pronoun.
- The object performs the **first / second** action shown by the **main verb / infinitive**.
- The object goes **between / after** the main verb and infinitive.
- To form a negative statement, *not* is placed **before / after** the infinitive.

>> FOR PRACTICE, PAGE 133

B What is the difference between the following sentences?

He ordered his orchestra to play the song with more feeling.

His orchestra was ordered to play the song with more feeling.

3 VIDEO TALK

A ▶03-15 Listen or watch. What is synesthesia?

B ▶03-15 Read the Note-taking Skill. Listen or watch again. Take notes in the chart.

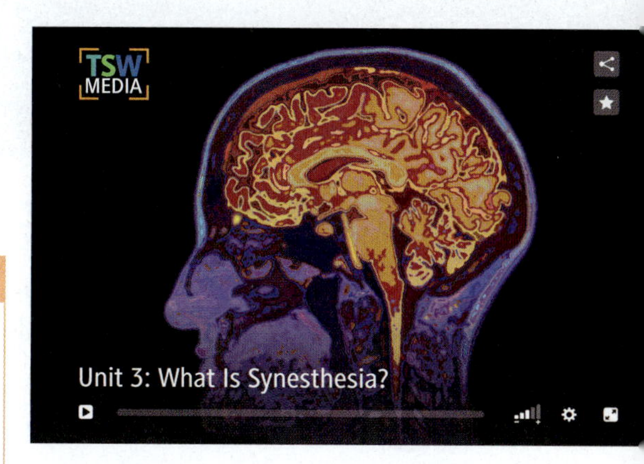

NOTE-TAKING SKILL Note unfamiliar names and words

Sometimes you will hear unfamiliar words and names in talks and lectures. Don't worry about spelling these correctly in your notes. Make your best guess or use abbreviations. You can add a question mark after the name or word as a reminder to yourself to look it up or ask about it afterward.

Artist	Profession	Type of synesthesia	Details
Liszt	composer	music / color	

C What does the speaker conclude about synesthesia?

D PAIRS REACT Which person do you think had the most interesting experience of synesthesia? Explain your choice.

4 DISCUSSION SKILL

Read the discussion skill. Which of these phrases do you use in your discussions now?

Summarize ideas to focus the conversation

After several ideas have been raised, remind the group of what has been said:

Three of us think that…

Maria and Tan both said…

So far none of us has…

5 TRY IT YOURSELF

A THINK If you could have synesthesia, which form would you choose? Would you like to hear music as colors, taste words, see letters or numbers as colors, or feel shapes and colors? What would be the advantages and disadvantages?

Type of synesthesia	Advantages	Disadvantages

B DISCUSS Compare your ideas in small groups. Identify which kind of synesthesia is most popular in the group. Talk about why you made the choices you did.

C EVALUATE Share your results with the class. Come to a consensus about which forms of synesthesia have the most advantages and disadvantages.

☐ I CAN TALK ABOUT DIFFERENT SENSES.

@KateS

Are you feeling uncreative? I found this discussion thread with some interesting ideas to get your creative juices flowing!

1 BEFORE YOU READ

A PAIRS Are you a creative person? What is it that makes some people more creative than others?

B ▶03-16 VOCABULARY Read and listen. Do you know these words?

writer's block	jump-start	amplify	a pose	on the threshold of
be purported to	clearheaded	inconsequential	a blindfold	doze

>> FOR DEFINITIONS, PAGE 158

2 READ

A PREVIEW Read the titles of the posts. What do you think the discussion thread is about?

B ▶03-17 Read and listen to the posts. Was your prediction correct?

Home | Discussion Board | Logout

Help! I'm out of ideas! Posted 5 hours ago

I'm taking a creative writing course and have a terrible case of writer's block. I read that novelist Brad Meltzer takes showers to boost his creativity. It's purported to work for a few reasons: the unconscious mind takes over and starts making lots of connections between ideas; the brain produces more dopamine, a chemical brain cells use to send 5 signals to each other; and the focus of the mind turns inward in the shower, allowing it to wander and, ideally, discover some great insights. So far, unfortunately, it hasn't helped. What other advice do famous people have for jump-starting creativity?

Novelist Brad Meltzer

Why not stand on your head? Posted 4 hours 21 minutes ago

That's what Igor Stravinsky, the famous composer, used to do. He said he felt rested and clearheaded afterward. As a yoga teacher, I can tell you that yoga boosts creativity in various ways. For example, the headstand pose causes the 10 brain to absorb more oxygen, which I think must amplify creativity. However, that's an advanced pose. Why not just try some yoga breathing? It increases the production of alpha brain waves, which are associated with creativity. Or you can give yoga meditation a try. It increases activity in the frontal lobe of the brain, which is also linked to creativity.

Try keeping a notebook. Posted 3 hours 14 minutes ago

Great ideas enter and leave our heads all day, but if we don't record them, some can be lost forever. Here's an idea I got from Richard Branson, the British entrepreneur: Keep a notebook with you wherever you go and write down all 15 your ideas as soon as you think of them, even ones that seem incomplete or inconsequential. So don't judge them! You can cross out the bad ones later. Just record them whenever and wherever they occur to you—even in the shower! Did you know they sell waterproof notebooks for that?

Dress for creativity! Posted 1 hour 9 minutes ago

What you wear matters. For example, psychologist Abraham Rutchick found that wearing formal clothes improved individuals' scores on tests of abstract thinking, which researchers believe enhances creative problem-solving. And 20 here's an unscientific idea: Some people find wearing different hats inspires different types of moods. Oh, and my favorite author, Jonathan Franzen, sometimes wears earplugs, earmuffs, and a blindfold while he writes to help him focus. Would that work for you?

>>

>

Creativity on the threshold of sleep Posted 12 minutes ago

The mind makes more connections between ideas when you're neither fully awake nor fully asleep (in the so-called hypnagogic state). The famous Spanish painter, Salvador Dali, used to spend his afternoons sitting in a
25 chair with a key between his thumb and finger over a plate. When he began to drift off, the key would drop onto the plate and wake him. Many of his paintings are inspired by ideas that came to him during these short naps. The inventor Thomas Edison also sought new ideas in the hypnagogic state. He would hold metal balls as he dozed in his armchair until they clattered onto the floor. Whichever method you use, be ready to write down your creative ideas when you open your eyes. Good luck!

C Read the Reading Skill. Then reread the discussion thread and follow these steps.

1. For each post, underline the main idea and draw an asterisk (*) beside each supporting idea.
2. Circle any words, phrases, or names you're unfamiliar with.
3. Write questions you have in the margin.
4. Compare and discuss your annotations with a classmate.

READING SKILL Annotate the text

You annotate a text by underlining, circling, and writing symbols and notes. This helps you engage more closely with the text, understand it in greater detail, and clarify aspects you're not sure about.

3 CHECK YOUR UNDERSTANDING

A Answer the questions according to the posts in the thread.

1. In what ways is showering purported to enhance creativity?
2. In what ways does yoga affect the brain?
3. Why does the third post recommend keeping a notebook all the time?
4. What are the effects of formal clothes, different hats, and earplugs?
5. What did Dali and Edison have in common?

B CLOSE READING Reread the lines. Then circle the correct answers.

1. In line 6, what does the word *ideally* imply?
   a. The wandering mind creates the perfect creative situation.
   b. This is the best reason of the three presented.
   c. It's possible great insights might not be discovered.
2. In lines 11–12, how is the second sentence connected to the first?
   a. It concedes that the pose may be difficult.
   b. It expresses encouragement to attempt the pose.
   c. It emphasizes that this pose amplifies creativity.

C PAIRS Summarize the discussion thread. Write one sentence for each post.

How creative are you? Search online for quizzes that claim to test creativity. Take one or two and see how you do!

4 MAKE IT PERSONAL

A THINK Which of the creativity-boosting methods you read about would be most effective for you? Why? What creative activity would you use it for? Take notes.

B GROUPS Present your method, reasons, and the activity you would use it for. Then discuss whether your classmates' ideas would work for you.

C EVALUATE In the same groups, decide together on your most practical ideas. Choose one person to present them to the class.

☐ I CAN READ ABOUT CREATIVITY-BOOSTING IDEAS.

1 BEFORE YOU WRITE

A Read about opinion essays.

In an opinion essay, the writer takes a position on a topic. In the introductory paragraph, the writer states the topic and a position for or against it. Then, in multiple body paragraphs, the writer provides detailed examples that support that opinion. Similar to a persuasive essay, in an opinion essay, the writer tries to convince the reader to agree with an opinion.

B Read the model. What is the writer's position on creativity?

The Creativity Gene: Truth or Myth?

Many people believe that creativity is an inherited quality. You are either born with a natural inclination towards creativity, or not. But anyone can be taught creativity, as long as they are willing to work at it.

Albert Einstein said, "Genius is 1% inspiration and 99% perspiration." Similarly, Malcolm Gladwell theorized that anyone who does something for 10,000 hours will become an expert. This "10,000-hour rule" might be oversimplified, but it makes an important point: If you put in enough quality practice, you can learn to do anything well. In turn, mastering a skill lets you experiment and improvise. My brother, a graphic designer, is one example. James has loved drawing ever since he was a child. He wasn't a child prodigy, but because he enjoyed drawing so much, he spent a lot of time doing it. He studied other people's drawings and gradually refined his skills. Today, many companies hire him to design their websites or product logos.

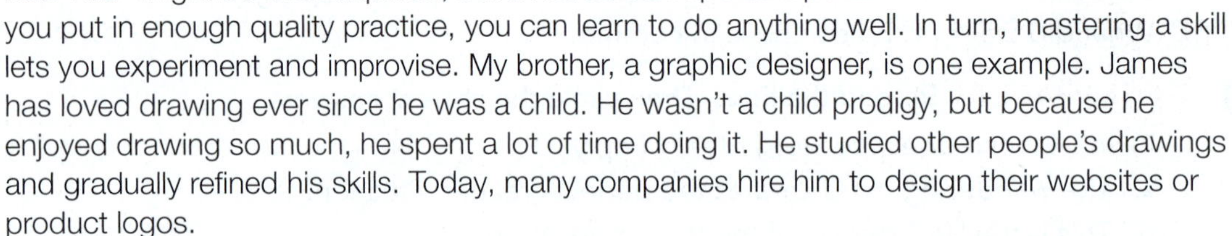

Businesses often invest in the idea that creativity can be taught. My company ran some so-called creativity workshops to help people start thinking outside the box. From one such workshop, I learned that 98% of children have a high level of creativity, but as they get older, this percentage drops. In other words, we are all born creative, but gradually we forget how to be creative. If we have all unlearned creativity, cannot we learn it again, with focus and training?

It is true that creativity often runs in families—especially "showbiz" families. Singer Enrique Iglesias is the son of Julio Iglesias, also a famous singer. Jaden and Willow Smith, who are both singers and actors, are the children of actors Will Smith and Jada Pinkett Smith. So, one might argue that there is a gene for creativity. But I believe there's another explanation. People whose parents are artists are more likely to consider the arts as a valid career choice for themselves. And also, they are more likely to be supported by their parents in pursuing such a career.

Many people may think that if you are not born creative, there is no point in trying to become creative. But I disagree. By approaching creativity as a skill that can be learned and by understanding that creativity is something useful in any job, we can really free ourselves to pursue more interesting, fulfilling, and yes, creative lives.

C PAIRS Did the writer convince you that creativity can be taught? Why or why not?

D Read the model again. Take notes in the chart.

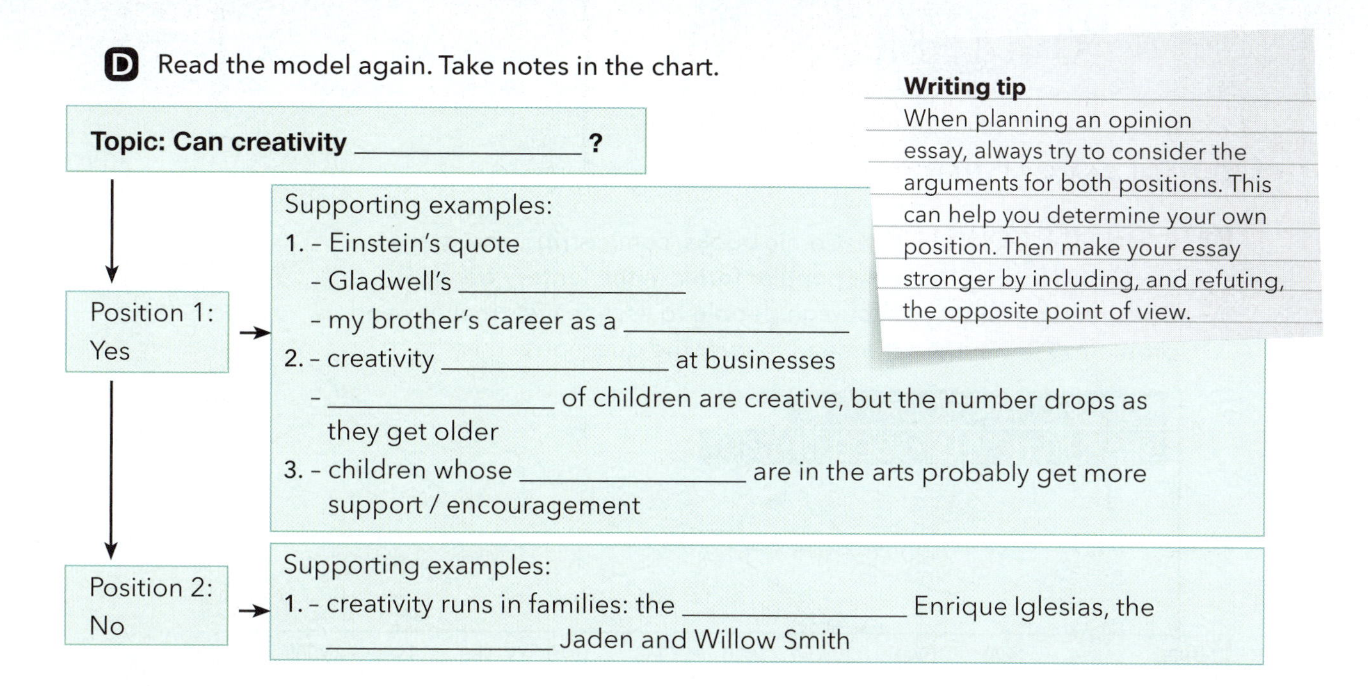

2 FOCUS ON WRITING

Read the Writing Skill. Then reread the opinion essay. Underline the supporting examples. Put an asterisk (*) next to the examples from outside sources.

WRITING SKILL Refer to outside sources

To make a strong case for your opinion, include not only personal examples, but use outside sources whenever possible. Referring to books, studies, and quotes from famous people are some ways to do this.

3 PLAN YOUR WRITING

A To work creatively, which is more important: having a daily routine, or being flexible and spontaneous? Create a chart like the one in 1D to organize your ideas.

B PAIRS Discuss your ideas.

I think routine is more important, because you need to work at something regularly before...

4 WRITE

Write a first draft of an opinion essay about whether routine or flexibility is more important to a creative life. Remember to cite outside sources when possible. Use the essay in 1B as a model.

5 AFTER YOUR FIRST DRAFT

A PEER REVIEW Read your partner's essay. Answer the questions.

- Does the essay state a clear opinion about the topic?
- Are sufficient supporting examples given?
- Do the supporting examples refer to outside sources? Can you add more?
- Does the essay include and refute an opposing argument?
- Does the conclusion say something bigger about the topic?

B REVISE Write another draft based on the feedback you got from your partner.

C PROOFREAD Check the spelling, grammar, and punctuation in your essay. Then read it through again for overall sense.

☐ I CAN WRITE AN OPINION ESSAY.

PUT IT TOGETHER

1 PROBLEM SOLVING

A **CONSIDER THE PROBLEM** Comic books, comic strips, and graphic novels are among the most popular forms in the fantasy genre. Does reading fantasy encourage people to escape life's realities and problems? Review the chart and answer the questions.

RISE OF COMIC BOOKS AND GRAPHIC NOVELS: GOOD OR BAD?

comic book
comic strip
graphic novel

1900 1910 1920 1930 1940 1950 1960 1970 1980 1990 2000

1. Why did comic strips peak in the 1940s? ______________________________
2. What happened to graphic novels after 2000? ______________________________
3. Why are comic strips dropping in popularity? ______________________________

B **THINK CRITICALLY** Are people overwhelmed by the problems of the real world? Could reading escapist literature lead to problems in society? Discuss with a partner.

C **FIND A SOLUTION** Consider the data, the problem, and possible solutions in small groups.

Step 1 **Brainstorm** Think of 3–5 arguments for or against people reading fantasy, such as comic books and graphic novels.

Step 2 **Evaluate** Choose the best ideas. Consider the political and economic impact of the world today.

Step 3 **Present** Explain the best argument to the class. Refer to the data to support your ideas.

2 REFLECT AND PLAN

A Look back through the unit. Check (✓) the things you learned. Highlight the things you need to learn.

Speaking Objectives
☐ Talk about what a genius is
☐ Talk about fictional worlds
☐ Talk about different senses

Vocabulary
☐ Words related to accomplishments

Conversation
☐ Defend arguments informally

Pronunciation
☐ Pronouncing *to* in infinitives

Listening
☐ Listen for definitions signaled by pauses

Note-taking
☐ Note unfamiliar names and words

Language Choices
☐ Verb + gerund vs. infinitive
☐ Gerund usage
☐ Verb + object + infinitive

Discussion
☐ Summarize ideas to focus the conversation

Reading
☐ Annotate the text

Writing
☐ Refer to outside sources

B What will you do to learn the things you highlighted?

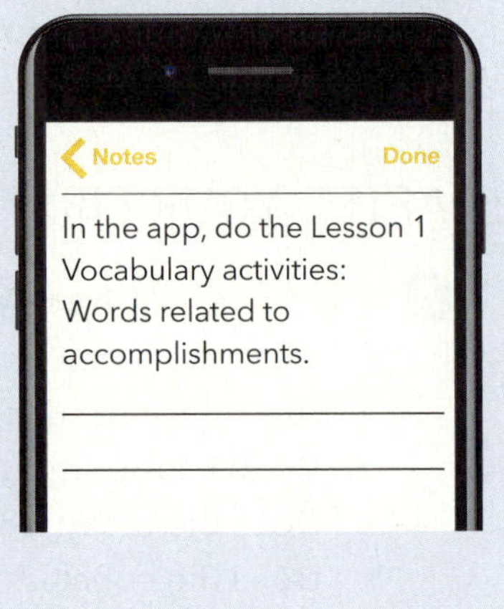

4 ARE YOU AN ANIMAL PERSON?

LEARNING GOALS

In this unit, you

- talk about animal videos
- discuss animal personalities
- discuss animal behavior
- read about animals that use language
- write a persuasive essay

GET STARTED

A Read the unit title and learning goals. What does it mean to be an animal person? Are you one? Why or why not?

B Look at the picture. The flamingos appear to be communicating, but are they talking? What's the difference?

C Read Hiro's message. How do people communicate with their animals? What are the most complicated ideas pets can express?

HIRO MATSUDA

@HiroM

My dogs have different barks, whines, and growls. I think each sound means something specific.

HIRO MATSUDA
@HiroM
Working from home today. Hope the puppy doesn't distract me!

1 VOCABULARY Words to describe unusual things

A Look at the pictures. Do you think the descriptions are accurate?

B ▶04-01 Read and listen.

exotic, unique, striking

cute, precious, adorable

weird, peculiar, bizarre, gross

magnificent, astonishing

>> FOR PRACTICE, PAGE 134 / DEFINITIONS, PAGE 158

2 LANGUAGE CHOICES Articles for general and specific nouns

A Nouns can be general or specific, depending on the context and how the speaker perceives them. Read the example sentences. Underline the nouns and circle the articles. Then complete the rules in the chart with the words *general* or *specific*.

Example sentences

1. **The lion** is **a magnificent animal**.
2. **A toucan** is **an exotic bird** with **a large, colorful bill**.
3. **Toucans** live in **the rainforest** in **South America**.
4. **Rainforests** are full of **unique animals**.
5. **A chameleon** can change **the color** of its skin.
6. Did you see **the cute new panda bear** at **the zoo**?
7. I watched **a video** of **elephants** eating **fruit** and playing in **the water**.

Articles for general and specific nouns

- A noun that refers to a particular member of a category is ______________ .
- A noun that refers to a category or to an undefined member of a category is ______________ .
- Use *the* with ______________ nouns that are singular, plural, or non-count.
- Use *a / an* or *the* with ______________ nouns that are singular.
- Use no article with ______________ nouns that are plural or non-count.

>> FOR PRACTICE, PAGE 134

B Underline the nouns in this sentence. For each noun, explain why the writer chose to use *the*, *a / an*, or no article. Is it possible to use different articles with these nouns?

A flying squirrel cannot fly like a bat or a bird, but it has the ability to glide between trees.

3 CONVERSATION SKILL

A ▶04-04 Read the conversation skill. Then listen. Notice how the speakers use circumlocution. Complete the sentences.

1. It's ____________________ and you move it with your body.
2. It's about the size ____________________ .
3. They weren't using ____________________ that people sit on when they ride a horse.

B PAIRS Student A: Think of an object or an animal. Use circumlocution to describe it. Student B: Guess the object or animal.

Use circumlocution when you don't know a word

When you aren't sure of a word for something, try to describe it. For example:
those things that...
it looks like a...
it's shaped like a...
it's about the size of a...

4 CONVERSATION

A ▶04-05 Listen. What do Hiro and Carla talk about?

B ▶04-05 Listen again. Answer the questions.

1. Which animals do Hiro and Carla discuss?
2. Which animal do Hiro and Carla feel differently about?
3. What happens in the video that Hiro describes?

C ▶04-06 Listen. Complete the conversation.

Carla: Puppies are so precious. I just saw this ________________ of one fetching a ball out of a pool without getting in the water.
Hiro: How did he manage that?
Carla: He jumps on a...on ________________ things that you float on...
Hiro: Like an inflatable mattress?
Carla: Yes, ________________ ! He stands on it, paddles over to the ball, grabs the ball in his mouth, and then paddles back to the edge.

5 TRY IT YOURSELF

A MAKE IT PERSONAL Think of an animal video you've seen. If you can't remember a real video, use your imagination. Take notes to prepare for describing it.

Type of animal	Words to describe it	What it does in the video

B GROUPS Tell your classmates about the video. Use circumlocution to describe things you don't know the words for. Come to a consensus about which video is the cutest, funniest, or most bizarre.

☐ I CAN TALK ABOUT ANIMAL VIDEOS.

HIRO MATSUDA

@HiroM

Listened to a podcast about dogs' personalities being like their owners'. My three dogs are pretty different. Not sure what the research would say about that!

1 BEFORE YOU LISTEN

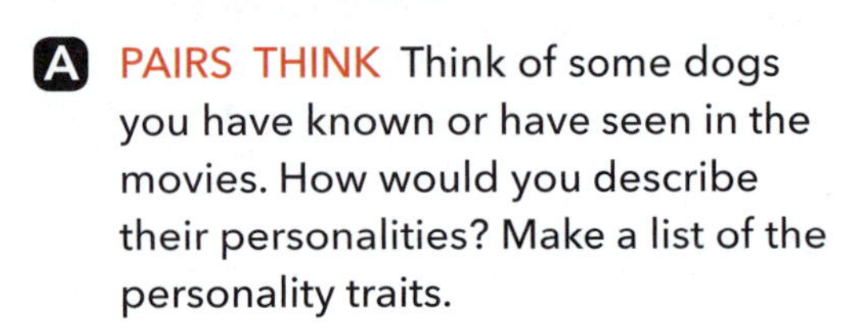

A PAIRS THINK Think of some dogs you have known or have seen in the movies. How would you describe their personalities? Make a list of the personality traits.

B ▶04-07 VOCABULARY Look at the words and listen to the sentences. Do you know these words?

conduct	extroverted	fearful	a lifespan
extensive	excitable	pessimistic	a shelter

>> FOR PRACTICE, PAGE 135 / DEFINITIONS, PAGE 158

2 LANGUAGE CHOICES Quantifiers with singular vs. plural verbs

A Read the example sentences. Circle the verb that goes with the quantifier. Is the verb singular or plural? In the chart, complete the rules by circling the correct answer.

Example sentences

1. **About 50 percent of** a dog's life is spent sleeping.
2. **At least half of** the researchers disagree with that information.
3. **Most of** the information has been proven false.
4. **A lot of** my friends have been adopting pets lately.
5. **Every one of / Each of / One of** her cats has a funny name.
6. **Both of** my dogs are house trained.
7. If **either of** the dogs barks loudly, separate them.
8. **None of / Neither of** my cats likes to go to the vet.

For *either*, *neither*, and *none*, a plural verb is commonly used in informal contexts:

If either of the dogs bark loudly, separate them.

None of / Neither of my cats like to go to the vet.

Quantifiers with singular vs. plural verbs

- Use a **quantifier / verb** to give information about the number or amount of something.
- With fractions, percentages, *most of, a lot of, some of*, and *all of*, the verb form is determined by the **noun / quantifier**.
- With *one of, each of*, and *every one of*, always use the **singular / plural** form of the noun and the **singular / plural** form of the verb.
- With *both of*, the form of the verb is **singular / plural**.
- With *either of, neither of*, and *none of*, use the **singular / plural** form of the verb in formal contexts.
- Use the **singular / plural** form of the verb with a quantifier + non-count noun.

>> FOR PRACTICE, PAGE 135

B Look at the verbs in this sentence. Are they singular or plural? What words determine subject-verb agreement? Notice the verbs after *a number of* and *the number of*.

A number of animal shelters **use** personality assessments to match prospective pet owners with the right cat or dog, and most of them **claim** that the number of successful matches **has** greatly **increased** as a result.

3 PRONUNCIATION

A ▶04-09 Listen. Read the pronunciation note.

B ▶04-10 Listen. Notice how the words in the underlined phrases blend together. Then listen and repeat.

Reductions in quantifier phrases

In quantifier phrases like *some of the animals* or *half of it*, the preposition *of* is unstressed and blends with the words around it. The quantifier before and the noun after *of* are usually stressed. *Of* is often reduced to /ə/ when the next word begins with a consonant sound: *neither of those* /niðərəðouz/. When the next word begins with a vowel sound, *of* is often pronounced /əv/: *half of it* /hæfəvɪt/.

1. Some of the animals in pet shelters have been abandoned by their owners.
2. Some animals are brought in by their owners, many of whom are moving.

C ▶04-11 Listen. Cross out the letter *f* in *of* when it's not pronounced.

some videos of my new dog
one of the cats
both of our cats
so many of the animals

4 LISTENING

A ▶04-12 Listen. What is the main idea of the podcast?

B ▶04-12 Read the Listening Skill. Listen again. Summarize the findings of Chopik and Weaver's research in the chart.

LISTENING SKILL Summarize

Immediately after listening, summarize the main ideas to help you remember information and gain a deeper understanding.

	Key findings	Details
1.		
2.		

C ▶04-12 Listen again. Note the details in the chart.

D PAIRS REACT Are you surprised by the results of the study? Why or why not?

5 TRY IT YOURSELF

A THINK Consider people you know (you can include yourself) who have had pets. Make a list of the pets. What was the pet's personality like?

Pet	Personality

B DISCUSS Did / Does the pet's personality resemble or not resemble that of its owner?

I have a friend who has a tarantula, a spider the size of your hand. In some ways, it resembles my friend because it spends most of its time being quiet and watching the world, and my friend is a quiet, observant person. On the other hand, the tarantula is very scary-looking and possibly dangerous, but my friend would never hurt anyone.

C ANALYZE In groups, brainstorm some things owners can do to have a positive or negative effects on a pet's personality. As a class, vote on three or four of the most important ideas.

☐ I CAN DISCUSS ANIMAL PERSONALITIES.

HIRO MATSUDA

@HiroM

You should watch this talk about amazing animal behaviors. They're so much more like us than people realize.

1 BEFORE YOU LISTEN

A PAIRS THINK Which wild animals are the most intelligent? What have you heard about them?

B ▶04-13 VOCABULARY Label the pictures with the words in the box. Then listen and check your answers.

grieve	mourn	howl	hold a grudge	dive-bomb	scold	be self-aware	feel guilty

>> FOR PRACTICE, PAGE 136 / DEFINITIONS, PAGE 158

2 LANGUAGE CHOICES Articles for known and unknown information

A Read the example sentences with articles for known and unknown information. Then complete the rules in the chart with *a / an, the,* or Ø (no article).

Example sentences

1. Could you please run to **the** store and pick up some food for **the** cat?
2. I hear dogs barking. It sounds like **the** dogs are really close to our house.
3. Harry recently got **a** pet snake. I think **the** snake is pretty creepy, but I really don't like snakes.
4. Slow down! Watch out for **the** deer.
5. Did you ever watch **the** animal show that I told you about?
6. **The** birds in that cage seem upset.

Articles for known and unknown information

- When it's clear that the speaker and the listener both know which specific person, place, or thing is being referred to, use ______ .
- When a singular noun is mentioned for the first time, use ______ .
- When a plural noun is mentioned for the first time, use ______ .
- When a noun has already been mentioned, use ______ .
- When the noun is made definite by an adjective clause or phrase that directly follows it, use ______ .

>> FOR PRACTICE, PAGE 136

B Which information in this sentence is known or unknown to the listener? How can you tell?

I looked out the window and watched the cat chase a squirrel around the tree.

3 VIDEO TALK

A ▶04-15 Read the Note-taking Skill. Listen or watch. What is the main idea of the talk? Write it in the chart.

NOTE-TAKING SKILL Identify a speaker's key examples

In talks and lectures, speakers often say a lot to engage or entertain you. You don't have to recreate their whole speech or descriptive scenes in your notes. Instead, first identify the main idea of the talk. (The title of the talk or lecture is often a good clue.) Then focus on capturing the key examples that support it.

Talk title: Animals Like Us

Main idea:

	Key examples	More details
1.	chimp greeting friend	
2.		
3.		
4.		

B ▶04-15 Listen or watch again. Add key examples and more details to the chart.

C What does the speaker conclude about animal behaviors?

D PAIRS REACT Which of the animal behaviors was most surprising to you? Why?

4 DISCUSSION SKILL

Read the discussion skill. Which of these phrases do you use in your discussions?

Tell an anecdote

An anecdote is a brief story that illustrates a point. You can begin an anecdote with phrases like these:

Did I ever tell you about the time I…?
I'll never forget the time I…
Here's a good one…
Believe me,…

5 TRY IT YOURSELF

A THINK What is an animal behavior that you have seen (in person or on video) that seemed humanlike. Take notes in the chart.

Type of animal	Description of behavior	Why it seemed humanlike

B DISCUSS Share your anecdotes in small groups. Do you think the animal and human behaviors just appear to be similar, or is there a deeper connection? Come to a consensus.

C SYNTHESIZE What conclusions can you draw about animal and human behavior? Share your ideas with the class.

☐ I CAN DISCUSS ANIMAL BEHAVIOR.

1 BEFORE YOU READ

A PAIRS What are some similarities and differences between the way animals and humans communicate?

B ▶04-16 VOCABULARY Read and listen. Do you know these words?

mimic	in the wild	deprived of	be suited to	nasal	ungrammatical
primitive	captivity	befriend	albeit	a cavity	intelligible

>> FOR DEFINITIONS, PAGE 159

2 READ

A PREVIEW Read the title and the interview questions only. What is the main topic?

B ▶04-17 Read and listen to the interview. Were your predictions correct?

Home I Technology I Work I Social Media

SCIENCE IN FOCUS: TALKING ANIMALS

Last weekend, I interviewed Jennifer Orsher, the curator of primates at the Stoneville Animal Conservation Center, about animals using human language. Here's what she had to say.

Dr. Francine Patterson and Koko

Q: Jennifer, why can some animals learn to mimic words while others can't?

A: Not many species have the capacity for vocal mimicry: among birds, only parrots, songbirds, and hummingbirds, and among mammals, only humans, bats, elephants, seals, and cetaceans—whales, dolphins, and the like.

Q: What makes these animals different?

A: Well, the biology of animals that are vocal mimics is different because the muscles that control their voices are directly connected to the forebrain. However, in most other animals, those voice-control muscles are connected to the brain stem, a more primitive part of the brain. Plus, all vocal mimics are social animals, and imitation is their way of interacting and bonding with one another in the wild.

Q: Why would animals want to mimic human speech?

A: In the wild, they rarely would, but most vocal mimicry goes on in captivity, where these normally social animals find themselves deprived of contact with others of their kind. It seems they befriend humans and mimic them as they would when joining a new group of animals of their own species.

Q: Do you know of any examples of the mammals you mentioned mimicking human language?

A: Not bats, but I've heard seals in aquariums use a few words. Talking elephants are quite rare as elephants' mouths aren't suited to mimicking human sounds. However, there is one named Koshik. He lives in Everland, South Korea's largest theme park. He inserts his trunk into his mouth to help make sounds resembling Korean words meaning *yes*, *no*, *sit*, *lie down*, and several others. Then there's Nack, a Beluga whale in Kamogawa Sea World, a marine park near Tokyo. He can imitate a few sounds and Japanese words, albeit not exactly, by over-inflating his nasal cavities.

Q: Do other primates have the ability to mimic or use language the way humans do?

A: Although their larynx (the organ in the throat that produces sound) is very similar to ours, they usually don't. Tilda, an orangutan at the Cologne Zoological Garden in Germany, surprised everyone by making humanlike sounds—but not words. Koko, a gorilla that was kept by researcher Francine Patterson in California, learned over 1,000 signs >>

>

in Gorilla Sign Language, a modified form of American Sign Language. Although she claimed that Koko used
30 signs to express herself much as humans do, Koko's signing was ungrammatical, and Dr. Patterson always had to interpret it.

Q: Do you think any animals will one day use language in a more intelligible way?

A: I'm not sure. It brings to mind a quotation from the philosopher Wittgenstein: "If a lion could talk, we wouldn't be able to understand it." He meant that we'd have too little in common to understand each other. So, perhaps it's primates that we would have the best chance of talking with since they are our closest animal relatives!

3 CHECK YOUR UNDERSTANDING

A Answer the questions according to the interview.

1. How does the biology of vocal mimics differ from that of most other animals?
2. Why did Koshik likely learn to say *sit* and *lie down*?
3. Why does Orsher doubt that Koko expressed thoughts like a human?
4. Why is Orsher unsure about animals ever using language more intelligibly?

B CLOSE READING Reread the lines. Then circle the correct answers.

1. In lines 9–12, how is the second sentence related to the first sentence?
   a. It provides a reason for direct connections.
   b. It explains a different type of connection.
   c. It describes the purpose of direct connections.
2. In line 16, what does the word *as* mean?
   a. because b. in the same way c. during the time

C Read the Reading Skill. Then reread the interview. Write the definition of each term.

1. cetaceans: ______________________
2. brain stem: ______________________
3. larynx: ______________________
4. Gorilla Sign Language: ______________________

READING SKILL Recognize definitions

After a new or difficult noun or noun phrase, look for a definition that clarifies the meaning of the term. It might be set off by a comma or dash or be in parentheses. Recognizing such definitions helps break some long sentences into easily understandable chunks.

D PAIRS Summarize the interview in six sentences. Write one sentence for each answer in the interview.

Visit Koko the gorilla's website and watch videos of her using Gorilla Sign Language. Does she use language meaningfully?

4 MAKE IT PERSONAL

A THINK How would it be useful for scientists to teach different species of vocal mimics to use human language and communicate with them? Think of as many benefits as you can. Take notes.

B GROUPS Discuss how they could be implemented and the advantages and disadvantages of having animals that are able to communicate with us.

C EVALUATE In the same groups, decide the biggest advantage and the biggest disadvantage. Choose one person to present your idea to the class.

☐ I CAN READ ABOUT ANIMALS THAT USE LANGUAGE.

HIRO MATSUDA

@HiroM

Why don't we treat animals better? 😠 Check out this piece I wrote for @AnimalLife...

1 BEFORE YOU WRITE

A Read about persuasive essays.

A persuasive essay is similar to an opinion essay in that the writer seeks to convince the reader to agree with the points that he or she is making. The language in a persuasive essay is usually stronger, as the writer takes a stand on a topic of importance. In the introductory paragraph, the writer states his or her position. Then, the writer provides reasons and examples to support that position and convince the reader to agree.

B Read the model. What does the writer want to be done about the use of wild animals in circuses?

Life in the circus is a terrible life for animals. It is hard to believe that in this day and age, we still accept animals being taken away from their natural environment and used for the sole purpose of entertainment. While some countries are taking steps in the right direction, far too many people still do not consider what a horrible way this is to treat animals. There is no question in my mind that the use of wild animals in circuses should be banned.

Most animals that are used in circuses are captured in the wild. They are taken away from their homes and families. Elephants in the wild live in herds, and numerous studies show that without their families, elephants often become depressed. Can you imagine being taken from your family and forced to travel and entertain others? Of course not; we would call this slavery. Animals also have emotions, and so humans have the responsibility to treat them fairly.

As part of the circus, the animals have to live in cages and travel all the time. Then they are forced to perform tricks that they would never do naturally. Perhaps people think that children can learn about animals by going to the circus, but what are they learning? That tigers will jump through a hoop if you make them? To get the animals to do these tricks, the trainers hit or poke them. The animals do the tricks out of fear, not because they want to do them. There is no reason in the world why people should be allowed to treat animals this way.

There are alternatives. Some circuses today do not use animals at all. The internationally famous Cirque du Soleil is a show with only people, performing acrobatic tricks of all kinds. It is much more astonishing to watch a show like this, seeing the amazing things that people are able to do; and it is also more enjoyable, knowing that every performer is there because they want to be. It would be a better world if all circuses were like this. Banning the use of wild animals in circuses is a no-brainer. In the meantime, it's up to all of us to make the right choices and not to support any show that uses wild animals for entertainment.

One circus has replaced real animals with holograms.

C PAIRS Has the writer convinced you that animals should not be used in circuses? Which argument in particular convinced you?

D Read the model again. Take notes in the chart.

Environment
animals taken from ___________
animals become ___________ without families

Treatment
animals forced to do ___________
trainers ___________ ___________ the animals

Position: The use of wild animals in circuses should be ___________.

Not educational
tricks aren't ___________
___________ don't learn about animals

Alternatives exist
some circuses have no animals
Example: ___________

2 FOCUS ON WRITING

Read the Writing Skill. Then reread the model. Underline language that you think is colloquial or emotional, rather than formal.

WRITING SKILL Use strong, emotional language

Although formal language makes a good impression, sometimes it is appropriate to use a more colloquial or conversational voice and appeal to your readers' emotions. In a persuasive essay, using emotional language can help readers relate to you and convince them that you mean what you say.

3 PLAN YOUR WRITING

A What animal rights issue is important to you? Choose an issue from the box or think of one yourself. Create a chart like the one in 1D to organize your ideas.

- abandoning or mistreating pets
- deforestation and/or development of land where many wild animals live
- factory farming
- hunting animals
- keeping animals in zoos
- testing products on animals
- wearing fur or leather

B PAIRS Discuss your ideas.

I'm going to write about factory farming. The animals on factory farms are...

4 WRITE

Write a first draft of a persuasive essay about an animal rights issue. Remember to use strong, emotional language. Use the essay in 1B as a model.

Writing tip
Start strong! Having a strong, declarative statement of position in your opening sentence will immediately draw readers in.

5 AFTER YOUR FIRST DRAFT

A PEER REVIEW Read your partner's essay. Answer the questions.

- Does the essay give a strong position on the topic?
- Does it start strong, with a clear leading sentence?
- Are sufficient supporting examples given?
- Does the essay use strong, emotional language?
- Is the essay persuasive to you? Do you have suggestions for improving it?

B REVISE Write another draft based on the feedback you got from your partner.

C PROOFREAD Check the spelling, grammar, and punctuation in your essay. Then read it through again for overall sense.

☐ I CAN WRITE A PERSUASIVE ESSAY.

PUT IT TOGETHER

1 PROBLEM SOLVING

A TYPICAL DISTRIBUTION OF INVASIVE SPECIES IN WESTERN CANADA

Animals: Invertebrates / Vertebrates

Animal	Type	%
Insects & Spiders	Invertebrates	50%
Molluscs	Invertebrates	33%
Freshwater Fish	Vertebrates	15%
Birds	Vertebrates	14%
Mammals	Vertebrates	12%
Amphibians & Reptiles	Vertebrates	4%

A CONSIDER THE PROBLEM Many invasive species threaten various ecosystems after being introduced by accident, such as when goods are shipped from one country or another, or deliberately, for example, when people adopt dangerous pets but later release them in the wild. Review the chart and circle the correct answers.

1. Insects and spiders are more likely to be an invasive species because they ______ .
   a. crawl great distances b. are shipped with goods c. can always fly
2. For fish to be considered invasive in lakes, they probably ______ .
   a. are dropped by birds b. arrive from oceans c. kill off other fish
3. Probably the easiest species to find and remove are ______ .
   a. spiders b. birds c. mammals

B THINK CRITICALLY Discuss why some creatures are more likely than others to become invasive species. Talk to a partner.

C FIND A SOLUTION Consider the data, the problem, and possible solutions in small groups.

Step 1 **Brainstorm** Think of 3–5 ideas to help avoid the spread of non-native species that can destroy fragile ecosystems.

Step 2 **Evaluate** Choose the best solution.

Step 3 **Present** Explain the best solution to the class. Refer to the data to support your ideas.

2 REFLECT AND PLAN

A Look back through the unit. Check (✓) the things you learned. Highlight the things you need to learn.

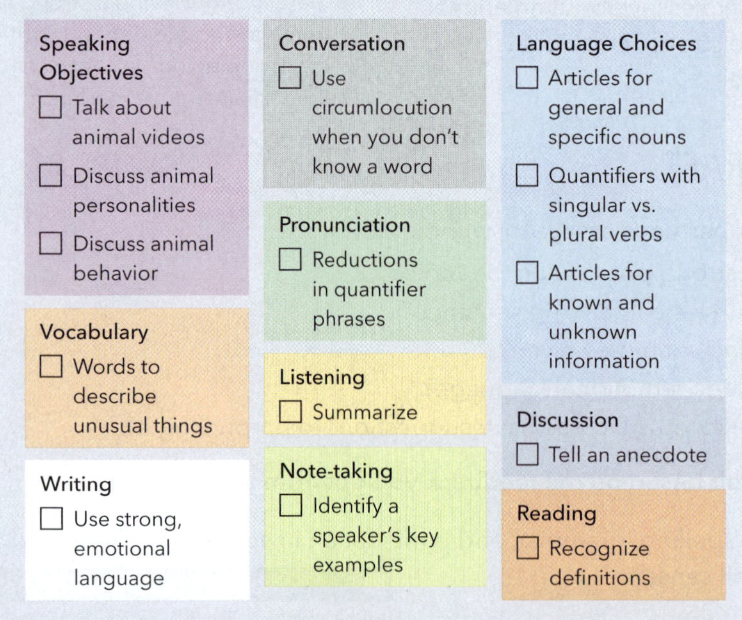

B What will you do to learn the things you highlighted?

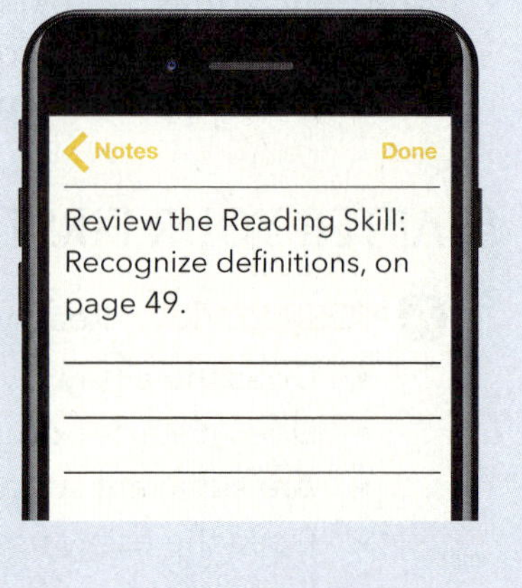

5 IS THIS GOING TO WORK?

LEARNING GOALS

In this unit, you

- talk about starting a small business
- talk about inventions
- talk about a success story
- read about alternative foods
- write an online review

GET STARTED

A Read the unit title and learning goals. Some people avoid innovation because there are more risks involved. Would you want to work at a job where innovation was required daily? Why or why not?

B Look at the picture. There's a concept that technology has the capacity to make each of us bigger, extending our abilities and influence. How does this image reflect that?

C Read Carla's message. How is technology helping people develop new businesses? Why might it be easier to start a business now than it was 100 years ago?

CARLA LUGO

@CarlaL

My friends started a new business. It's up and running already. Technology is making it easier than ever before.

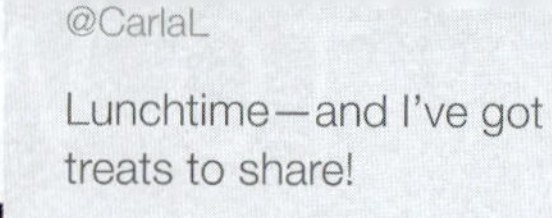

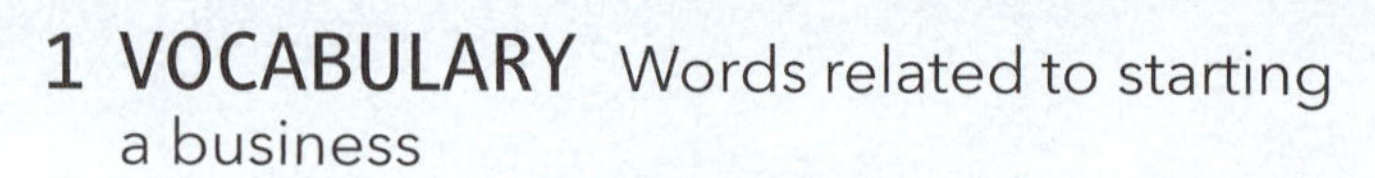

1 VOCABULARY Words related to starting a business

A Read the information about starting a business. Which points are generally good, or positive, for starting a business? Which are not?

B ▶05-01 Read and listen. Notice the words in bold.

>> FOR PRACTICE, PAGE 137 / DEFINITIONS, PAGE 159

2 LANGUAGE CHOICES Reported speech patterns

A Read the example sentences. Circle the reporting verb and underline the information that is being reported. Then write the example numbers next to the correct pattern in the chart.

Example sentences

1. John's friends **told him that** his business might flop.
2. They **talked about hiring** some more employees.
3. We **asked the office assistant to contact** the supplier about the missing invoice.
4. Our investors **said we need** to come up with some new ideas.
5. Mariko **decided not to create** a new expense report.
6. I **suggest not forming** a partnership at this time.
7. William **worried that his company might not break** even this year.
8. Dana **reassured us we'll be** in the black again soon.

Reported speech patterns

Reported speech pattern		Example sentences
subject + reporting verb	+ (*that*) + clause	
	+ direct object + (*that*) + clause	
	+ (*not*) infinitive	
	+ direct object + (*not*) infinitive	
	+ (*not*) gerund	

>> FOR PRACTICE, PAGE 137

B Does the meaning of this sentence change when you change the pattern?

Mika suggests tracking our cash flow with this new app.

3 CONVERSATION SKILL

A ▶05-04 Read the conversation skill. Then listen. Write the words the woman uses to show interest in the conversation.

1. ____________ 2. ____________ 3. ____________

B PAIRS Student A: Imagine that you are going to open a restaurant. Describe what it will be like. Student B: Show interest in your partner's ideas by using the words and sounds from the conversation skill box.

Show interest in a conversation

You can use words and sounds like these to show someone that you are listening to and interested in what they are saying.

Right.	*Really?*
For sure.	*Huh.*
OK.	*Uh-huh.*

4 CONVERSATION

A ▶05-05 Listen. What do Carla and Kate talk about?

B ▶05-05 Listen again. Answer the questions.

1. How did Carla's friend get started in the food-truck business?
2. What challenges did she encounter?
3. Why do you think Kate says, "I'll be happier to eat this knowing that they didn't cut corners"?

C ▶05-06 Listen. Complete the conversation.

Kate: This is delicious! Your friend knows what she's doing!

Carla: Yep, she sure does. For a while she doubted ____________, but I knew she'd do well once people tasted her food.

Kate: ____________!

Carla: Actually, the truck is so profitable now that they're thinking about buying a second one.

5 TRY IT YOURSELF

A THINK Imagine that you are going to form a partnership and open a new business together. What kind of business will it be? Write some ideas for your business plan.

Type of business	Supplies / Equipment	Type / Number of employees	Location / Space

B GROUPS Share your business plan with another group. Make a list of the biggest challenges for each business.

A: For our restaurant to be successful, we'll need to lease a building in a central area, and that will be expensive.
B: Right.
A: We'll need to ask someone to lend us...

☐ I CAN TALK ABOUT STARTING A SMALL BUSINESS.

CARLA LUGO
@CarlaL
Sometimes a simple idea can make someone a ton of money. Wish I could think of something like that!

1 BEFORE YOU LISTEN

A PAIRS THINK Brainstorm 5-7 modern inventions. Which ones do you think are the most useful?

B ▶05-07 VOCABULARY Look at the words and listen to the sentences. Do you know these words?

a sketch	tinker	land	pitch	cite
scribble	go broke	an entrepreneur	publicity	

>> FOR PRACTICE, PAGE 138 / DEFINITIONS, PAGE 159

2 LANGUAGE CHOICES Changes in reported speech

A Read the example sentences with quoted speech and reported speech. Then circle the correct words to complete the rules in the chart.

Quoted speech	Reported speech
He said, "**I want** to land a job in Japan."	He said **that he wanted** to land a job in Japan.
She said, "**Running** a business **is** hard work."	She said that **running** a business **is** hard work.
They said, "**We're working** on something new."	They said **they were working** on something new.
She said, "**I tinkered** with the settings."	She said **she had tinkered** with the settings.
He said, "**My sister was sketching** ideas."	He said that **his sister had been sketching** ideas.
She asked, "**Have you gotten** any lucky breaks?"	She asked me **if / whether I had gotten** any lucky breaks.
They asked, "**Had you pitched** the idea before?"	They asked **if / whether we had pitched** the idea before.
He asked, "**Where will you** advertise?"	He asked us **where we would** advertise.
I asked her, "**How can you gain** publicity?"	I asked her **how she could gain** publicity.
He said, "**Be strong. Don't give up**."	He said **to be strong** and **not to give up**.

Changes in reported speech

- When reporting a situation from before the time of speaking, **change / don't change** the verb.
- When reporting a general truth, **change / don't change** the verb.
- Change verbs in the present form to **the past / modals** when reporting a situation from the past.
- *Can* becomes ***can't / could***, and *will* becomes ***would / were***.
- Change the word order in **statements / questions**.
- Introduce *Yes / No* questions with ***that / if* or *whether***, and information questions with ***that /* a question word**.
- Change imperatives to **gerunds / infinitives**.
- Change the pronoun *we* to ***they / us***, and the pronoun *I* to ***he* or *she / they* or *we***.

>> FOR PRACTICE, PAGE 138

B What changes need to be made to rewrite this sentence as reported speech?

Before I started my own business, my parents asked me, "What do you think you need to do before you can become a successful entrepreneur?"

3 PRONUNCIATION

A ▶05-09 Listen. Read the pronunciation note.

B ▶05-10 Listen. Notice how the bold words are stressed. Then listen and repeat.

A: Where's your **uncle**?

B: In the **kitchen.** He's tinkering with his new meatless **burger**.

A: A **veggie** burger? But there are already so **many**.

> **Sentence stress in conversations**
>
> The most important word in a sentence receives sentence stress. At the beginning of a conversation, sentence stress is often on the last content word of the sentence: a noun, verb, adjective, or adverb. Words representing new information often receive sentence stress.
>
> *In the last podcast, we talked about a new* ***medical*** *device.*
>
> *The inventor sold it for almost a* ***billion*** *dollars.*

C ▶05-11 Listen. Circle the words that have sentence stress.

1. My uncle is going to the stadium next week. There's a convention for inventors.
2. He's taking his veggie burgers. Someone might want to invest in them.

4 LISTENING

> **LISTENING SKILL Selective attention**
>
> Listening for a particular piece of information can help you focus on and understand the information you are looking for.

A ▶05-12 Listen. What is the topic of the podcast?

B ▶05-13 Read the Listening Skill. Read the questions below. Focus on answering the questions as you listen to the introduction of the podcast again.

1. What is a Ring doorbell? ____________________
2. Who is Ben Thompson? ____________________
3. Who is Jamie Siminoff? ____________________

C ▶05-12 Listen again. Take notes about Siminoff's story.

How he got the idea:
First lucky break:
Company growth:
The end of the story:

D PAIRS REACT Do you think luck or hard work was more important to Siminoff's success? Explain your point of view.

5 TRY IT YOURSELF

A THINK You have invented a new product. Prepare to convince investors to back it.

Product name and function	What makes it special	Why it will be successful

B PAIRS Help your partner prepare to present his or her product by asking questions about it.

C EVALUATE In groups, present your products. When not presenting, evaluate your classmates' products. Consider how expensive the product would be to make and how easy it would be to sell. Decide which products you will fund and explain your reasoning.

☐ I CAN TALK ABOUT INVENTIONS.

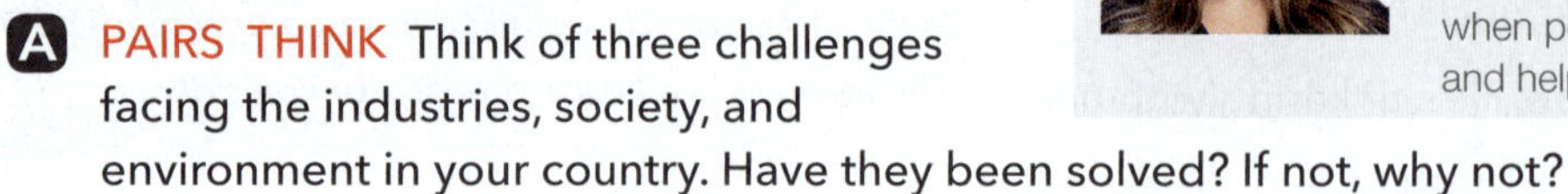

1 BEFORE YOU LISTEN

A PAIRS THINK Think of three challenges facing the industries, society, and environment in your country. Have they been solved? If not, why not?

B ▶05-14 VOCABULARY Match the adjectives with the nouns. Then listen and check your answers.

1. a diesel	a. project	5. kinetic	e. background
2. a hydroelectric	b. generator	6. noxious	f. country
3. an underrepresented	c. dam	7. a developing	g. fumes
4. an infrastructure	d. community	8. a diverse	h. energy

>> FOR PRACTICE, PAGE 139 / DEFINITIONS, PAGE 160

2 LANGUAGE CHOICES Common reporting verbs

A Read the example sentences with common reporting verbs. Then match the group of verbs with the reported speech pattern in the chart. (Hint: Many verbs can take more than one pattern. The verbs in bold are used in only one pattern.)

Example sentences

1. She **maintains that** she wouldn't have been successful without her team.
2. We **recommend replacing** the old generator.
3. They **instructed us to continue** with the project.
4. I **assure you that** we'll finish the work by the end of the month.
5. He **claimed to have** a new solution to the problem.
6. We **agreed not to use** any machines that produce noxious fumes.

Common reporting verbs

Patterns	Common reporting verbs
verb + (*that*) + clause ______	a. admit (to), deny, insist on, mention, propose, recommend, report, suggest
verb + direct object + (*that*) + clause ______	b. advise, ask, beg, convince, **encourage**, **forbid**, **instruct**, **invite**, **order**, **persuade**, remind, tell, **urge**, warn
verb + infinitive ______	c. admit, agree, **announce**, answer, claim, complain, confirm, decide, deny, explain, insist, **maintain**, mention, promise, propose, reply, report, say, suggest
verb + direct object + infinitive ______	d. advise, **assure**, convince, **inform**, notify, persuade, promise, **reassure**, remind, tell, warn
verb + gerund ______	e. agree, ask, claim, decide, demand, offer, promise, propose, **refuse**, request, threaten

>> FOR PRACTICE, PAGE 139

B What other verbs can replace the reporting verb in this sentence without significantly changing the meaning? Is it necessary to change the sentence pattern?

She told us that she wanted to address bigger problems.

3 VIDEO TALK

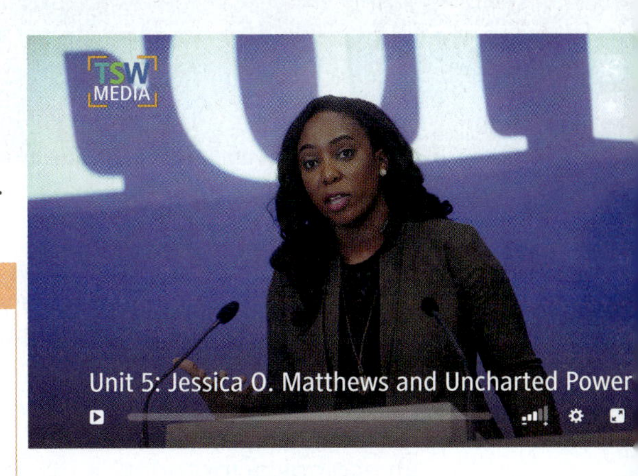

A ▶05-16 Listen or watch. Who is Jessica O. Matthews?

B ▶05-16 Read the Note-taking Skill. Listen or watch again. Write down key questions and take notes in the chart.

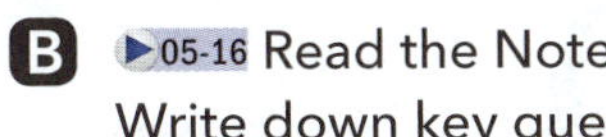

NOTE-TAKING SKILL Use Cornell Notes

Use Cornell Notes to help you remember information from a lecture.

- Take notes on the right side of the page.
- After you listen, write questions or key words on the left side of the page to help you focus on the important information.
- Write a short summary of the most important ideas at the bottom of the page.

Key questions	Notes
What is the Sockket?	
Summary:	

C What is Jessica O. Matthews's motto? What do you think it means?

D PAIRS REACT Why do you think Matthews has received so much recognition for her work?

4 DISCUSSION SKILL

Read the discussion skill. Which of these phrases do you use in your discussions now?

Build on what others have said

Use phrases like these:

I'd also say…	*In fact,…*
It's also true that…	*Another…*

5 TRY IT YOURSELF

A THINK In what ways do Matthews's inventions and her company benefit others? Take notes in the chart.

How the products help others	
How the company helps others	

B DISCUSS In small groups, talk about your ideas. Use examples. Discuss the most important way that Matthews helps other people.

C CATEGORIZE Share the ideas from your group. As a class, make a list of short-term and long-term benefits that a company like Matthews's can have on a community.

☐ I CAN TALK ABOUT A SUCCESS STORY.

CARLA LUGO
@CarlaL
I've never been a picky eater, but I'm not sure if I'm ready for this!

1 BEFORE YOU READ

A PAIRS Are you now or have you ever considered becoming a vegetarian? Why or why not?

B 05-17 VOCABULARY Read and listen. Do you know these words?

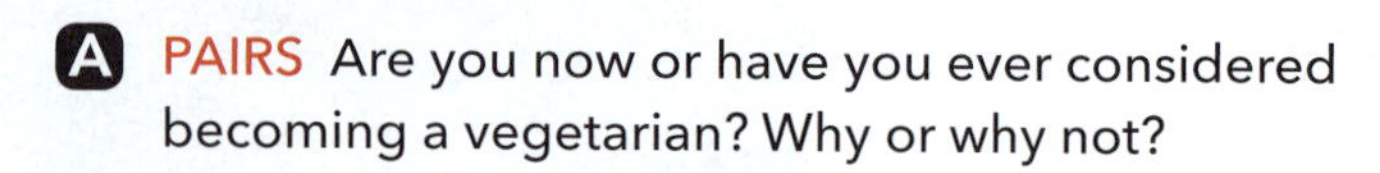

an ecological footprint	culinary	a biopsy	a serum	a hurdle
culture	a stem cell	incubate	proliferate	recoup

>> FOR DEFINITIONS, PAGE 160

2 READ

A PREVIEW Read the title, look at the picture, and read the caption. What do you think the blog post will be about?

B 05-18 Read and listen to the blog post. Was your prediction correct?

Blog | About | Food | Contact Logout

A Food Alternative

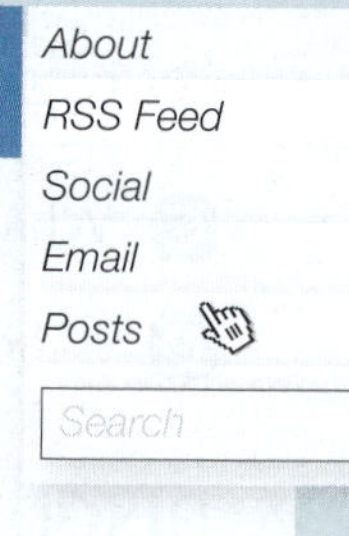

About
RSS Feed
Social
Email
Posts
Search

One of the latest developments in the food industry is "clean meat," which is essentially producing meat in a lab. I know meat grown in a laboratory may not appeal to everyone, but I find the idea fascinating and have been studying developments in the "clean meat" industry very closely. It promises, in the near future, to supply meat that's raised with a much smaller ecological footprint, 5 though it isn't without controversy.

The idea of clean meat—also known as *cultured meat*, *lab-grown meat*, *in-vitro meat*, *cell-based meat*, or *alt-meat*—is not new. In fact, the growing of animal parts in laboratories was predicted by Winston Churchill as early as 1930. However, it wasn't until 1999 that the first patent for a meat-culturing process was granted. In the 2000s, millions of research dollars began to flow into projects aimed at creating meat, fish, and even leather by 10 culturing animal cells. Recently, start-ups have appeared that are creating prototype clean meat products, and they're betting that this new type of meat has a bright future.

One such company, Just, Inc. of San Francisco, has begun to allow culinary reporters to taste their prototype chicken nuggets, which begin as stem cells taken from a chicken by means of a humane biopsy. These stem cells are then transported to a lab and incubated in a 15 warm, nutrient-rich serum, where they continue to proliferate indefinitely. After about two weeks, the technicians at Just, Inc. harvest several kilograms of chicken muscle, fat, and connective tissue cells and combine them in the correct proportions to create the "ground chicken" from which they make their tasty—if slightly mushy—chicken nuggets.

Indeed, getting the texture right is one of the hurdles standing in the way of mass 20 acceptance of clean meat, but developers remain confident that perfect chicken breasts, beef steaks, and lamb chops are just a few years away. A thornier issue is production costs, which are not yet competitive with farm-raised meat. One solution is to produce high-priced food items such as bluefin tuna and wagyu beef to recoup research and development expenditures. Another is to avoid the high cost of the serum the cells grow in by switching to 25 one that is derived from plants. However, even if these challenges are overcome, the process still requires an enormous amount of energy, which may leave clean meat unable to compete with farm-raised alternatives.

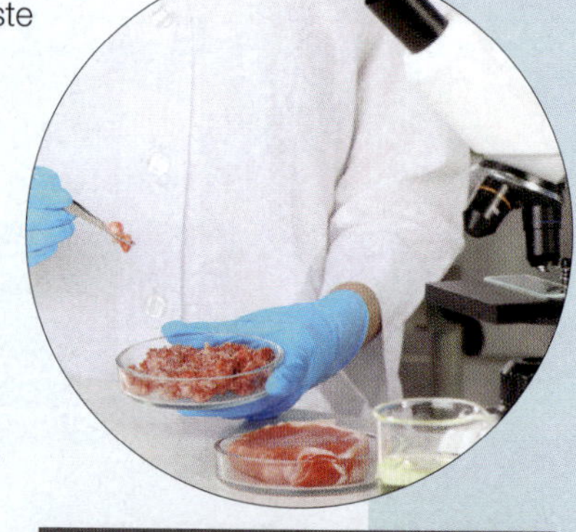

Clean meat, also known as *cultured meat*, *lab-grown meat*, *in-vitro meat*, *cell-based meat*, and *alt-meat*

> Although there are critics who say that clean meat offers no advantages over traditional meat in terms of its impact on the climate as well as vegetarians who say it encourages people to continue eating meat instead of 30 switching to a healthier vegetable diet, I'm still optimistic. Even though I became a vegetarian a few years ago, I can still appreciate the potential benefits of lab-produced meat for both people and animals.

3 CHECK YOUR UNDERSTANDING

A Answer the questions according to the article.

1. What key events in the history of clean meat research advanced its development?
2. How do chicken stem cells become "ground chicken" at Just, Inc.?
3. What obstacles stand between clean meat and mass acceptance?
4. What objections do critics have to clean meat?

B CLOSE READING Reread the lines. Then circle the correct answers.

1. In lines 6–8, how is the second sentence connected to the first?
   a. It differentiates between an older idea and the one in the first.
   b. It explains the origins of the terms presented in the first.
   c. It adds more detailed information about the point made in the first.
2. In lines 15–21, how is the second sentence connected to the first?
   a. It presents the results of the process described in the first.
   b. It highlights an issue presented in the first.
   c. It provides a reason for the issue described in the first.

C Read the Reading Skill. Choose a challenging excerpt of several lines to paraphrase. Then follow the steps below.

1. Reread the excerpt until you feel you fully understand it.
2. Close your book and imagine explaining the excerpt.
3. Write a paraphrase of the excerpt.
4. Exchange paraphrases with a partner and compare them with the original excerpts.
5. Does your partner's paraphrase accurately reflect the excerpt?
6. Is it written in your partner's own style and not just a rearrangement of the words in the original excerpt?

READING SKILL Paraphrase

Paraphrasing is restating information in your own words. The ability to paraphrase text confirms and demonstrates that you understand it. Paraphrasing also allows you to take and use information from a source while avoiding plagiarism.

D PAIRS Summarize the blog post in 3–5 sentences.

Learn more about vegetable-based meat, chicken, and fish substitutes.

4 MAKE IT PERSONAL

A THINK Imagine the government is planning to massively fund clean meat production and completely ban the raising of animals for food. Think of positive and negative aspects of the plan. Take notes.

B GROUPS Share your ideas and compile one list of the best points for the plan and another of the best points against it.

C EVALUATE In the same groups, decide together which list is the most convincing. Choose one person to present the list to the class.

☐ I CAN READ ABOUT ALTERNATIVE FOODS.

1 BEFORE YOU WRITE

CARLA LUGO

@CarlaL

Love my coffee but HATE when it gets cold before I finish it! Has anyone heard of an EverWarm mug? Reading some reviews now…

A Read about online reviews.

Everyone informally reviews things, explaining to friends and family the advantages and disadvantages of new products and services. Reviews can be more formal, such as on websites and online consumer magazines. When writing a review, it is helpful to categorize the different features of the product–for example design, performance, and usability.

B Read the online review. Does the reviewer recommend purchasing this item?

The EverWarm Mug: Is a hot cup of coffee worth it?

We've all been there: You make a hot cup of coffee, but ouch! It's too hot to drink. You put it down and go back to your work. When you pick it up again, it's cold. Now you have to decide: Do you drink it cold? Do you dump it out? Do you put it in the microwave, compromising the flavor? The EverWarm mug proposes to fix this age-old problem. By using an integrated heating element, it keeps your drink the exact temperature you want. But it does come at a price: It's far more expensive than a normal coffee cup.

How does it work?

Like everything these days, the EverWarm mug works with an app. After downloading the app, you use Bluetooth to connect your mug to the app. I found this process very straightforward and smooth.

The cup itself needs to be turned on and charged, using the charging coaster that comes with it. After charging and connecting, you use the app to set the temperature you want for your drink. The mug will turn on as soon as it senses liquid in the cup. It will keep your coffee at the set temperature, even if there's not much left inside. When the cup is empty, it turns itself off—a great feature.

But does it actually perform? I'm happy to say, yes. I tested my coffee with a thermometer, and it was exactly the temperature I had set. And it stayed warm until I was finished. Happy customer!

Design and specs

The EverWarm mug is a great-looking mug. It comes in a range of rainbow colors—choose your favorite. But it doesn't hold quite enough liquid. I would prefer a 280 ml mug instead of a measly 200 ml. Also, it's a little heavier than an ordinary mug. Still, the main issue I have with the design is that you have to wash the mug by hand. It would be great to see a dishwasher-safe model in the future.

Pricing

Here we go. Currently priced at $99.99, this is not a cheap mug. But, it's true that *you get what you pay for.* I really can't complain. The features are amazing, and for someone like me, totally worth it to get a hot cup of coffee, every single time.

Was this review helpful? 

No 2

C PAIRS Would you buy this mug? Why or why not?

D Read the model again. Take notes in the chart.

Benefits	Drawbacks
• process of ______ is straightforward	• doesn't hold enough ______
• cup maintains ______ even when ______	• ______ than an ordinary mug
• when empty, it ______	• you have to ______ it by hand
• great-looking and comes in ______	• at $99.99, the mug is ______

2 FOCUS ON WRITING

Read the Writing Skill. Then look at the sentences from the model. Under which subtitle does each sentence fit? Write *A*, *B*, or *C*. Check your answers against the model.

Subtitle A: How does it work?

Subtitle B: Design and Specs

Subtitle C: Pricing

___ 1. When the cup is empty, it turns itself off—a great feature.

___ 2. Also, it's a little heavier than an ordinary mug.

___ 3. After downloading the app, you use Bluetooth to connect your mug to the app.

___ 4. Currently priced at $99.99, this is not a cheap mug.

___ 5. It comes in a range of rainbow colors—choose your favorite.

WRITING SKILL Use titles and subtitles

A catchy title draws your readers in and helps inform them about what information they will learn. Using subtitles helps organize information and make it clear to readers. Besides reviews, long essays and reports also benefit from this kind of organization.

3 PLAN YOUR WRITING

A Choose an innovative product or service that you would like to review. You can choose a product from the box or think of another one. Create a chart of benefits and drawbacks. Use the chart in 1D as a model.

- a drone
- a personal assistant / smart speaker
- a robot vacuum
- a sleep tracker
- a reusable notebook
- a medical chatbot
- a hoverboard scooter
- a new transportation device

B PAIRS Discuss your ideas.

I'm going to write a review of a drone. I just got my first one and it's great!

4 WRITE

Write a first draft of an online review of an innovative product. Remember to use a title and subtitles. Use the review in 1B as a model.

5 AFTER YOUR FIRST DRAFT

A PEER REVIEW Read your partner's review. Answer the questions.

- Is there a catchy title?
- Are the features categorized and clearly marked with subtitles?
- Are the benefits and drawbacks of the product clear?
- Is there a conclusion that includes a recommendation on whether or not to buy the product?

Writing tip

Read your first draft out loud—to a partner, if possible. This will help you to be sure that what you have written is clear, at the right level of formality, and not missing any important information.

B REVISE Write another draft based on the feedback you got from your partner.

C PROOFREAD Check the spelling, grammar, and punctuation in your review. Then read it through again for overall sense.

☐ I CAN WRITE AN ONLINE REVIEW.

PUT IT TOGETHER

1 PROBLEM SOLVING

A CONSIDER THE PROBLEM
Sometimes it takes years for even the greatest business ideas to become successful, as defined by finding a market and turning a profit. Review the chart and circle the correct answers.

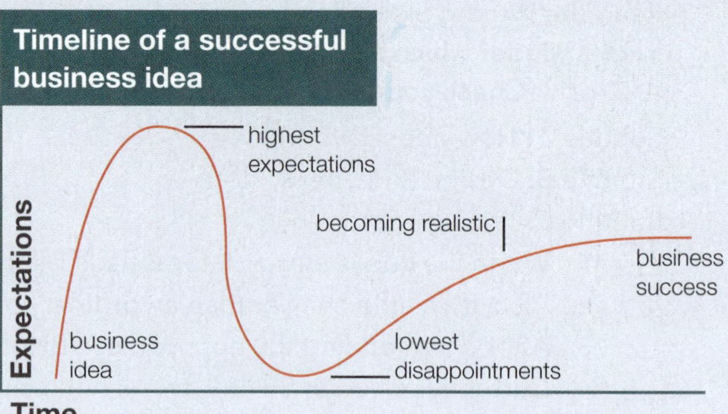

1. It's probably important to have high expectations when you have a new business idea because it's when you ______ .
   a. see the most potential b. are unemployed c. need investors
2. It's normal to have high expectations when starting a business because you ______ .
   a. have less energy b. see few challenges c. have had no failures
3. A businessperson who does not become realistic probably won't ______ .
   a. be disappointed b. have a successful business c. change jobs

B THINK CRITICALLY **What are some of the challenges of starting a new business? Do you think most businesses go through the same cycle? Discuss with a partner.**

C FIND A SOLUTION **Consider the data, the problem, and possible solutions in small groups.**

Step 1 **Brainstorm** Think of one or two things entrepreneurs could do at each stage in the timeline to help ensure that their business will be a success.

Step 2 **Evaluate** Decide which ideas would provide the most support for entrepreneurs and assurance of success.

Step 3 **Present** Explain the best idea to the class. Refer to the data to support it.

2 REFLECT AND PLAN

A **Look back through the unit. Check (✓) the things you learned. Highlight the things you need to learn.**

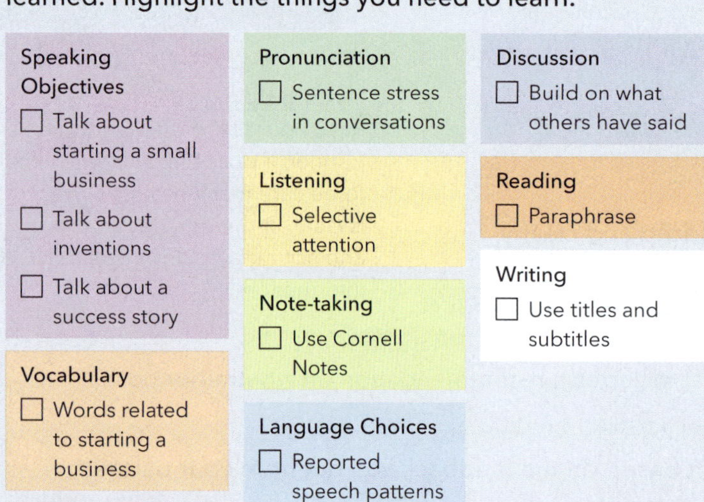

Speaking Objectives
- ☐ Talk about starting a small business
- ☐ Talk about inventions
- ☐ Talk about a success story

Vocabulary
- ☐ Words related to starting a business

Conversation
- ☐ Show interest in a conversation

Pronunciation
- ☐ Sentence stress in conversations

Listening
- ☐ Selective attention

Note-taking
- ☐ Use Cornell Notes

Language Choices
- ☐ Reported speech patterns
- ☐ Changes in reported speech
- ☐ Common reporting verbs

Discussion
- ☐ Build on what others have said

Reading
- ☐ Paraphrase

Writing
- ☐ Use titles and subtitles

B **What will you do to learn the things you highlighted?**

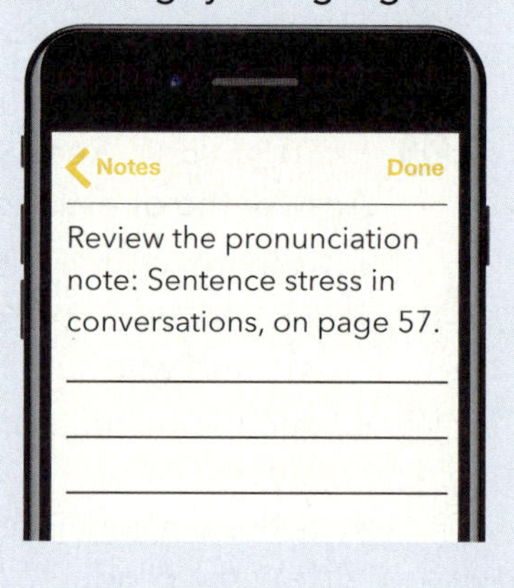

6 CAN I HAVE A RAISE?

LEARNING GOALS

In this unit, you
- talk about compensation
- talk about the gender pay gap
- discuss wealth inequality
- read about a job market trend
- write a compare and contrast essay

GET STARTED

A Read the unit title and learning goals. Getting paid fairly for work can be difficult to negotiate. What is the best way to assess someone's worth to do a job?

B Look at the picture. Why is a ladder often used as a symbol for progress in the workplace? In what way is this image a metaphor?

C Read Mateo's message. Should a company always improve salary and benefits if it adds responsibilities? Why or why not?

MATEO ROMERO

@MateoR

My friend's company cut staff and increased her responsibilities, but they're not offering her a better salary or benefits. Is that fair?

MATEO ROMERO
@MateoR
Bad news in my inbox today. 😔

1 VOCABULARY Words related to work and compensation

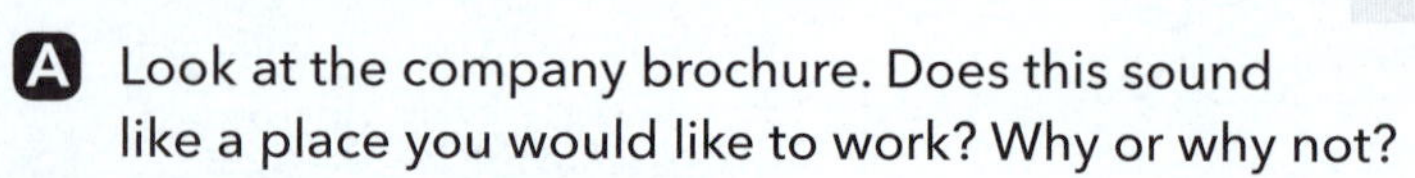

A Look at the company brochure. Does this sound like a place you would like to work? Why or why not?

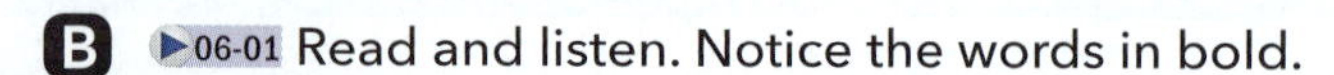

B ▶06-01 Read and listen. Notice the words in bold.

At QUEST, all of our **personnel** receive competitive wages and generous paid **time off**, as well as **incentives** such as **merit raises** and end-of-year **bonuses**. We also offer excellent **commission** rates for sales staff. **Perks** include a retirement package with a high employer **contribution**.

But QUEST employees aren't just happy on payday.

We offer **flextime** for many positions and the possibility to **transfer** to one of our hundreds of locations around the world. Our commitment to reasonable **workloads** and employee satisfaction means that we have one of the lowest **turnover** rates in the business.

Get your future started. Apply today!

>> FOR PRACTICE, PAGE 140 / DEFINITIONS, PAGE 160

2 LANGUAGE CHOICES Subject-verb agreement: Review and expand

A Read the example sentences. Complete the rules in the chart with *singular* or *plural*.

Example sentences

1. **Employee satisfaction has always been** our first priority.
2. **Our company offers** competitive wages and lots of perks. It's a great place to work.
3. **The educated have** more economic opportunities.
4. **Two weeks** of vacation a year **wasn't** enough for him, so he changed his job.
5. Are you sure you want to buy that phone? **A thousand dollars is** a lot of money.
6. **The United Nations is** an international organization.
7. **The good news is** that we're getting a raise next month.

Subject-verb agreement: Review and expand

- Collective nouns, like *staff*, usually take ______________ verbs.
- Proper nouns that end in *-s* take ______________ verbs.
- Non-count nouns always take ______________ verbs.
- *The news* always takes a ______________ verb.
- Units of time, distance, volume, and money take ______________ verbs.
- Collective adjectives, like *the rich and famous*, always take ______________ verbs.

>> FOR PRACTICE, PAGE 140

B PAIRS Discuss these questions. Pay attention to subject-verb agreement in your responses.

What are the responsibilities of a good company and good personnel?

What is a reasonable distance to commute to work?

3 CONVERSATION SKILL

A 06-04 Read the conversation skill. Then listen. Notice the expressions the speakers use to soften their opinions. Complete the sentences.

1. It's time to hire someone, ______________ .
2. It would save money in the long run, ______________________________ .
3. ______________ she'd be willing to listen to you.

Add comments to soften an opinion

You can add expressions like these to soften a statement of opinion, or make it sound less forceful or strong. These phrases can appear at the beginning or end of the statement:

I think *I assume*

Don't you think...? / ,...don't you think?

If you ask me,... / ..., if you ask me.

These phrases usually appear at the end of the statement:

..., at least that's what I think.

..., if I do say so myself.

B PAIRS Student A: Make a statement of opinion about your school, community, or job. Use one of the expressions from the conversation skill box to soften your opinion. Student B: Agree or disagree with your partner's statement.

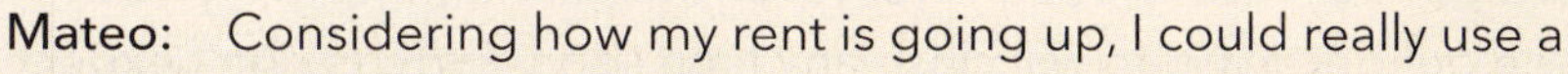

4 CONVERSATION

A 06-05 Listen. What do Mateo and Tae-ho talk about?

B 06-05 Listen again. Answer the questions.

1. Why isn't Mateo happy about merit raises?
2. What does Tae-ho plan to negotiate for?
3. Why does Tae-ho think Mateo doesn't have to worry?

C 06-06 Listen. Complete the conversation.

Mateo: Considering how my rent is going up, I could really use a raise right about now.

Tae-ho: I know! But they said they'll give more merit raises, and the majority of us qualify, ________________ ?

Mateo: I hope so.

Tae-ho: I mean, the staff here is pretty fantastic, ________________ .

5 TRY IT YOURSELF

A THINK If you were going to negotiate for perks, what are three things you might ask for? Why? Take notes in the chart.

Perk	Reason
1.	
2.	
3.	

B PAIRS Share your ideas. Choose the most valuable perk and explain your choice to the class.

A: Paid time off is the best job perk because it means you have more time to travel and do other things besides work. At least that's what I think.

B: I agree that's important, but what about...

☐ I CAN TALK ABOUT COMPENSATION.

1 BEFORE YOU LISTEN

A PAIRS THINK Brainstorm a list of jobs typically done by men and typically done by women. What are the education and training requirements for each job?

B ▶06-07 VOCABULARY Listen to the sentences. Do you know these words?

a gap	equivalent	bring to light
a factor	sanitation	hesitate
workforce	tend to	turn down

>> FOR PRACTICE, PAGE 141 / FOR DEFINITIONS, PAGE 161

2 LANGUAGE CHOICES Probability and certainty in the future

A Read the example sentences with the expressions of probability and certainty in the future. Use these expressions to complete the chart.

Example sentences

1. We're **likely to** get a pay increase this year. We get an increase almost every year.
2. It's **doubtful** that the gender pay gap will close any time soon. Experts don't **expect** it **to** close for another 200 years.
3. Adrienn is **on the verge of** quitting her job. She'll **probably** find a better position with another company.
4. Chiara applied for a promotion, but there's **not much chance** she'll get it.
5. Things are **bound to** change soon. They're **unlikely to** stay this way for a long time.
6. We're **certain to** have a meeting this afternoon. The company is **about to** make some big announcements.

Probability and certainty in the future

- To indicate an action is imminent, or going to happen very soon, use these expressions: _______________ , _______________
- To indicate certainty that something will happen at some point in the future, use: _______________ , _______________
- To indicate some degree of certainty, but not 100%, use: _______________ , _______________ , _______________
- To indicate something is probably *not* going to happen, use: _______________ , _______________ , _______________

>> FOR PRACTICE, PAGE 141

B Look at the sentences. How certain is the writer? How can you change the future expressions to show more certainty or less certainty?

Men at that company are certain to advance more quickly than women. It is highly unlikely that this trend will change in the near future.

3 PRONUNCIATION

A ▶06-09 Listen. Read the pronunciation note.

B ▶06-10 Listen. Notice the heavy stress and higher pitch on the words in bold. Then listen and repeat.

1. The **work**force is **well** paid, even in **entry**-level positions.
2. The **pay** gap between **support** staff and **department** supervisors is large.

> **Stress in compounds**
>
> Compounds are two words used together with a new meaning, for example: ***work****force* and ***safety*** *issues*. The first word has heavy stress and a higher pitch ♪. The second word has less stress and a lower pitch:
>
> ***safety*** *issues*
>
> Some adjective-noun expressions also have compound stress:
>
> ***black****board* ***elementary*** *school* ***well****-paid jobs*

C ▶06-11 Listen. Underline the compounds. Place a dot over the most heavily stressed syllable.

1. Many people join the workforce when they are in high school.
2. Requests for pay raises by women are often turned down.
3. High-paying jobs are more likely to be filled by well-educated applicants.

4 LISTENING

A ▶06-12 Listen. What is the main idea of the podcast?

B ▶06-12 Read the Listening Skill. Listen again. What does the speaker want his listeners to do?

> **LISTENING SKILL Infer goals**
>
> Sometimes speakers don't say directly that they expect a reaction from an audience. You need to infer it from what they do say.

C ▶06-12 Listen again. Take notes in the chart.

What is the gender pay gap?	
How long will it take to close it?	
Explanation for the gap	
Reasons the explanation isn't sufficient	1. 2. 3. 4. 5.
Conclusion	

D PAIRS REACT How does the speaker feel about the gender pay gap? Do you feel the same way? Why or why not?

5 TRY IT YOURSELF

A THINK How well do the ideas in the podcast relate to people you know? Take notes.

B GROUPS Share your information. As a group, decide whether the experience of women you know suggests that things are changing or staying the same.

C EVALUATE Present your conclusion to the class. As a class, make some predictions about what will happen with the gender pay gap in your area.

☐ I CAN TALK ABOUT THE GENDER PAY GAP.

MATEO ROMERO
@MateoR
This talk about wealth inequality has some pretty crazy statistics!

1 BEFORE YOU LISTEN

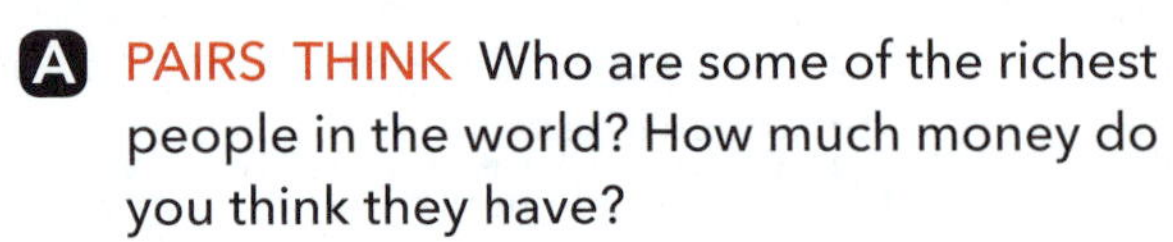
A PAIRS THINK Who are some of the richest people in the world? How much money do you think they have?

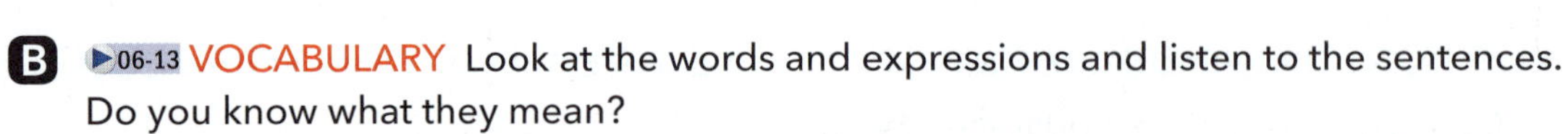
B 06-13 VOCABULARY Look at the words and expressions and listen to the sentences. Do you know what they mean?

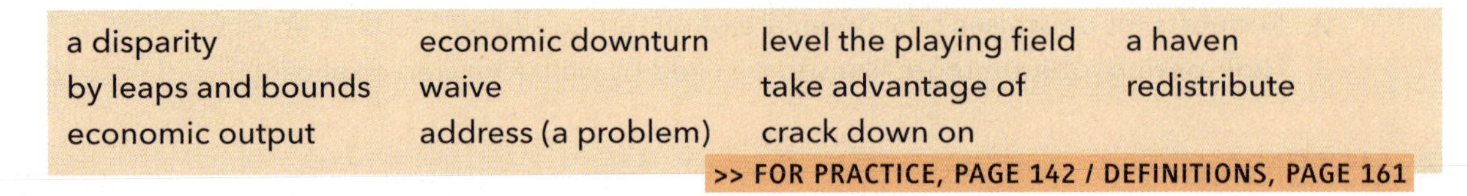

a disparity	economic downturn	level the playing field	a haven
by leaps and bounds	waive	take advantage of	redistribute
economic output	address (a problem)	crack down on	

>> FOR PRACTICE, PAGE 142 / DEFINITIONS, PAGE 161

2 LANGUAGE CHOICES Expressing future time

A There are many ways to express future time. Read the example sentences. Then match the explanations with the correct verb form in the chart.

Form	Example sentences
Simple future with *will*	The government **will** likely **waive** taxes on childcare expenses, but it **won't go** into effect until the end of the year.
Simple future with *be going to*	The new tax code **is going to level** the playing field.
Present continuous	We **are meeting** next week to discuss pay increases.
Simple present	The meeting **begins** at 9:00 tomorrow morning.
Future continuous	We**'ll be making** several changes in the upcoming weeks.
Future perfect	By next year, the new tax code **will have gone** into effect.

Expressing future time

- To state future actions or make predictions, use ______ .
- To talk about a scheduled event in the future, use ______ .
- To show that an action will happen before another action, use ______ .
- To show that an action will be in progress in the future, use ______ .
- To talk about future plans and fixed arrangements, usually made by more than one person, use ______ .

a. the simple future
b. the present continuous
c. the simple present
d. the future continuous
e. the future perfect

>> FOR PRACTICE, PAGE 142

B Underline the verbs. Name each tense and discuss what it expresses.

I leave for Shanghai next Friday. I'm attending another economics conference. It's the third conference I will have attended this year, but I think this one is going to be especially interesting. The keynote speaker will be discussing new research on wealth inequality.

3 VIDEO TALK

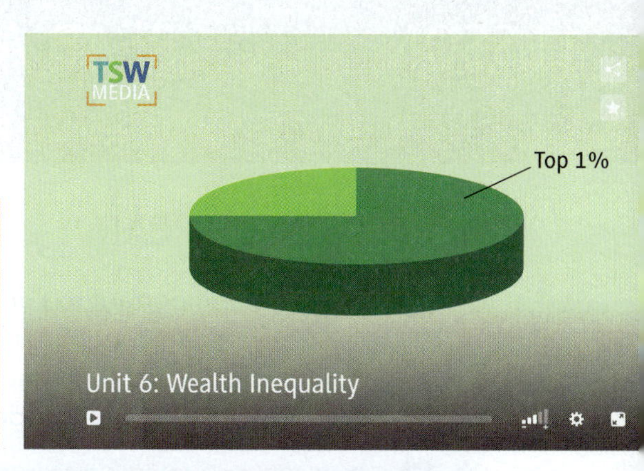

A Read the Note-taking Skill and the title of the talk. Complete the K and W columns of the chart.

NOTE-TAKING SKILL Use a KWL chart

You can use a KWL chart to help you focus on and retain information from a talk. Before you listen, complete the first two columns with what you know (K) and what you want to know (W). After you listen, take notes on what you learned (L) in the last column.

K	W	L

B ▶06-15 Listen or watch. Did the speaker include any of the information you knew or wanted to know?

C ▶06-15 Listen or watch again. Take notes in the L column of the chart.

D PAIRS REACT Were you surprised by any of the speaker's information? Why or why not?

4 DISCUSSION SKILL

Read the discussion skill. Which of these phrases do you use in your discussions now?

Acknowledge others' contributions

In a group discussion, acknowledge other people's contributions with phrases like these:

That's a good point.

That's an interesting idea.

I agree with what ______ said about…

I think ______ is making a good point.

5 TRY IT YOURSELF

A THINK Imagine you work for the government and your partner is a billionaire. Have a conversation about things you should or shouldn't do to help people in poverty. Write your ideas in the chart.

	Should	Shouldn't
Government		
Wealthy people		

B DISCUSS In small groups, talk about your ideas. Make a list of persuasive arguments about what governments and wealthy people should or shouldn't do to address wealth inequality.

C EVALUATE Share your most persuasive arguments with the class. Come to a consensus about the top three actions that should be taken or avoided.

☐ I CAN DISCUSS WEALTH INEQUALITY.

MATEO ROMERO
@MateoR
The working world is changing so fast! I need to keep up with employment trends—just in case!

1 BEFORE YOU READ

A PAIRS How important to you are rate of pay, physical working conditions, possibilities for advancement, a flexible schedule, and employee benefits? Rank them from 1 (most important) to 5 (least important).

B ▶06-16 VOCABULARY Read and listen. Do you know these words?

disciplined	an advocate	sidestep	streamlined	size up
the advent of	sweeping	the lion's share of	indispensable	a prerequisite

>> FOR DEFINITIONS, PAGE 161

2 READ

A PREVIEW Read the title, look at the picture, and read the caption. What do you think the article is about?

B ▶06-17 Read and listen to the article. Was your prediction correct?

PROS AND CONS OF THE GIG ECONOMY

WANTED: workers who can't stand a boss breathing down their necks or the stress of conforming to corporate culture. Must be comfortable with unsteady workloads and no benefits. If you're independent, disciplined, and desire a flexible schedule to create your ideal work-life balance and make room for your interests and passions, apply now!

Ridesharing is booming in the gig economy.

If this sounds good to you, you're not alone. Increasingly, people choose not to work as company employees and instead take on work one gig (temporary project) at a time as freelancers or temporary staff. Gig work is more accessible than ever thanks to the advent of online platforms such as Uber (which connects drivers with people who need rides), Upwork (which connects various types of freelancers with clients), and TaskRabbit (which connects workers with people who need everyday jobs done). According to Staffing Industry Analysts, Inc., this expanding global economic sector represents as many as 20 percent of workers and perhaps $3.7 trillion annually.

The gig economy also has some desirable aspects for companies. Providing employees with benefits such as guaranteed salaries, paid vacations, and health insurance is a large part of corporate budgets. A gig-work approach eliminates much of that burden. Moreover, only hiring workers with the skills needed to work on clearly defined tasks means no more wasteful employee downtime, possibly enhancing corporate productivity.

Nevertheless, workers' rights advocates are suspicious of these sweeping changes. To them, the gig economy is a gravely concerning trend that could endanger over 100 years of hard-earned worker protections. They suggest that many corporations wish to classify employees as independent contractors primarily to stop paying for their insurance, save on taxes, sidestep wage laws, and avoid dealing with workers' unions.

There is also reason for small businesses to be concerned. In the gig economy, not only are fewer people taking on full-time work with a company but also the limited number of top-performing freelancers are hugely in demand. In this situation, large corporations are better positioned to attract the lion's share of the available and talented candidates. Some companies even lose market share to streamlined gig-work platforms (for example, Uber's impact on local taxi companies),

>>

which larger enterprises can deal with more easily than smaller ones can. Additionally, in 50 the gig economy, it's often useful to assemble teams of freelancers living in different regions or countries; however, keeping a geographically dispersed team running smoothly can involve additional administrative staff, software tools, or 55 financial incentives. This is more difficult for smaller companies, which likely have tighter budgets.

For better or for worse, the gig economy appears to be here to stay. If there's gig work in your future, here are a few key skills you'll need to thrive. First, 60 critical thinking skills and logic are indispensable. With only yourself to rely on, the task of sizing up situations and asking the right questions is yours alone. Second, top gig workers need the skills sought by corporate human resource departments, 65 such as a positive attitude, communication skills, teamwork, and efficient work procedures. Third, since you'll be handling your own taxes, savings, and budgets, a good understanding of finance is a basic prerequisite. If you need brushing up in these 70 areas, it might be time to take some online courses so you can face the fierce competition of the gig economy with confidence.

C Read the Reading Skill. Then reread the article and underline the hedging expressions. Compare the expressions you underlined with a partner's.

READING SKILL Recognize hedging

Hedging expressions (for example, *seems*, *could*, *possibly*, *suggests*) signal the writer's caution about whether the information presented is factual or only an approximation, opinion, or claim. By recognizing hedging, you will avoid taking something as a confirmed fact when it is not.

3 CHECK YOUR UNDERSTANDING

A Answer the questions according to the article.

1. What trend does the phrase *gig economy* refer to?
2. In what two areas can firms benefit in the gig economy? How can they do so?
3. Why are workers' rights advocates worried about the shift to the gig economy?
4. What skill sets are necessary to thrive in the gig economy?

B CLOSE READING Reread the lines. Then circle the correct answers.

1. What does the sentence in lines 45–49 imply about Uber?
   a. It is losing market share to streamlined gig-work platforms.
   b. It is taking market share from local taxi companies.
   c. It is fighting to save market share for local taxi companies.
2. In lines 59–63, how is the second sentence connected to the first?
   a. points out an exception b. provides an explanation c. supplies a comparison

C PAIRS Summarize the article in 3–5 sentences.

Search online to find the gig-work platforms mentioned in the article. Determine whether you would be eligible to obtain work through them. 

4 MAKE IT PERSONAL

A THINK How does gig work compare to traditional employment in terms of pay, physical working conditions, benefits, career path, scheduling, and work-life balance? Take notes.

B GROUPS Discuss gig work versus traditional employment for young, middle-aged, older, married, and single people.

C EVALUATE In the same groups, decide together on the best and worst aspects of gig work. Choose one person to present your ideas to the class.

☐ I CAN READ ABOUT A JOB MARKET TREND.

MATEO ROMERO

@MateoR

Found this interesting article on what criteria to use in choosing a job. For those of us who sometimes wonder about what "might have been"...

1 BEFORE YOU WRITE

A Read about compare and contrast essays.

A compare and contrast essay looks at two different things or ideas and analyzes the similarities and / or differences between them. It seeks to draw readers' attention to the advantages and disadvantages of each side, allowing readers to determine which idea is preferable.

B Read the model. What two things is the writer comparing? What are some advantages of each side?

The Great Jobs Debate: Passion vs. Pay

When you are looking for a new job, or perhaps for your first job, there are a lot of questions to consider. How can you decide what will be the right career move? One of the biggest decisions you will need to make is whether to choose a job based on your passion, or whether to choose a job based on practical features such as salary. If you follow your passion, will you make enough money to live? If you choose a job for the salary, will you be happy? It's important to consider the ramifications of both options.

"Following your passion" means choosing a job based on your innermost desires. When you choose a job because it's something you love—teaching, for example, or playing a musical instrument—you can be pretty sure that the job will make you happy. You are less likely to lose interest in the work over time. On the other hand, there may be fewer jobs in your area of interest. The salary may be low, and the benefits may not be great. And, of course, for many people, even figuring out what they are passionate about can be a challenge!

Choosing a more practical job can solve some of these problems, but it can raise other problems. If you can find a job with a good, steady salary, you are likely to feel less stressed. And if you have a steady job, you might have time to pursue your hobbies or passions outside of work. But if you are not happy about going to work every day, you will not feel motivated to do a great job; and then you might get stuck, and not be able to move ahead in your career.

Perhaps the best solution is a happy medium. Don't feel pressured to choose a job based on your passion, but do choose a job that seems interesting to you. Don't choose a job based solely on the salary, but do choose a job that makes enough money to cover your expenses. In the end, if you put enough energy and effort into your work, it's possible that your work will become your passion. And then you have the best of both worlds.

Writing tip

It's OK if you don't know your conclusion when you start writing your first draft. Writing is a process of discovery. Writers often figure out how they feel about the topic only after they have written out the details in the body paragraphs.

C PAIRS Do you agree with the writer's conclusion? Why or why not?

D Read the model again. Take notes in the chart.

Choosing a job based on ____________	
Pros	*Cons*
- the job will make you happy - you will not ____________ over time	- fewer jobs - lower ____________ - fewer ____________ - not always easy to figure out what your passion is

Choosing a job based on ____________	
Pros	*Cons*
- better salary - less ____________ - time to pursue ____________ outside of your job	- less ____________ - you might get ____________

2 FOCUS ON WRITING

Read the Writing Skill. Then reread the model. Underline the examples of parallel structure.

WRITING SKILL Use parallel structure

Parallel structure in writing means repeating the same grammatical form within a sentence or across several related sentences. Using parallel structure to compare items or ideas throughout your essay makes the writing fluent, clear, and easy to read.

3 PLAN YOUR WRITING

A Imagine that you have to choose between two jobs. One job sounds like the perfect job, but you would have to move far away. The other job is not your perfect job, but you can stay in your hometown. Create a chart to compare and contrast the two options. Use the chart in 1D as a model.

B PAIRS Discuss your ideas.

A: I wouldn't want to move far away. I would choose a job closer to home.
B: I can see benefits to both sides...

4 WRITE

Write a first draft of a compare and contrast essay about choosing a job far away versus choosing a job closer to home. Remember to use parallel structure. Use the essay in 1B as a model.

5 AFTER YOUR FIRST DRAFT

A PEER REVIEW Read your partner's essay. Answer the questions.

- Does the essay clearly present the two sides being compared?
- Are the advantages and disadvantages of each side presented in the body paragraphs?
- Are there examples of parallel structure?
- Does the writer come to a clear conclusion?

B REVISE Write another draft based on the feedback you got from your partner.

C PROOFREAD Check the spelling, grammar, and punctuation in your essay. Then read it through again for overall sense.

☐ I CAN WRITE A COMPARE AND CONTRAST ESSAY.

PUT IT TOGETHER

1 PROBLEM SOLVING

Unemployment Percentages, Based on Education Level

	Unemployment rate (%)
Less than a high school diploma	5.6
High school diploma	4.1
Some college, no degree	3.7
Bachelor's degree	2.8
Master's degree	2.2
Professional degree	1.5
PhD degree	1.6

A CONSIDER THE PROBLEM Education can be difficult to obtain, time-consuming, and expensive, but it could lead to better employment opportunities. How can students know how far they should go in their education? Review the chart and circle the correct answers.

1. Someone with less than a high school diploma is **2** / **10** / **3.5** times as likely to be unemployed than someone with a PhD degree.
2. Having less education means that there may be more **cooperation in** / **competition for** / **confrontation about** a job.
3. Professional degrees may make someone more employable than a PhD because they prepare people for work that is more **practical** / **theoretical** / **interesting**.

B THINK CRITICALLY Is education always the most important factor for good employment opportunities? What other factors are important? Talk with a partner.

C FIND A SOLUTION Consider the data, the problem, and possible solutions in small groups.

Step 1 **Brainstorm** Think of 3–5 reasons for or against getting additional education.

Step 2 **Evaluate** Choose the best solution. Consider a variety of jobs and other factors for increasing employment opportunities.

Step 3 **Present** Explain the best solution to the class. Refer to the data to support your ideas.

2 REFLECT AND PLAN

A Look back through the unit. Check (✓) the things you learned. Highlight the things you need to learn.

Speaking Objectives
- ☐ Talk about compensation
- ☐ Talk about the gender pay gap
- ☐ Discuss wealth inequality

Vocabulary
- ☐ Words related to work and compensation

Conversation
- ☐ Add comments to soften an opinion

Pronunciation
- ☐ Stress in compounds

Listening
- ☐ Infer goals

Note-taking
- ☐ Use a KWL chart

Language Choices
- ☐ Subject-verb agreement: Review and expand
- ☐ Probability and certainty in the future
- ☐ Expressing future time

Discussion
- ☐ Acknowledge others' contributions

Reading
- ☐ Recognize hedging

Writing
- ☐ Use parallel structure

B What will you do to learn the things you highlighted?

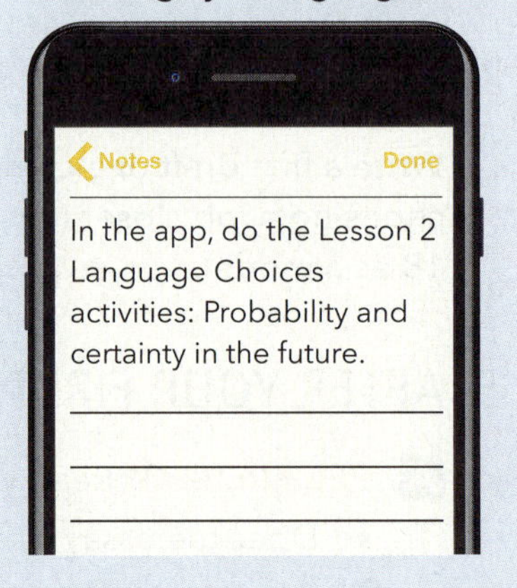

7 WHAT ARE YOU GOING TO DO ABOUT IT?

LEARNING GOALS

In this unit, you

- talk about making a difference
- talk about citizen journalism
- discuss the impact of social media
- read about environmental solutions
- write a petition

GET STARTED

A Read the unit title and learning goals. There are many social problems in the world, some of which you cannot solve. What social problem might you be able to solve?

B Look at the picture. Phones and the internet have led to citizen journalism. What kinds of events do citizen journalists report on?

C Read Esra's message. What skills do you have and what are three ways you could you use them to volunteer and help others?

ESRA KARA

@EsraK

Does anyone know where I could volunteer some of my time and skills in New York City? Any ideas?

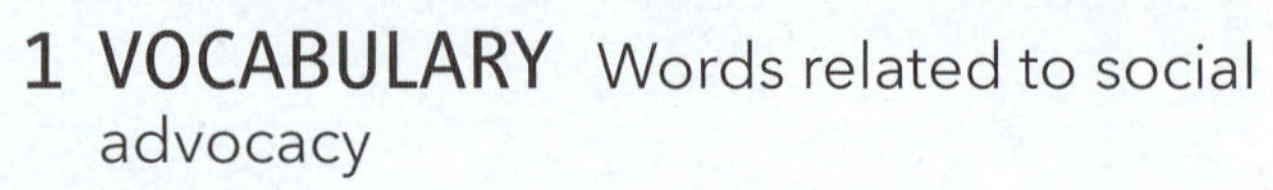

1 VOCABULARY Words related to social advocacy

@EsraK

My brother is always trying to save the world. Anyone want to donate? 🙂

A Look at the website. What kinds of issues do you think they raise money for?

B ▶07-01 Read and listen. Notice the words in bold.

http://www.ActionNowCampaigns.org/about

Search

At Action Now **Campaigns** we can help you **raise awareness** *and* funds for the **causes** you care about. Our team has ten years of experience in:

- social media **fundraisers** (We'll help you go viral!)
- engaging celebrity advocates (Check our past campaigns to see some familiar faces!)
- finding **sponsors** in the business community (Big businesses make big changes!)

"I used to be **cynical** about progress. I thought it was too late to get our community **back on track**. But Action Now helped me see that by working together, we can all **make a difference**."

Rebecca Solis, ANC partner

To volunteer for an existing campaign, or just to **kick in** some money, go to our donations page.

>> FOR PRACTICE, PAGE 143 / DEFINITIONS, PAGE 162

2 LANGUAGE CHOICES Passive voice: Form and use

A Read the example sentences. Then complete the rules by circling the correct answers. More than one answer may be correct.

Example sentences

1. The homeless shelter **is sponsored** by local businesses.
2. A fundraiser **is being held** to raise money for the hurricane victims.
3. Advocates for the charity **have been featured** in several media sources.
4. Contributions **can be made** on our website.
5. A lot of clothes **get donated** to the shelter.

The **agent** is the person or thing that performs the action stated by a verb. The agent is the subject in an active sentence.

Passive voice: Form and use

- Use the passive voice when the agent is **not known** / **obvious or unimportant** / **missing**.
- To form passive sentences, use a form of ***be*** / ***get*** / ***have*** and the past participle.
- In a passive sentence, the object of the active verb becomes the **agent** / **focus** / **subject** of the passive verb.
- Passive voice occurs **only in the past tense** / **in all tenses** / **only in simple verb tenses**.

>> FOR PRACTICE, PAGE 143

B Read the sentence. Why do you think the writer used the passive voice? Where would you expect to see or hear such a sentence? Can the sentence be changed to active voice?

When the study on homelessness was published, real commitment was brought to the issue.

3 CONVERSATION SKILL

Identify gaps between thought groups

A *thought group* is a set of several words that go together as a phrase or sentence. Avoid interrupting a speaker by listening for pauses that indicate the end of a thought group.

A ▶07-04 Read the conversation skill. Then listen. Does the second speaker listen for the gap between thought groups before interrupting? Circle *Yes* or *No*.

1. Yes / No
2. Yes / No
3. Yes / No
4. Yes / No
5. Yes / No

B PAIRS Student A: Talk about a cause that you think is important, for example, the environment, poverty, health, education, or the arts. Student B: Listen and respond with statements or questions. Be sure to wait for gaps between thought groups.

4 CONVERSATION

A ▶07-05 Listen. What do Esra and Hiro talk about?

B ▶07-05 Listen again. Answer the questions.

1. What does Esra think about the fundraiser?
2. Why does Hiro think the fundraiser is worthwhile?
3. What do you think the phrase "glass half full" means?
4. What does Hiro mean when he says, "Got to put my money where my mouth is"?

C ▶07-06 Listen. Complete the conversation.

Esra: You haven't heard about it? It's ______________ that was started by a group that fights homelessness. A bunch of people are walking a hundred kilometers on June 30th.

Hiro: Oh yeah.

Esra: You know, they get friends ______________ them per kilometer, and then they're all going to post photos along the way and all that.

Hiro: I think I did see something about that.

5 TRY IT YOURSELF

A THINK Make a list of charity challenges and other fundraisers that you have heard about and then describe them.

Type of charity or fundraiser	What do you know about it?

B DISCUSS Share the information from your chart. Talk about why fundraisers are successful or not successful. Remember to listen for pauses as your partners speak to avoid interrupting.

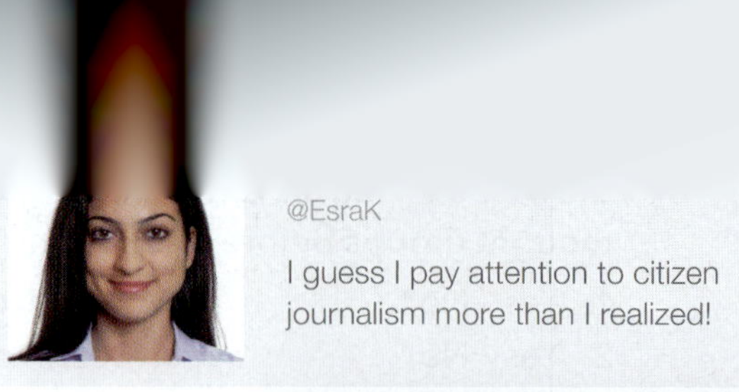

1 BEFORE YOU LISTEN

A PAIRS THINK Sometimes people find important news stories on their cell phones. Why might people prefer to watch news on their phones than on other devices?

B 07-07 VOCABULARY Look at the words and listen to the sentences. Talk to a partner about what these words mean.

feed	a bystander	consume	clickbait
breaking	break down	a fraud	biased
footage	accompany	agitate	a perspective

>> FOR PRACTICE, PAGE 144 / DEFINITIONS, PAGE 162

2 LANGUAGE CHOICES Passive voice: Reporting structures

A Read the example sentences and match them with the sentence patterns. Then circle the words to complete the rules in the chart.

Example sentences

1. It **was thought** that citizens would play a role in the production of professional news.
2. It **has been announced** the story is not true.
3. The story **is known** to be a rumor.
4. A bystander **is believed** to have captured a video on her phone.
5. The journalist **is expected** to be interviewing local residents at this time.
6. The footage **is said** to have been filmed on a tablet.
7. A rise in population **is presumed** to be accompanied by a rise in crime.

We can use passive reporting when we don't know if something is true or not.

Passive voice: Reporting structures

Pattern	Example sentence
• *It* + passive reporting verb (+ *that*) + clause	
• Subject + passive reporting verb + infinitive	
• Subject + passive reporting verb + *to be* + *-ing*	
• Subject + passive reporting verb + *to have* + past participle	

1. The reporting verb may be **past tense only / any verb tense**.
2. *To be* + *-ing* shows the reported action is **simultaneous with / previous to** the reporting.
3. *To have* + past participle shows the reported action is **simultaneous with / previous to** the reporting.

>> FOR PRACTICE, PAGE 144

B Look at the pairs of sentences. Which sentences sound more professional? Explain why passive voice is useful in reporting news stories.

They say that the doctor was a fraud.	Everybody knows those apps are full of clickbait.
It is said that the doctor was a fraud.	Those apps are known to be full of clickbait.

3 PRONUNCIATION

A ▶07-09 Listen. Read the pronunciation note.

B ▶07-10 Listen. Notice the pronunciation of *-ate* in the underlined words. Then listen and repeat.

Pronunciation of *-ate* endings

The *-ate* ending, as in *advocate* and *graduate*, is pronounced differently depending on whether the word is used as a verb, or as a noun or adjective. As a verb ending, *-ate* is pronounced /eit/: *to advocate* /ædvokeit/. As a noun or adjective ending, *-ate* is reduced to /ət/: *an advocate* /ædvokət/.

-ate is /eit/	*-ate* is /ət/
Citizen journalism fascinates me.	Climate change is an immediate problem.
She's going to graduate soon.	She's in graduate school.
They advocate for more objective news.	He's an advocate of digital newspapers.

C ▶07-11 Listen. Circle the words where *-ate* is pronounced /ət/.

1. Why do we read social media news when it is known to exaggerate or be inaccurate?
2. Can we depend on social media companies to regulate inappropriate content?
3. How can checking alternate sources of a news story help you evaluate its truth?

4 LISTENING

A ▶07-12 Listen. What is the topic of the podcast?

B ▶07-12 Read the Listening Skill. Listen again. The speaker uses tone of voice to indicate that one sentence isn't true. Check (✓) the sentence that the speaker doesn't believe.

LISTENING SKILL Tone of voice

Speakers sometimes use tone of voice to indicate that they don't think something is true or credible.

☐ 1. Thousands of bloggers and vloggers could be described as citizen journalists.
☐ 2. Research shows this fruit can cure cancer.
☐ 3. Citizen journalism is here to stay.

C ▶07-12 Listen again. Take notes in the chart.

What citizen journalists do:
Why people enjoy citizen journalism:
Criticism:
Conclusion:

D PAIRS REACT Do you agree with the speaker that "citizen journalism is here to stay"? Why or why not?

5 TRY IT YOURSELF

A THINK Consider a breaking news event, for example a giant storm or a fire. How might its coverage by a citizen journalist be different from that of a professional? Make notes.

B DEBATE In groups, choose an event and take sides for and against citizen journalism as a means of reporting on it. Decide which side has the strongest arguments.

C ANALYZE As a class, make a list of the most important advantages and disadvantages of citizen journalism. Support your ideas with any examples you know of from real life.

☐ I CAN TALK ABOUT CITIZEN JOURNALISM.

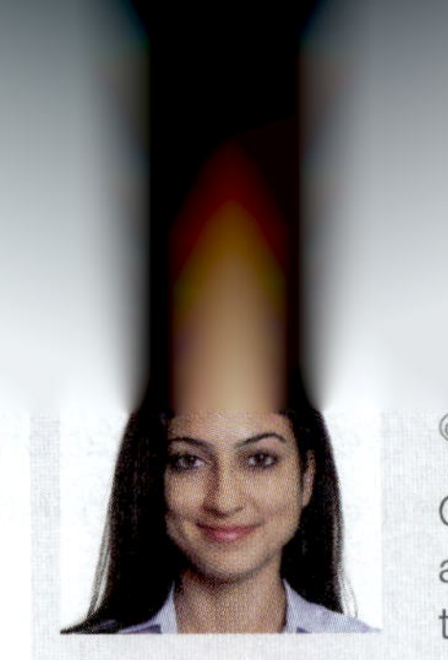

@EsraK

OK, I confess. I love funny animal pictures. If I see one that makes me laugh, I share it!

1 BEFORE YOU LISTEN

A PAIRS THINK What kinds of information spread rapidly on social media? Why?

B ▶07-13 VOCABULARY Look at the words and expressions and listen to the sentences. Do you know what they mean?

a fad	provoke	convey	spread like wildfire	at (the very) least
a phenomenon	empathy	self-expression	a positive force	

>> FOR PRACTICE, PAGE 145 / DEFINITIONS, PAGE 162

2 LANGUAGE CHOICES Passive infinitives and causatives

A Read the example sentences. Then read the rules in the chart. Are the statements true (*T*) or false (*F*)? Correct the false rules.

Example sentences: passive infinitives

1. The photo of the polar bear continues **to be** widely **used** in ad campaigns.
2. What message do you want **to be conveyed** in this ad?
3. We didn't expect the joke **to be shared** outside our office.
4. The politician was upset **to be featured** in the news story.
5. Emma is thrilled **to have been chosen** to present at the conference.
6. Many false stories appear **to have been started** on social media platforms.
7. Her profile seems **not to have been updated** for many years.

Example sentences: causatives

8. We recently **had** our website **updated** with a more modern look.
9. You need to **get** this story **fact-checked** by an expert.

Passive infinitives and causatives

- In passive infinitives and causatives, it is necessary to mention the agent. ______
- We use passive infinitives after adjectives or verbs that go with infinitives. ______
- An adverb can be placed between *to be* and the verb to describe the infinitive. ______
- We can make negative statements by using *not* with the main verb or by adding *not* before the infinitive. ______
- Use *to have been* + past participle to show that an action is happening now. ______
- Passive causatives with *get* or *have* express the idea that the speaker will ask someone else to perform the action. ______

>> FOR PRACTICE, PAGE 145

B What is the difference between these sentences?

This story needs to be reviewed. We need to have this story reviewed.

3 VIDEO TALK

A ▶07-15 Listen or watch. What is the speaker's main idea?

B ▶07-15 Read the Note-taking Skill. Listen or watch again. Take notes in the chart.

NOTE-TAKING SKILL Include key definitions and examples

When a speaker defines a key term, label the definition and any examples in your notes.

Key word:	**Definition:** **Examples:**
Why are memes powerful?	
1.	
2.	
3.	
4.	

C What is the speaker's point about the polar bear meme?

D PAIRS REACT Do you ever share memes like the ones mentioned in the video? Why or why not?

4 DISCUSSION SKILL

Read the discussion skill. Which of these phrases do you use in your discussions now?

Interrupt politely

When you want to interrupt someone, wait for the person to pause. Then use an expression like one of these:

Can I interrupt for a second?
Can I jump in here?
Can I just mention something?

5 TRY IT YOURSELF

A THINK Recall two or three memes you have seen or have heard about. How would you explain their meanings? What do you know about them (for example, how they got started, how long they've been around, or how they are used)?

Description of meme	What it means	Other information

B DISCUSS In small groups, talk about and, if possible, show your memes. Are any of them related to important topics, or would you categorize them as "silly"?

C ANALYZE Based on the memes you discussed, do you think the speaker is right about the need to be cautious about sharing them? Discuss your ideas with the class. If you want to interrupt, be sure to do so politely.

☐ I CAN DISCUSS THE IMPACT OF SOCIAL MEDIA.

@EsraK

I've always wanted to launch a start-up, so I admire these guys a lot. And it's for such a good cause!

1 BEFORE YOU READ

A PAIRS Is there a place near you with an air pollution, water pollution, or trash problem? What, if anything, is being done about it?

B ▶07-16 VOCABULARY Read and listen. Do you know these words?

strewn with	haul in	bear	gender-neutral	novel
a lifeguard	daunting	settle on	custom	rest on your laurels

>> FOR DEFINITIONS, PAGE 163

2 READ

A PREVIEW Read the title, look at the picture, and read the caption. What do you think the article will be about?

B ▶07-17 Read and listen to the article. Was your prediction correct?

4ocean: A Solution to Plastic Pollution

Ninety-seven percent of plastic waste is not recycled.

In 2015, American teenagers Andrew Cooper and Alex Schulze flew to Bali with one thing on their minds: surfing. However, when they arrived, they were disappointed to see its world-class surfing beaches strewn with plastic trash. A lifeguard explained that the beaches were cleaned every morning; the problem was that so much plastic continually floated in that by afternoon, they were covered again. The pair then spoke to local fishermen, who said that when they hauled in their nets, they always discovered a lot of unwanted plastic with the fish, but they simply threw it back into the ocean because it was worthless to them. Inspired rather than discouraged, Andrew and Alex began to think about business models, hoping somehow to make clearing the beaches and ocean of plastic litter profitable.

These two young entrepreneurs were taking on a daunting task. Although much plastic waste bears a recycling symbol, 97 percent is not recycled; the equivalent of one trash truck full of plastic waste is dumped into the sea every minute, which amounts to 8 million tons per year. The situation is made worse by the fact that once it is dumped into the ocean, the plastic is swept around the world and concentrated in many different areas by ocean currents, making tracking it down and collecting it an extremely challenging task, to say the least.

Back in Florida, Andrew and Alex brainstormed ideas with their families. They settled on selling a product made from recycled plastic to fund beach cleanup efforts. They considered gender-neutral products, so as not to leave anyone out, and finally decided on a bracelet. The next year was spent planning. The first step was to develop a prototype of the bracelet. They then needed to find a manufacturer willing and able to take on the job. After that, they had a custom logo and website created for their company, which they named 4ocean. Finally, they built a social media presence to introduce their novel concept to the public.

4ocean was an overnight success. For each $20 bracelet sold, the company promised to clean up 1 pound of trash, and they sold twenty bracelets the first day, 250,000 the first year and, at last count, have removed over 4.5 million pounds of trash. Of the money they take in, 45% goes to fund cleanup operations and 10% to charity partners who work with marine life. Andrew and Alex pay themselves an average wage, and the rest goes to business expenses and expansion.

Not content to rest on their laurels, Andrew and Alex plan to collect more and more trash each year; in fact, they hope to become the largest ocean-cleaning company in the world. Recently, they started selling additional products to fund their business, including steel water bottles and T-shirts with their company logo. Check them out and consider helping to fund this worthwhile cause. As it says on the 4ocean website, "Let's end the ocean plastic crisis together."

3 CHECK YOUR UNDERSTANDING

A Answer the questions according to the article.

1. How would clearing plastic from the ocean affect beach cleanup and fishermen in Bali?
2. How has plastic trash in the ocean become such a huge problem?
3. Before starting up, how did they plan to reach a large number of people?
4. What does the way 4ocean's money is used say about the owners' priorities?

B CLOSE READING **Reread the lines. Then circle the correct answers.**

1. Which sentence is closest in meaning to the sentence in lines 13–16?
   a. They were inspired to think of profitable business models.
   b. They were inspired by business models that made plastic profitable.
2. Which sentence is closest in meaning to the sentence in lines 52–55?
   a. Despite their great success, they still think number one is within reach.
   b. They are ambitious to grow their company and aspire to be number one.

C Read the Reading Skill. Complete the flow chart with the steps taken in the development and launch of the 4ocean start-up.

READING SKILL Create a process flow chart

Creating a process flow chart can help you reflect on the steps in a process and organize your thoughts by making them visible. The steps are usually written in rectangular boxes connected by arrows.

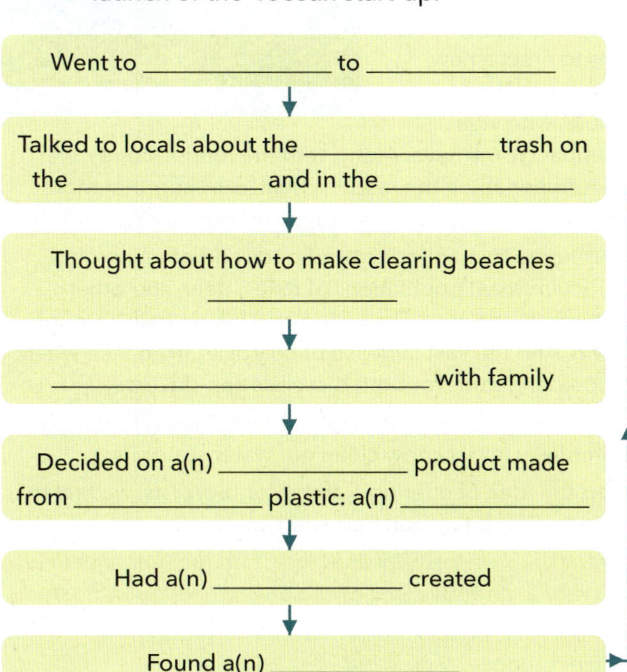

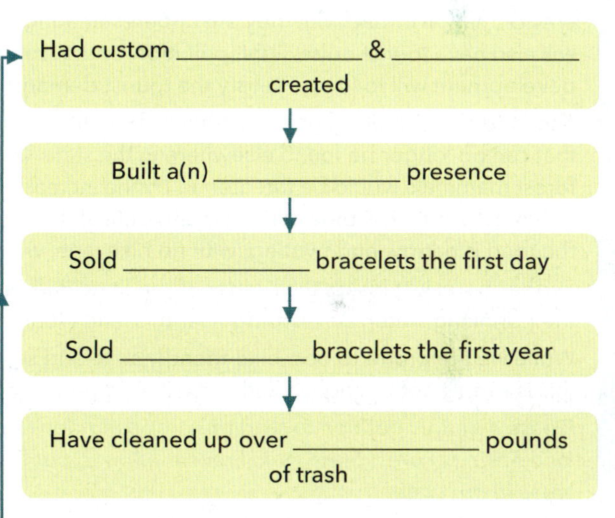

D PAIRS Summarize the article in 3–5 sentences.

Visit the 4ocean website to find out how many tons of trash they have cleaned up by now and more about their mission and products. 

4 MAKE IT PERSONAL

A THINK Consider an environmental cause that you are interested in. Why is it important, and what needs to be done to improve the situation?

B GROUPS Tell the group about the cause and your approach(es) to dealing with it. Ask the group to contribute suggestions.

C EVALUATE Choose one environmental cause with the best suggestions and have one person present the ideas to the class.

☐ I CAN READ ABOUT ENVIRONMENTAL SOLUTIONS.

@EsraK

Now here's a petition I can get behind. From a friend who lives near this beautiful park. Please help save it!

1 BEFORE YOU WRITE

A Read about petitions.

> A petition is a formal written request submitted to an authority, such as a government or a private company. Petitions ask for a particular action to be taken; the text of the petition includes the reasoning behind the request. Petitions can be circulated as paper documents or online, and they are usually signed by many people who support the action to be taken.

B Read the model. What is the action that the writer is requesting?

Save our state park!

As concerned citizens of Pine Springs, we call upon our city to reject the development plan for a biking resort near the entrance to the Pine Springs Forest State Park.

Pine Springs Development Company has submitted plans to erect a new biking resort directly across from the entrance to the forest park. The developer argues that it will bring tourist money to our state, with little environmental impact. But they are underestimating the impact it will have. Along with the tourist money, we will also have tourist noise, light, pollution, and garbage. Additionally, if the resort is built, it is likely that more development will follow, to satisfy the tourist demand for more services such as shops and restaurants.

The State Park has long been a protected wildlife area. It is home to many species of birds and other animals that can no longer be found elsewhere in the state. In particular, local populations of foxes, deer, and other forest mammals would be threatened by the increase of traffic in the area. The hiking and biking trails through the forest would become overused and difficult to maintain. And the vast increase of bicyclists, in an area where the road is narrow and twisting, with no bike lane, would be dangerous for both bicyclists and drivers.

Furthermore, just inside the border of the State Park is the reservoir from which several surrounding towns get their drinking water. Developing near this land would potentially impact how clean our water supply is.

While we are proud to be a bike-friendly state and support the idea of offering a resort for bicyclists, we feel that this is simply not the right location for it. Alternative locations must be researched and considered!

Please sign this petition to stop the proposed development of a bike resort just across from the entrance to Pine Springs Forest State Park. Prevent harm to our local wildlife and save one of the few remaining protected areas in our state.

This petition is to be submitted to the Town Council of Pine Springs.

C PAIRS Is the petition effective? Would you sign this petition? Why or why not?

D Read the model again. Take notes in the chart.

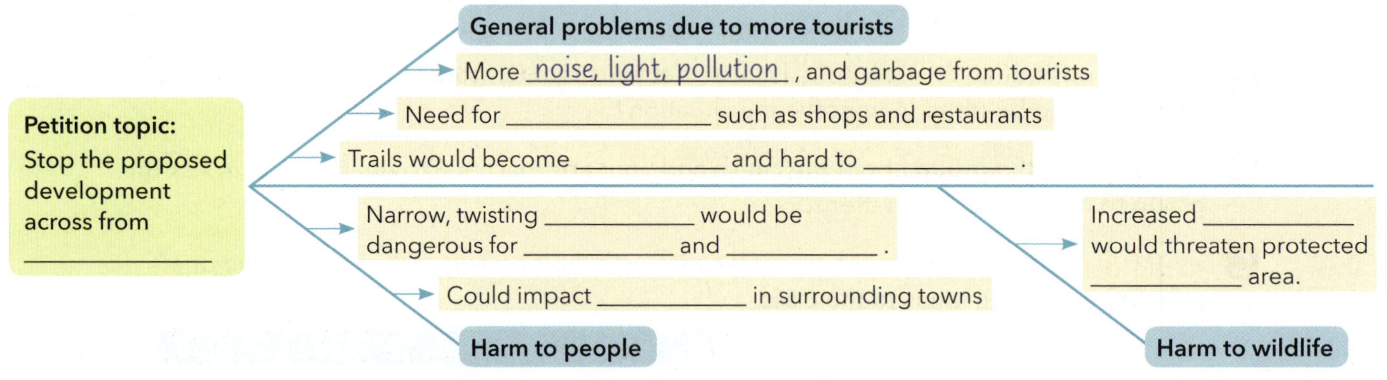

2 FOCUS ON WRITING

Read the Writing Skill. Then read the model again. Are these sentences examples of formal or emotional language? Check (✓) your answers.

WRITING SKILL Consider your audience

Thinking about who will read your writing helps you determine choices such as formality and emotional appeal, as well as what information you choose to include. A petition is a hybrid form of writing with two audiences: the signers of the petition and the authority to whom the petition is submitted. Therefore, it must be both emotional and formal, and it must include any information that either audience needs to know.

	Formal	Emotional
1. As concerned citizens of Pine Springs, we call upon our city to reject the development plan for a biking resort...	☐	☐
2. Pine Springs Development Company has submitted plans to erect a new biking resort directly across from the entrance to the forest park.	☐	☐
3. But they are underestimating the impact it will have.	☐	☐
4. The State Park has long been a protected wildlife area.	☐	☐
5. Alternative locations must be researched and considered!	☐	☐

3 PLAN YOUR WRITING

A Choose an issue, either local or global, which you would like to petition for or against. Create a chart to organize your ideas. Use the chart in 1D as a model.

B PAIRS Discuss your ideas.

There's a really dangerous road crossing downtown. I want to start a petition to add a traffic light and a crosswalk.

4 WRITE

Write a first draft of a petition. Remember to consider your audience. Use the petition in 1B as a model.

Writing tip

Sometimes you have to write on behalf of a group. A petition is a good example of this. If you are the person writing, make sure you discuss your ideas first with other interested parties. This way you can be sure to reflect everyone's ideas and consider all important aspects of the topic.

5 AFTER YOUR FIRST DRAFT

A PEER REVIEW Read your partner's petition. Answer the questions.

- Does the petition provide solid evidence in support of the cause?
- Does it have both emotional language and formal language?
- Does it include all the necessary information that all readers would need?
- Does the ending sum up the important points?
- Were you convinced to support this cause?

B REVISE Write another draft based on the feedback you got from your partner.

C PROOFREAD Check the spelling, grammar, and punctuation in your petition. Then read it through again for overall sense.

☐ I CAN WRITE A PETITION.

PUT IT TOGETHER

1 PROBLEM SOLVING

Where People Get Their Digital News

Source	Percentage
news websites	36%
online search	25%
social media	23%
email	6%
mobile alerts	5%
other	5%

A CONSIDER THE PROBLEM **People today get their news quickly from a lot of different sources, but not all sources are as reliable and accurate as others. Review the chart and circle the correct answers.**

1. The most reliable news is likely to be from ______ .
   a. news websites
   b. online searches
   c. social media
2. People are likely to do online news searches in order to find ______ .
   a. more details b. old stories c. fun facts
3. People are likely to ask for mobile alerts on news stories that are ______ .
   a. oversees b. forgotten c. ongoing

B THINK CRITICALLY **Why do you think some news sources are more or less reliable and accurate than others? Discuss with a partner.**

C FIND A SOLUTION **Consider the data, the problem, and possible solutions in small groups.**

Step 1 **Brainstorm** Think of 3–5 ways that we can make sure that the news we get is reliable and accurate.

Step 2 **Evaluate** Choose the best solution. Consider the problems that can be caused when news is not reliable or accurate.

Step 3 **Present** Explain the best solution to the class. Refer to the data to support your ideas.

2 REFLECT AND PLAN

A **Look back through the unit. Check (✓) the things you learned. Highlight the things you need to learn.**

Speaking Objectives
- ☐ Talk about making a difference
- ☐ Talk about citizen journalism
- ☐ Discuss the impact of social media

Vocabulary
- ☐ Words related to social advocacy

Conversation
- ☐ Identify gaps between thought groups

Pronunciation
- ☐ Pronunciation of *-ate* endings

Listening
- ☐ Tone of voice

Note-taking
- ☐ Include key definitions and examples

Language Choices
- ☐ Passive voice: Form and use
- ☐ Passive voice: Reporting structures
- ☐ Passive infinitives and causatives

Discussion
- ☐ Interrupt politely

Reading
- ☐ Create a process flow chart

Writing
- ☐ Consider your audience

B **What will you do to learn the things you highlighted?**

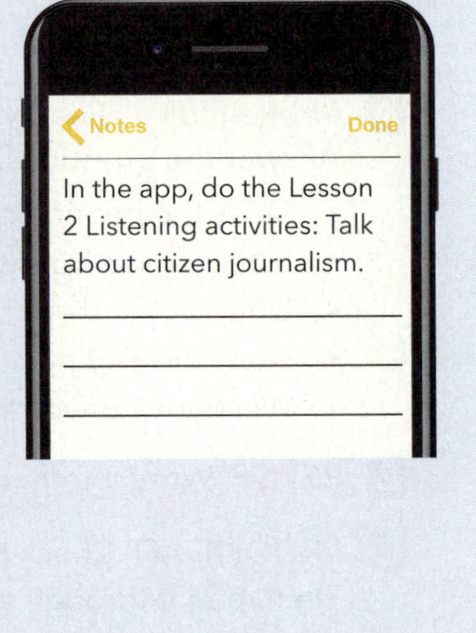

8 WHAT'S OUR STORY?

LEARNING GOALS

In this unit, you

- talk about a solution to a problem
- talk about promotion strategies
- talk about corporate origin stories
- read about deceptive marketing
- write a personal essay

GET STARTED

A Read the unit title and learning goals. Marketing can be defined as promoting someone or something. How has the internet made it easier to market ideas?

B Look at the picture. The photo shows employees holding a variety of icons. Choose three. How does each one relate to the concept of marketing?

C Read Carla's message. What might be some of the challenges of reaching out to customers of different ages?

CARLA LUGO
@CarlaL
Our client needs to connect with adults of every age group. It's a challenge to reach out to all of them!

1 VOCABULARY Marketing words

A Look at the advertisement for a marketing firm. Would you hire this company? Why or why not?

B ▶08-01 Read and listen. Notice the words in bold.

Here at NextLevel, it's our business to help your business! We have proven **strategies** for building your **social media presence**, creating clever ad campaigns that will increase awareness of your **brand**, and planning spectacular **product launches** and **promotional materials** for every new product or service you offer. We understand the importance of **customer interaction** and can help you with **damage control** for any challenges you've faced in the past. Call us! We'll pitch ideas that **stand out** from the competition and work with you to take your business to the next level.

>> FOR PRACTICE, PAGE 146 / DEFINITIONS, PAGE 163

2 LANGUAGE CHOICES Modifying relative clauses

A Read the example sentences. Then read the rules in the chart. Are they true (*T*) or false (*F*)? Correct the false rules.

Example sentences

1. We've had to do a lot of damage control, **some of which has been effective**.
2. Our marketing team pitched several ideas, **only three or four of which we liked**.
3. Let's translate this ad for our overseas clients, **the majority of whom don't speak English**.
4. We can learn a lot from that competitor, **most of whose product launches have been successful**.
5. We need help creating an ad campaign, **a task in which we have little experience**.
6. I'm pleased to announce our new sales director, **a person for whom I have great respect**.
7. Scott is leaving his job at Solutions, **the company at which he has worked for ten years**.

Modifying relative clauses

- Modifying relative clauses modify the whole sentence. ______
- A modifying relative clause can't be a sentence by itself. ______
- Some relative clauses follow this pattern: quantifier + *with* + relative pronoun. ______
- Some relative clauses begin with noun + preposition + relative pronoun. ______
- In a relative clause with a quantifier or noun + preposition, the relative pronoun can be *who, whom, whose, which,* or *that.* ______
- Clauses with a quantifier or noun + preposition must be separated by a comma. ______

>> FOR PRACTICE, PAGE 146

B Look at other ways to write example sentence 5 in 2A. Then rewrite sentences 6 and 7.

We need help creating an ad campaign, a task which we have little experience in. (formal)
We need help creating an ad campaign, a task (that) we have little experience in. (informal)

3 CONVERSATION SKILL

A 08-04 Read the conversation skill. Then listen. Write the words they use to speculate about the future.

1. I think _______________ your idea _______________ the right way!
2. _______________ she's going to save this company.

Speculate about the future

Use expressions like these to speculate—or guess—about what will happen:

It's (quite) possible that...

I suppose...

[They] might...if...

B PAIRS The shoe company you work for is failing.
It is considering spending the last of its budget on an expensive marketing campaign. Speculate about how this might affect the future of the company.

4 CONVERSATION

A 08-05 Listen. What do Carla and Hiro talk about?

B 08-05 Listen again. Answer the questions.

1. What are the two problems with the BeautyTree account?
2. Why don't they want to spend money on social media?
3. What solution does Hiro suggest?

C 08-06 Listen. Complete the conversation.

Hiro: I mean, in the end, they are going to spend their money however they want to, no matter what we think about it.

Carla: True. _______________ listen if I focus on damage control instead of trying to build their social media presence.

Hiro: _______________ a good compromise.

5 TRY IT YOURSELF

A THINK Imagine that in your company there is a disagreement about advertising. One person wants to spend more money on local TV advertising and the other wants to focus on social media. Think about the pros and cons for each. Take notes in the chart.

	Pros	Cons
Social media		
TV advertising		

B PAIRS Use the details in your chart to negotiate the best choice or think of another solution.

A: If we spend too much on television, then we might not have enough resources for a proper social media campaign.

B: It's true, but we could...

☐ I CAN TALK ABOUT A SOLUTION TO A PROBLEM.

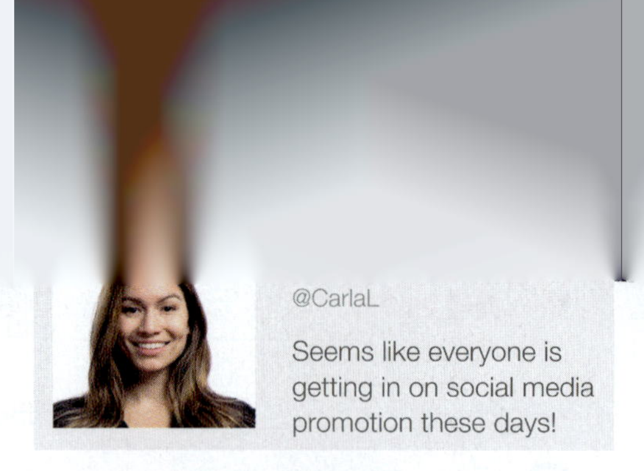

1 BEFORE YOU LISTEN

A PAIRS THINK What kinds of products do you see celebrities promoting on social media? Do they make you want to buy things?

B ▶08-07 VOCABULARY Look at the words and listen to the sentences. Do you know these words?

vouch for	authenticity	put off
plug	word of mouth	turn into
computer-generated	an endorsement	
get in on	engage	

>> FOR PRACTICE, PAGE 147 / DEFINITIONS, PAGE 163

#makeup #style #ad

2 LANGUAGE CHOICES Participle clauses

A Read the example sentences. Then circle the correct words to complete the rules in the chart.

Adverb clause example sentences	Participle clause example sentences
When I'm reading his posts, I get tired of all the advertising hashtags.	**Reading** his posts, I get tired of all the advertising hashtags.
Because she's a nanoinfluencer, she gets a lot of free products.	**Being** a nanoinfluencer, she gets a lot of free products.
After we got in on social media promotion, we nearly doubled our sales.	**Having gotten** in on social media promotion, we nearly doubled our sales.
Since I've used their products for years, I can vouch for their quality.	**Having used** their products for years, I can vouch for their quality.
Because I was impressed by their ad campaign, I joined the new gym.	**Impressed** by their ad campaign, I joined the new gym.
Since it's located downtown, that coffee shop is always busy.	**Located** downtown, that coffee shop is always busy.

Participle clauses

- Use *-ing* participle clauses to emphasize the **present / past**.
- Use *having* + past participle clauses to emphasize the **present / past**.
- Adverb clauses can be changed to participle clauses only when the subject of the adverb clause and the main clause are **the same / different**.
- Participle clauses that begin with a past participle usually replace **an active / a passive** adverb clause.

>> FOR PRACTICE, PAGE 147

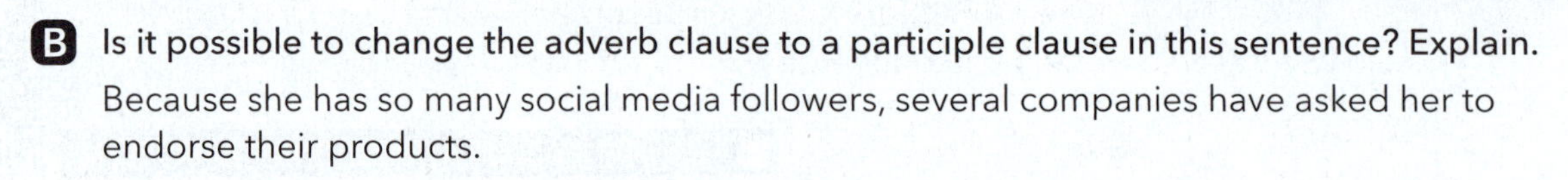

B Is it possible to change the adverb clause to a participle clause in this sentence? Explain.

Because she has so many social media followers, several companies have asked her to endorse their products.

3 PRONUNCIATION

A ▶08-09 **Listen. Read the pronunciation note.**

B ▶08-10 **Listen. Notice stress and blending. Then listen and repeat.**

A: Wow, Eva just got in on a great opportunity using her blog.
B: Yeah, Ana's new restaurant, right? It's just about to open and Eva's come up with a creative idea for promoting it.
A: Yeah. She has amazing social media ideas. I really look up to her.

Phrasal prepositional verbs

Phrasal prepositional verbs are expressions that consist of a verb followed by two prepositions, for example: *get out of*. Some expressions may have an object after the verb: *help me out with*. The first preposition is usually stressed, and the second one is unstressed. The verb can also be stressed. The words in these expressions are blended together:
I have to get out of class early today.

C ▶08-11 **Listen. Complete the conversation. Mark the stressed preposition in the phrasal verb with a dot over the stressed vowel. Then check your answers with your partner.**

A: Let's hurry and ______________ Chang. He can give us a ride back.
B: Oh, Chang. I don't really ______________ him. He always argues.
A: I know what you mean. Just ______________ him for half an hour.

4 LISTENING

LISTENING SKILL Anticipate words

When you hear a title or part of a talk, try to anticipate–or guess–related words and ideas that you might hear. Anticipating content in this way can help you understand and remember what you hear.

A ▶08-12 **Read the Listening Skill. Then listen to the beginning of a podcast. List more words you anticipate hearing as the podcast continues.**

B ▶08-13 **Listen to the whole podcast. As you listen, check (✓) any of the words on your list that you hear.**

C PAIRS **How many of the words you anticipated did you hear in the podcast? What is the topic?**

D ▶08-13 **Listen again. Take notes in the chart.**

What influencers do	
Benefits of nanoinfluencers to companies	1. 2.
Being a nanoinfluencer	Pros: Cons:
Conclusion	

E PAIRS REACT **Would you like to be a nanoinfluencer? Why or why not?**

5 TRY IT YOURSELF

A THINK **Imagine that you are going to be a nanoinfluencer. What product could you promote to your friends? How would you make it seem appealing? Take notes.**

B PAIRS **Help improve your partner's strategy by asking questions about the product.**

C EVALUATE **In groups, take turns sharing your products and promotion strategies. Choose two or three of the best ideas. Share them with the class and explain why they are effective.**

☐ I CAN TALK ABOUT PROMOTION STRATEGIES.

@CarlaL

Well, I learned something new about a couple of very famous companies today!

1 BEFORE YOU LISTEN

A PAIRS THINK What kinds of stories do businesses tell about how they got started? Think of the story of a famous company. Tell what you know about how it got started.

B ▶08-14 VOCABULARY Look at the words and expressions and listen to the sentences. Do you know what they mean?

stumble upon	a peer	iconic	hit it big	a stretch
expertise	dream up	designate	the premises	captivating

>> FOR PRACTICE, PAGE 148 / DEFINITIONS, PAGE 164

2 LANGUAGE CHOICES Infinitive clauses

A Read the example sentences. Then circle the correct answers to complete the rules in the chart. More than one answer is correct.

Example sentences

1. We decided **not to start a business together**.
2. They expected us **to have a more interesting origin story**.
3. **To make mistakes** is human. / It is human **to make mistakes**.
4. We left early **(in order) to beat the traffic**.
5. They rented a garage to **use as a lab**.
6. We were happy **to stumble upon this great place for brunch**.
7. It's normal for a business **not to hit it big right away**.
8. It's nice for us **to have some time off this week**.
9. They relocated their headquarters **to save money**.

Infinitive clauses

- Infinitive clauses can follow ______ .
  a. prepositions b. certain verbs c. nouns or pronouns d. adjectives
- Infinitive clauses can function as ______ .
  a. main verbs b. subjects c. objects d. sentences
- Infinitive clauses can be used to ______ .
  a. express purpose b. make a comment c. explain why d. show quantity
- An infinitive always ______ .
  a. has the word *to* b. has a noun c. has a verb d. comes last in a sentence

>> FOR PRACTICE, PAGE 148

B Infinitive clauses expressing purpose can often be replaced by *so (that)* + subject clause. Look at this example. Then look at the example sentences in 2A. In which example sentences can the infinitive clause be replaced by *so that*?

He took summer classes **in order to** graduate early.

OR:

He took summer classes **so that he would** graduate early.

3 VIDEO TALK

A ▶08-16 Listen or watch. What two stories does the speaker talk about?

B ▶08-16 Listen or watch again. Take notes in the chart.

Reason for corporate origin stories:

Company	Story	Truth

C ▶08-16 Read the Note-taking Skill. Then listen again and complete the sentences.

In essence, ______________________________ .

To sum up, ______________________________

______________________________ .

NOTE-TAKING SKILL Listen for restatement

Speakers use a variety of expressions to restate or summarize an important point. Listen for signal expressions like these, and make a note of what is said:

in essence	*in brief*
in other words	*on the whole*
that is to say	*to sum up*
in short	*in conclusion*

D PAIRS REACT Are you surprised that the corporate origin stories are exaggerated?

4 DISCUSSION SKILL

Read the discussion skill. Which of these phrases do you use in your discussions now?

Ask follow-up questions

One way to demonstrate interest in a conversation or discussion is to ask follow-up questions like these to get more information.

What happened next? *Why / How did they…?*

5 TRY IT YOURSELF

A THINK Read the beginnings of origin stories for three businesses. Choose one and take notes about its founder(s) and the business.

Restaurant: A woman learned to cook in her grandmother's kitchen. Then neighbors helped her attend a famous cooking school...

A clothing store: A man worked in his parents' tiny store as a teenager and had an idea to sell their specialty clothes online...

A car company: Two people who loved cars used to draw them after school. They went to work at a dealership and then went to engineering school together…

B PAIRS Work with someone who chose the same business. Share your ideas and develop the origin story together.

C EVALUATE Present your origin story to the class. Vote on which one is the most compelling and discuss why.

☐ I CAN TALK ABOUT CORPORATE ORIGIN STORIES.

CARLA LUGO
@CarlaL
I always try to buy *natural products*, but does anybody know what that really means?

1 BEFORE YOU READ

A PAIRS *All natural*, *organic*, *sustainable*, *recyclable*, and *eco-friendly* are buzzwords often found on so-called "green" products. Discuss their meanings.

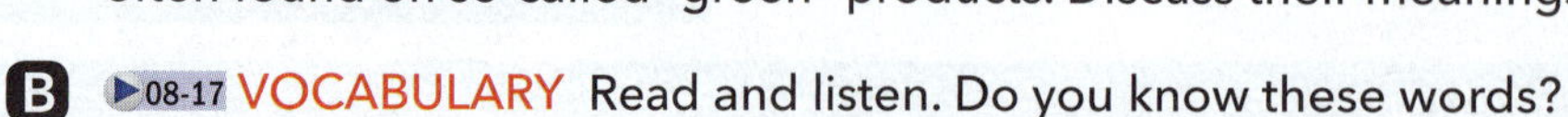

B ▶08-17 VOCABULARY Read and listen. Do you know these words?

wrongdoing	mislead	biodegradable	a municipality	disintegrate
deceptive	abhorrent	reassuring	detrimental	suggestive

>> FOR DEFINITIONS, PAGE 164

C Read the Reading Skill. Skim the article. Then check (✓) the topics that you think the article will cover.

- ☐ the definition of *greenwashing*
- ☐ why green products are inferior
- ☐ how to find bargains
- ☐ the origins of greenwashing
- ☐ green buzzwords
- ☐ examples of greenwashing
- ☐ advice to shoppers
- ☐ tips on how to greenwash

READING SKILL Skim

Skimming is a type of speed reading that involves glancing over a text and only pausing to read the title, look at images and read their captions, and read just the first and last sentences of each paragraph. It's a time-saving way to get the main idea and an overall impression of the text.

2 READ

▶08-18 Read and listen to the article. Were your predictions correct?

Greenwashing: Don't Be Fooled!

Most people know that one meaning of *green* is *eco-friendly*, but are you familiar with *greenwashing*, a verb that entered dictionaries in the late '90s? Patterned on words like *brainwashing* (making people 5 believe what you want by controlling information) and *whitewashing* (covering up wrongdoing with deceptive information), greenwashing occurs when a company misleads customers about its negative impact on the environment by attempting to 10 convince them otherwise through advertising and publicity. In the '60s and '70s, before we had a name for this phenomenon, the chemical, automobile, and energy industries were already greenwashing their products and services to calm fears about the 15 dangers of air pollution, chemical and oil spills, and nuclear energy technology.

In the '80s, several ecological catastrophes, including massive chemical and oil spills and a nuclear disaster, prompted various greenwashing campaigns 20 by powerful corporations. This was the start of the corporate environmentalism movement. As a consequence of the severe damage inflicted on the environment, a company's reputation for eco-friendly practices had never been more important. Opinion 25 polls at the time revealed that more than 70% of those surveyed were swayed by environmental issues when they shopped, and over 80% viewed environmental offenses as the most abhorrent of all corporate crimes.

30 The '90s brought various buzzwords, many of which still appear on packaging today, such as *recyclable*, *biodegradable*, *environmentally friendly*, and *all natural*. In recent years, *sustainable*, *renewable*, and *organic* are frequently seen. While it is reassuring to 35 see such language on the packaging of the products we buy, whether it is simply a case of greenwashing depends on the meaning of the terms. For example, *green*, *pure*, and *natural* are essentially meaningless when they do not correspond to any legal or 40 industrial standards. There have also been cases

when *organic* and *sustainable* have only referred to one component of a product, whereas the other components were neither organic nor sustainable.

45 The terms *recyclable* and *biodegradable* have been particularly controversial. In order to reduce its ecological footprint, one bottled water brand switched from plastic bottles to Tetra Pak packaging

50 made of paper, aluminum, and plastic. The problem was that although Tetra Pak cartons are labeled *recyclable*, not all municipalities are equipped to recycle them; thus, the switch may have had a

55 detrimental environmental impact. In another case, a large retailer was forced to pay a fine of nearly $1 million for labeling plastic bottles *biodegradable*. Although technically correct, the bottles could

60 take up to 1,000 years to disintegrate in landfills, which did not meet local standards for products labeled that way.

To conclude, here are four tips to help you avoid being fooled by greenwashing.

65 • Learn to recognize abused and inappropriately used buzzwords.

• Watch out for "green" products made by companies that pollute. An internet search using a company's name and *greenwashing* as search terms can be useful to check this.

• Look past suggestive labeling with natural images of birds,
70 flowers, and trees that create a "green" impression.

• Think critically about product claims. For example, if a company claims it is "greener" than its competitors, it does not mean much if those competitors are terrible polluters.

Green buzzwords are common these days, but what exactly do they mean?

3 CHECK YOUR UNDERSTANDING

A Answer the questions according to the article.

1. How was the word *greenwashing* derived?
2. Why was a green reputation so important to companies in the 1980s?
3. How can *pure*, *natural*, *organic*, or *sustainable* be deceptive?
4. How have companies used *recyclable* and *biodegradable* deceptively?

B CLOSE READING **Reread the lines. Then circle the correct answers.**

1. Which sentence is closest in meaning to the sentence in lines 34-37?
   a. Green buzzwords are reassuring, whether or not greenwashing is present.
   b. Although they can be misused for greenwashing, green buzzwords are reassuring.
   c. People are reassured by green buzzwords in simple cases of greenwashing.
2. In lines 55-62, how is the second sentence connected to the first?
   a. It ignores a small point then provides an example of a fine.
   b. It emphasizes slight wrongdoing then provides a reason for the fine.
   c. It concedes a minor point then provides a reason for the fine.

C PAIRS **Summarize the article in 3-5 sentences.**

Search online for cases of greenwashing. Present them to the class.

4 MAKE IT PERSONAL

A THINK **Think of a "green" product (for example, a food, a device, clothing, a vehicle) and write a short advertisement for it that includes green buzzwords.**

B GROUPS **Present your advertisement. Have the group identify the buzzwords and discuss what they mean in the context of each advertisement.**

C EVALUATE **Decide which buzzwords could have been used deceptively in the ads and discuss why. Choose one person to present them and the reasons to the class.**

☐ I CAN READ ABOUT DECEPTIVE MARKETING.

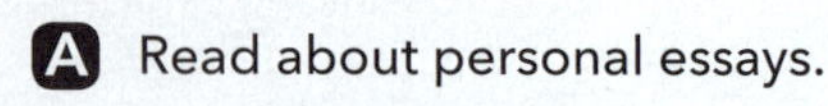

CARLA LUGO

@CarlaL

Sometimes we have to promote ourselves! I'm helping my friend Anant write a personal essay for his grad school application.

1 BEFORE YOU WRITE

A Read about personal essays.

A personal essay is a narrative essay about your life or interests. Personal essays are often required as part of the college admissions process. Sometimes they may be submitted with a job or scholarship application. If a specific topic is not provided, choose one that relates to something meaningful about yourself, such as something that taught you a lesson or contributed to your world view.

B Read the model. What was the incident that changed the writer's perspective?

When I was 13 years old, I learned a powerful lesson about finding the hidden talents within any person, including myself.

Up until then, I had been a shy child. I did well enough in school, and I had a few friends. But I did not consider myself particularly talented at anything.

When I started the eighth grade, there was a new boy at school named David. He had some learning problems; I now understand that he was autistic. Social interactions were difficult for him, so he did not have many friends. Unfortunately, children in my class often teased and bullied him. Although I did not participate in this bullying, I also did not intervene; instead, I stood aside.

One day, in math class, some of my classmates were again teasing David. The teacher saw what was happening. His reaction surprised all of us. He left the room without saying anything. When he came back five minutes later, he was holding a guitar. He set up a chair at the front of the classroom and asked David to sit in it. He handed him the guitar, and the boy started playing and singing. To our surprise, he had an amazing voice and could play the guitar like a professional. It was the most touching music I had ever heard.

From that day on, everyone treated David differently. My classmates and I finally started to accept him for who he was. We understood that although he was different from us, he still had something beautiful to offer the world.

That was not the only lesson I learned on that day. It also marked a turning point in my own life, when I started to look more deeply for the potential inside myself. That year I took up the piano. It was not easy; I had to practice every day. But I understood that the process of learning was just as important as the result. I did not have to be perfect; I just had to believe in myself and have the confidence to keep trying. This belief has pushed me to try many new things, to apply myself 100% to everything I do. Since that day many years ago, I have believed that everyone, including myself, has the potential to contribute something beautiful to the world.

C PAIRS Do you think that the lesson the writer discusses would be of value in a grad school program or a new job?

D Read the model again. Take notes in the chart.

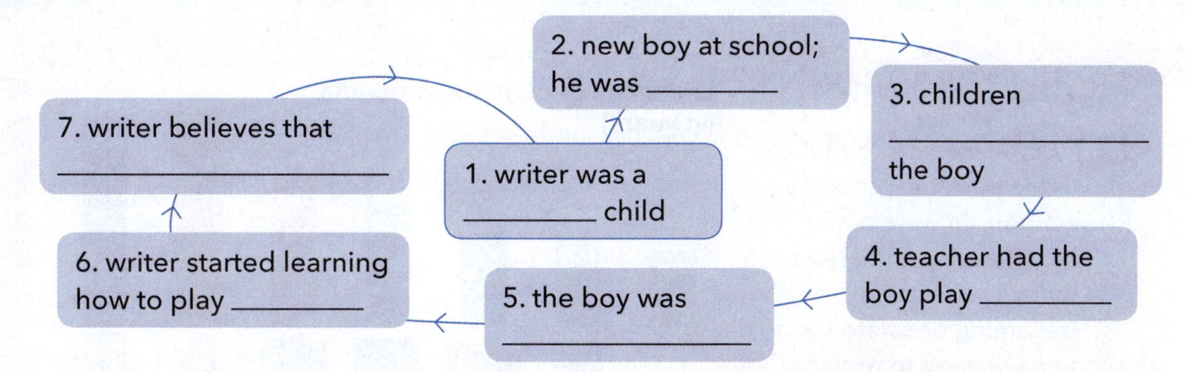

2 FOCUS ON WRITING

Read the Writing Skill. Then read the model again. Underline the sentences that state or restate the main ideas.

WRITING SKILL Use redundancy

Redundancy is stating a point over and over. If you restate your thesis at different points in the essay, it can help readers understand the connections between your ideas and remember your main idea.

3 PLAN YOUR WRITING

A If you had to promote yourself as a candidate for a job or a university program, what would your focus be? Think of a time in your life when you learned an important lesson. Create a chart to organize your ideas. Use the chart in 1D as a model.

B PAIRS Discuss your ideas.

I learned the importance of generosity when I was...

Writing tip

Think associatively. Let your mind wander and come up with an incident that you remember for some reason. Then think about why you remember the incident. Why was it important, and how did it change you? Keep a journal or take some notes on these ideas and use them as a starting point for your essay.

4 WRITE

Write a first draft of a personal essay. Remember to use redundancy. Use the essay in 1B as a model.

5 AFTER YOUR FIRST DRAFT

A PEER REVIEW Read your partner's essay. Answer the questions.

- Is there a lesson clearly stated in the introduction and then restated in other places in the essay?
- Is the narrative arranged in a clear chronological order?
- Does the essay explain clearly and concisely how the lesson was learned?
- Can you see how the lesson would be valuable for grad school or for a job? If not, can you suggest ways the writer can make this lesson more clearly of value?

B REVISE Write another draft based on the feedback you got from your partner.

C PROOFREAD Check the spelling, grammar, and punctuation in your essay. Then read it through again for overall sense.

☐ I CAN WRITE A PERSONAL ESSAY.

PUT IT TOGETHER

1 PROBLEM SOLVING

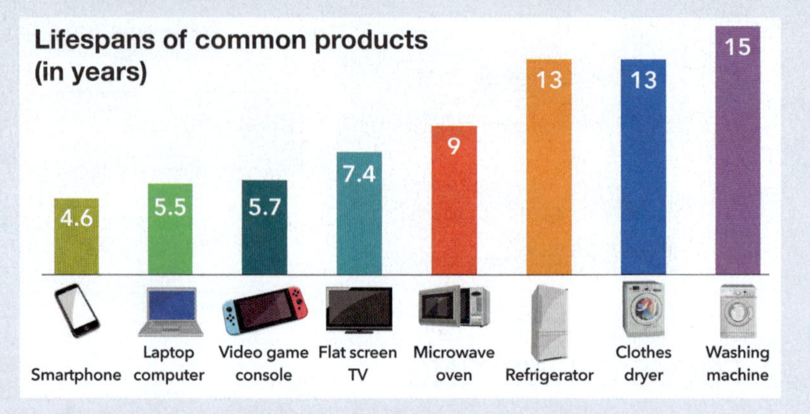

A CONSIDER THE PROBLEM In the past, the products we bought were made to last a long time. Now many products are becoming obsolete faster, and we need to replace them at a more rapid rate. Review the chart and circle the correct answers.

1. Since the 1950s, companies have purposely tried to make products that ______ .
   a. last longer b. cannot fail c. break down sooner
2. The difference in the lifespans between a washer and dryer means when the washer breaks down, many people may _____ .
   a. try to repair it b. replace both c. rent one
3. Smartphones are likely to become obsolete quickly because ______ .
   a. they no longer work b. consumers want new features c. they can't be repaired

B THINK CRITICALLY Why don't products last as long now as they used to? Talk with a partner.

C FIND A SOLUTION Consider the data, the problem, and possible solutions in small groups.

Step 1 **Brainstorm** Think of 3–5 consequences of products not lasting as long as they used to.

Step 2 **Evaluate** Choose the best solution. Consider the negative consequences and what could be done about them.

Step 3 **Present** Explain the best solution to the class. Refer to the data to support your ideas.

2 REFLECT AND PLAN

A Look back through the unit. Check (✓) the things you learned. Highlight the things you need to learn.

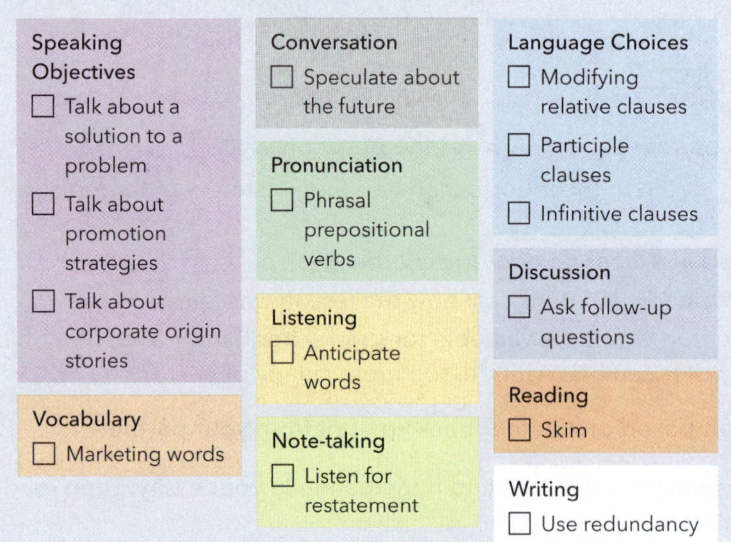

B What will you do to learn the things you highlighted?

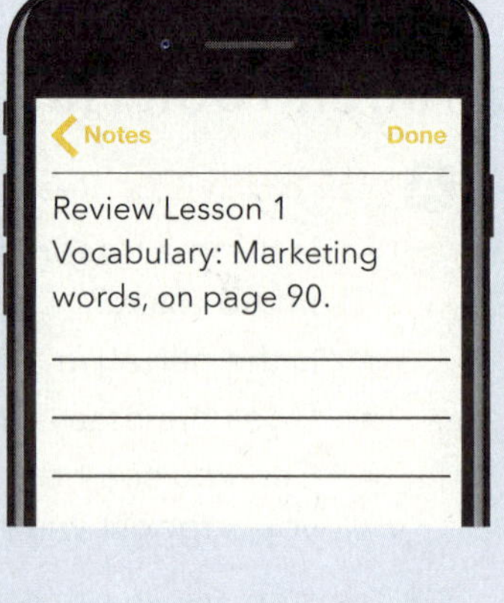

9 DO YOU FOLLOW ANY SPORTS?

LEARNING GOALS

In this unit, you

- talk about athletic competition
- talk about esports
- talk about what a sport is
- read about sports fans
- write a set of instructions

GET STARTED

A Read the unit title and learning goals. Following a sport means watching it as well as keeping up with other news about it. Which sport interests you, either to watch or play? Why do you like it?

B Look at the picture. The photo appears to be open-water swimming and might be part of a triathlete competition, also involving running and cycling. Why might people do these activities?

C Read Tae-ho's message. Do people generally like to play the sport that they are fans of? Why or why not?

TAE-HO KANG

@Tae-hoK

I love to watch soccer, but I'm not very good at it. Anyone interested in a fantasy soccer league?

@Tae-hoK

I think there was an employee baseball game yesterday. Funny no one in the office is talking about it!

1 VOCABULARY Athletic abilities

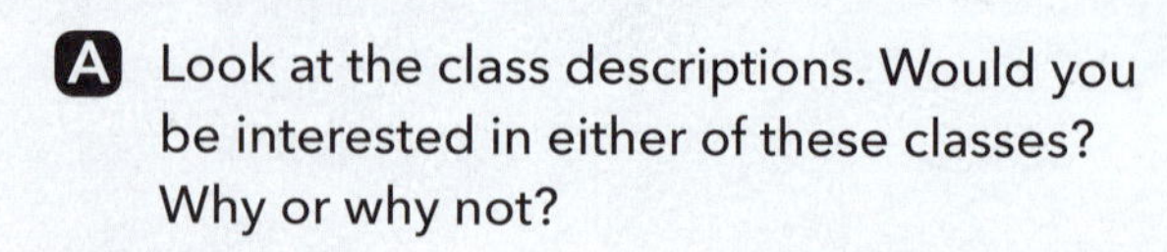

A Look at the class descriptions. Would you be interested in either of these classes? Why or why not?

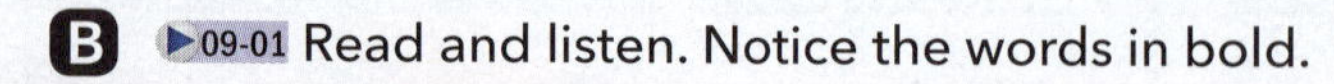

B ▶09-01 Read and listen. Notice the words in bold.

KP Sports Center

New! Classes to boost your **athletic abilities**!

Our top trainer, Pau Pujol, is offering these short-term classes to help you improve your skills.

CLASS 1 **Hand-Eye Coordination**

Do you feel like you're too **uncoordinated** to play sports well? Have trouble hitting the ball with your bat or racket? This class will teach training exercises you can do to build those skills. You'll be winning points and **scoring runs** before you know it.

CLASS 2 Building **Competitive Spirit**

In order to win any game, you need to **play your heart out** and do your best to **demolish your opponent** (without cheating, of course–everyone wants to **win fair and square**!). But sometimes we have trouble tapping into our competitive potential. In this class you'll learn some critical psychological tricks to really help you get your game on.

>> FOR PRACTICE, PAGE 149 / DEFINITIONS, PAGE 164

2 LANGUAGE CHOICES Modals for speculation and expectation

A Read the example sentences. Then complete the rules in the chart with the correct modals and word forms.

Example sentences

1. That team never loses. They **must** have some really good players.
2. The retirees won the game? You **must be kidding**, right?
3. They won by only 1 point. It **must have been** an exciting game.
4. You **can't** eat that entire pizza by yourself. It's enough for five people!
5. Where is everybody? They **can't be playing** softball. The weather is terrible.
6. We've been practicing all week, so our team **should** definitely win the next game.
7. I don't know where Scott is. He **might** have a softball game today, or he **may** be in his office.
8. Our team is getting better and better. We **could** win the next game. We'll see.

Modals for speculation and expectation

- Use ______________ to show you are quite certain that a situation is true.
- Use ______________ to express disbelief.
- Use ______________ to talk about a situation that you expect to happen.
- Use ______________ , ______________ , or ______________ to show you are not certain.
- Use a modal + *be* + ______________ to show the situation is happening now.
- Use a modal + *have* + ______________ to show the situation was in the past.

>> FOR PRACTICE, PAGE 149

B How certain are the speakers about these statements? Is it possible to change some modals to make them more certain or less certain?

"Joe's team can't be practicing again! They must have practiced a hundred hours this week."
"Don't worry. They might have improved, but our team should still win the next game."

3 CONVERSATION SKILL

Build empathy with active listening

You can use expressions like these to show that you understand how another person feels.

I see why you're ______ .
I hate / love that feeling.
That's a great / terrible feeling.
I know the feeling / how that feels.

A ▶09-04 Read the conversation skill. Then listen. Write the expressions that the woman uses to express empathy.

1. ______________________________
2. ______________________________
3. ______________________________

B PAIRS Student A: Imagine that you are nervous or excited about something that is going to happen.
Student B: Listen and express empathy. Give any advice you can think of.

4 CONVERSATION

A ▶09-05 Listen. What do Tae-ho and Carla talk about?

B ▶09-05 Listen again. Answer the questions.

1. Who was playing in the softball game?
2. What was the result of the game?
3. What reason does Carla give for the outcome?

C ▶09-06 Listen. Complete the conversation.

Tae-ho: Oh you wouldn't have wanted me ______________ .
I'd just have made things worse.
Carla: They could hardly have been worse.
Tae-ho: Seriously. Hiro tried to recruit me, but ______________ .
Carla: You look fit to me.
Tae-ho: Well, I run and swim, but I have zero hand-eye coordination. No ball sports for me.
Carla: OK, ______________ .

5 TRY IT YOURSELF

A THINK Choose one sport and think of three aspects of it that you like and three that you don't like.

Sport: ______________________	
What I like about it	**What I don't like about it**

B PAIRS Explain what you like and don't like about the sport you chose. Express empathy with your partner's point of view.

A: Baseball is so boring, especially in the outfield. You spend so much time standing around waiting for the ball to come to you...
B: I feel that way sometimes, too, but it's so exciting when all of a sudden you have to catch it!

TAE-HO KANG

@Tae-hoK

I'm pretty good at video games, but there's no way I could play esports professionally!

1 BEFORE YOU LISTEN

A PAIRS THINK Do you like to play video games? Do you think professional esports would be an interesting career? Why or why not?

B 09-07 VOCABULARY Complete the phrases with the words in the box. Then listen and check your answers.

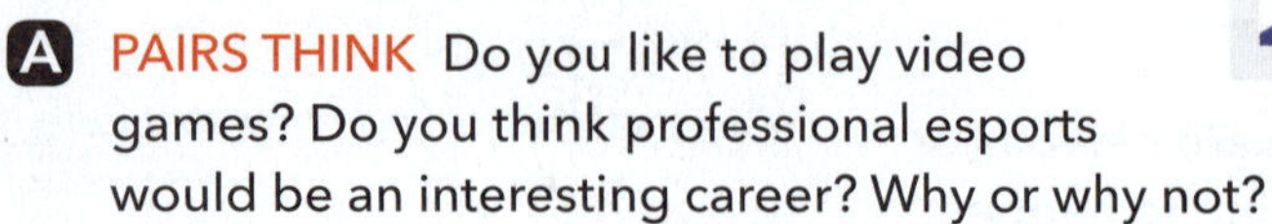

times	pro	risk	money	mind	decision
with	~~gig~~	head	humor	plan	back

>> FOR PRACTICE, PAGE 150 / DEFINITIONS, PAGE 165

1. get a paying ___gig___
2. keep in ___________
3. make big ___________
4. kick ___________
5. keep up ___________
6. have fast reaction ___________
7. go ___________
8. take a calculated ___________
9. make a split-second ___________
10. keep a cool ___________
11. have a good sense of ___________
12. have a backup ___________

2 LANGUAGE CHOICES Expressing necessity and obligation

A Read the example sentences. Then circle the correct words to complete the rules in the chart.

Example sentences

1. We**'ve got to** remember this is just a game. We **don't need to** be so competitive.
2. You **needn't** be a professional to enjoy playing this game.
3. I worked from home yesterday because I **didn't need to** go to the office.
4. Thanks for the coffee! You **didn't need to** do that, but I really appreciate it.
5. The birthday gift from my colleagues was nice, but they **needn't have** gotten me anything.
6. We **must** figure out a solution as soon as possible.
7. Participants are **required to** register before the competition.
8. You **don't have to** go to the show tonight. It's up to you.
9. I **had to** make a quick decision or I would lose points.

Expressing necessity and obligation

- Use *must*, *have to*, *need to*, and *have got to* to express **responsibility / speculation**.
- Use *don't need to* or *needn't* to show an action is **unnecessary / impossible**.
- Use *didn't need to* or *needn't have* to show something **wasn't required / was prohibited.**
- Use *don't have to* to show an action is **optional / prohibited**.
- Use *required to* to show an action is **a suggestion / an obligation**.
- To express past necessity, use ***had to / must have***.

>> FOR PRACTICE, PAGE 150

B Look at example sentences 3–5 in 2A. What is the difference in meaning? Is it possible to use *needn't have* or *didn't need to* in all three sentences?

3 PRONUNCIATION

A ▶09-09 Listen. Read the pronunciation note.

B ▶09-10 Listen. Notice the blended pronunciations of the underlined verbs. Then listen and repeat.

1. To be a professional dancer, first of all, you <u>have to</u> love dancing—because you <u>need to</u> give up a lot for the career.
2. A professional dancer <u>has to</u> train for several hours a day, six days a week, for almost the whole year.
3. Athletes who play seasonal sports <u>don't have to</u> practice so much and have more time off.

Expressions of necessity

Have to, has to, had to, need to, needs to, and *needed to* have blended pronunciations: /hæftə/, /hæstə/, /hædtə/, /nidtə/, /nidztə/, and /nidədtə/. The final /d/ in *had, need*, and *needed* and the /t/ of *to* blend into a single sound. In the words *don't, doesn't*, and *didn't*, /t/ is often silent: *don't have to* /donhæftə/.

C ▶09-11 Listen. Complete the sentences with the words you hear.

Playing for a professional esports team, Miko thought he __________________ study, but his coach said he __________________ finish high school. After the championships, he knew he __________________ save money for next season. He __________________ wait long before he got offers to promote gaming equipment.

4 LISTENING

A ▶09-12 Listen. What is the main idea of the podcast?

B ▶09-12 Read the Listening Skill. Listen again. Who is the intended audience for this talk?

LISTENING SKILL **Infer the target audience**

We can often tell from a speaker's language who the intended, or target, audience is. For example, if you hear very formal language about a particular field of study, you might deduce that the target audience is an academic one.

C ▶09-12 Listen again. Take notes in the chart.

Introduction:
1st:
2nd:
3rd:
4th:
Finally:

D PAIRS REACT Were you surprised by any of the information in the podcast? Why or why not?

5 TRY IT YOURSELF

A THINK Imagine that you have your heart set on becoming a professional gamer, but your friend wants to talk you out of it. What points could you make in favor of this choice? Write three ideas.

B PAIRS Student A: Try to convince your friend that professional gaming is a good career choice for you. Student B: Using your notes from 4C and your own ideas, try to talk your friend out of trying to going pro.

C EVALUATE Decide which are the most compelling arguments in favor of a gaming career. Share your ideas with the class.

☐ I CAN TALK ABOUT ESPORTS.

TAE-HO KANG

@Tae-hoK

Do you think ice dancing is a sport? What about bowling?

1 BEFORE YOU LISTEN

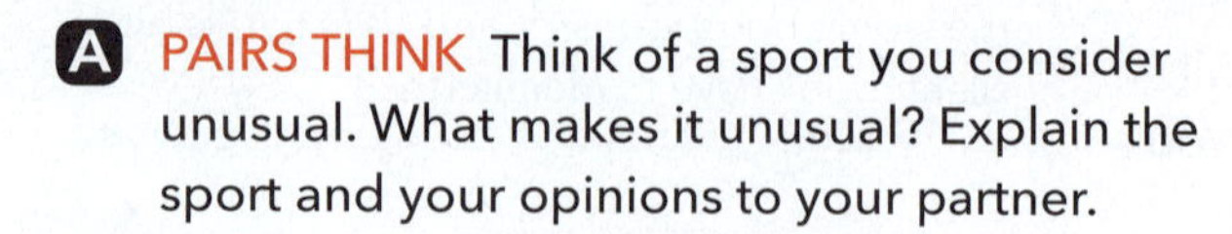

A PAIRS THINK Think of a sport you consider unusual. What makes it unusual? Explain the sport and your opinions to your partner.

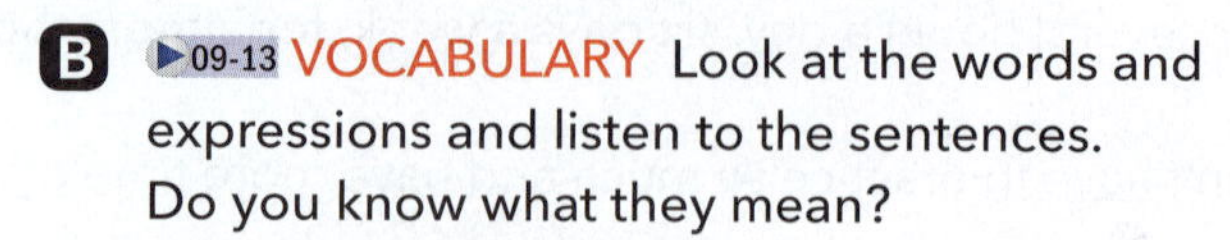

B ▶09-13 VOCABULARY Look at the words and expressions and listen to the sentences. Do you know what they mean?

call for	fetch	eliminate
as opposed to	a tournament	enlightening
play catch	regard as	

>> FOR PRACTICE, PAGE 151 / DEFINITIONS, PAGE 165

capoeira

2 LANGUAGE CHOICES Permission, strong advice, and prohibition

A Read the example sentences. Look at the words in bold expressing permission, strong advice, and prohibition. Then write those words in the correct categories in the chart.

Example sentences

1. You **ought to** rest the night before a big game.
2. We **should** wait for instructions before we begin.
3. You**'re allowed to** take breaks between games.
4. We**'re not allowed to** use our phones during the trivia game.
5. You **had better** stretch before the game begins.
6. We**'re supposed to** arrive an hour early.
7. Athletes **must not** use non-prescription drugs.
8. You **may** join our team if you'd like, or you **can** choose another team.
9. You **can't** park your car there.

Permission	Strong advice	Prohibition

>> FOR PRACTICE, PAGE 151

B PAIRS Discuss the differences in meaning in these sentences. Describe situations in which they might be used.

1. You're not allowed to participate with a sprained ankle.
2. You can't participate with a sprained ankle.
3. You must not participate with a sprained ankle.
4. You had better not participate with a sprained ankle.
5. You're not supposed to participate with a sprained ankle.

3 VIDEO TALK

A ▶09-15 Listen or watch. What is the tone of this lecture?

B ▶09-15 Read the Note-taking Skill. Listen or watch again and complete the chart.

NOTE-TAKING SKILL List a series of arguments

Sometimes a speaker will present a series of arguments and counterarguments when trying to answer a conceptual question. The counterarguments explain why each potential answer is incorrect or insufficient. In your notes, list each potential answer and the counterarguments against it.

What makes a sport a sport?	Counterarguments
Playing with a ball	
Playing on a team	
Playing competitively	
Using physical skill and coordination	
Being included in the Olympics	

C What does the speaker conclude?

D PAIRS REACT Which of the speaker's criteria do you think are most important in defining something as a sport? Why?

4 DISCUSSION SKILL

Read the discussion skill. Which of these phrases do you already use in your discussions?

Express strong opinions

In a group discussion, express strong opinions with phrases like these:

Obviously...

It seems clear to me...

There's no doubt...

5 TRY IT YOURSELF

Read online about hot-air ballooning, tug-of-war, and motor boating. What do these activities look like?

A THINK The activities in the chart were included in the Olympics at least once. List an argument for and against each one being considered a sport.

	For	Against
Hot-air ballooning		
Tug-of-war		
Motor boating		

B DISCUSS In small groups, present your arguments.

C EVALUATE Decide which are the strongest arguments for and against each activity being considered a sport.

TAE-HO KANG
@Tae-hoK
I'm a big soccer fan and go to a lot of games. Who likes to paint their face or wear team colors?

1 BEFORE YOU READ

A PAIRS What are some of the ways fans express support for their favorite sports teams?

B ▶09-16 VOCABULARY Read and listen. Do you know these words?

strut	prioritize	ostracize	eccentric	monotonous
eye-catching	disproportionate	manifest	contradictory	take its toll

>> FOR DEFINITIONS, PAGE 165

2 READ

A PREVIEW Read the title, look at the picture, and read the caption. What do you think the interview will be about?

B ▶09-17 Read and listen to the interview. Was your prediction correct?

An Interview with

Alan Harris

Author of *Sports Superfans*

Sports superfans supporting their teams

We've all seen them strutting or dancing around at sporting events wearing colorful, eye-catching clothes or costumes and body paint in their team's colors. They spare no expense buying team souvenirs and traveling across the country to attend games. They prioritize attending team events over personal obligations, including weddings and funerals, and may even name a child after their team's coach. They're sports superfans, the subject of the new book by Alan Harris, whom I had the pleasure of interviewing.

Q: Alan, what is the motivation behind the disproportionate enthusiasm of sports superfans that you document in your book compared to that of average fans?

A: Fundamentally, I think it stems from a strong desire to be part of a group. It's related to our survival instinct. In ancient times, if your group ostracized you, it often meant death. In the case of sports superfans, the intensity of this primitive instinct manifests itself as a display of allegiance to sports teams in a big way.

Q: I see. But, doesn't such eccentric behavior put superfans at risk of being ostracized?

A: While it's certainly true that the behavior of superfans is eccentric, in their private lives, they're generally people who fit into society very well. One concept that helps to explain this two-sided personality is the theory of optimal distinctiveness, which holds that people have two conflicting needs: to fit in and to be distinctive. Everyone finds a compromise between these two contradictory impulses. Most people seek a balance that allows them to satisfy both needs in a reasonable way. Sports superfans, however, are different in that they seek to make a spectacle of themselves while still gaining acceptance from the group.

Q: Isn't transitioning between extremely extroverted behavior at weekend sporting events and a monotonous office job during the week difficult for sports superfans?

A: Research confirms that it is. The intense personal investment that superfans feel for their team can cause chemical changes in the body. Studies on soccer professionals and soccer superfans have revealed that the increased hormone levels after a win and the decreased levels after a loss are the same in both groups. One fan I spoke with explained that when his team wins, the high lasts a week, but that after a loss, he can't sleep as memories of the game keep running through his head over and over, so he goes to work exhausted the next day.

>>

>

Q: Wow! That must really take its toll. Don't you think superfans are taking things too far?

A: I know what you mean, but I have a more positive take on them. Professional sports have assumed a central place in the social life of modern societies. They're one of the few 55 things that everyone can connect with. In the diverse and inclusive world of sports fans, the enthusiasm of superfans is constructive energy that can really benefit society by helping to build bridges between all kinds of people.

3 CHECK YOUR UNDERSTANDING

A Answer the questions according to the interview.

1. How is the behavior of a sports superfan related to that of ancient humans?
2. What is the theory of optimal distinctiveness and how does it apply to superfans?
3. What are the physiological effects of a superfan's behavior?
4. What is Harris's positive view of the role of sports superfans in society?

B CLOSE READING Reread the lines. Then circle the correct answers.

1. What follows the colon (:) in the sentence in lines 24–27?
   a. a more exact purpose for the previous phrase
   b. a more precise explanation of the previous phrase
   c. a new piece of evidence for the previous phrase
2. In lines 39–46, how is the second sentence connected to the first?
   a. a relevant anecdote b. supporting evidence c. a contrasting opinion

C Read the Reading Skill. Then circle the correct answers.

1. In line 9, who does *whom* refer to?
   a. Alan Harris
   b. superfans
2. In line 13, what does *that* refer to?
   a. the motivation
   b. the disproportionate enthusiasm
3. In line 22, what does *it* refer to?
   a. that superfans are eccentric
   b. no referent
4. In line 39, what does *it* refer to? a. extroverted behavior b. transitioning
5. In line 54, what does *They* refer to? a. professional sports b. modern societies

READING SKILL Understand referential cohesion

Referential cohesion is the way some parts of a text refer to other parts. Personal and demonstrative pronouns (for example, *he*, *they*, *this*, *those*) are often used for this purpose as they avoid repetition. Understanding the referents of such pronouns is essential to a correct understanding of nearly any text.

D PAIRS Summarize the interview in 3–5 sentences.

Search online for videos of sports superfans doing their thing. Share the link with the class.

4 MAKE IT PERSONAL

A THINK In what ways do you try to be part of groups? In what ways do you try to be distinctive? Take notes.

B GROUPS Share your ideas. Then assign each person a score from 1 to 10 for "need to fit in" and for "need to be distinctive." Based on the two scores, decide who would most likely enjoy being a sports superfan.

C EVALUATE In the same groups, discuss how well your score ratio predicts your actual feelings about becoming a sports superfan.

☐ I CAN READ ABOUT SPORTS FANS.

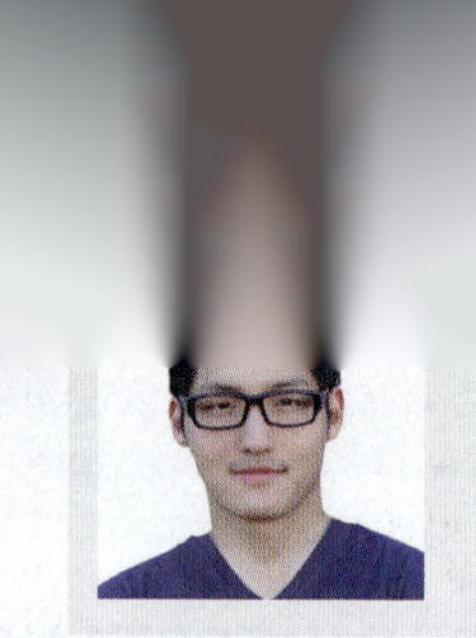

1 BEFORE YOU WRITE

A Read about "how-to" instructions.

When you are writing instructions for how to do something, you need to be sure they are clear and easy to follow. At the same time, you want to make sure not to forget any steps. Instructions for how to play a sport should include information on the number of players, any equipment needed, the rules for playing the game, and how to win the game.

B Read the instructions on how to play bossaball. What are some differences between bossaball and volleyball?

Bossaball Rules

Bossaball is a relatively new game which was invented in Spain. It is similar to volleyball, but with some important differences. It is meant to be played with music; its name is associated with the Brazilian music *bossa nova*.

Players and Equipment

To play bossaball, you need two teams of four players. Male and female players can be mixed.

For equipment, you need a bossaball court and a ball. You can buy your own court, but it is probably easier to rent one at a beach club or resort, where the sport is popular. The court is an inflatable surface around 45 meters long and 25 meters wide. There is a 3-meter-high net across the center of the court. On each side of the net, there is a trampoline in the center of the inflatable surface. One player is always on the trampoline.

Object of the Game

The goal is to score as many points as possible by hitting the ball over the net. You may hit the ball with any part of your body—the more creative, the better!

Playing the Game

One team serves, and then the rally begins. Each team may only touch the ball up to five times before the ball must go over the net. If the team does not succeed, the opposite team wins points (see "Scoring Points") and it also gets the next serve. Each time a team scores, the players rotate so that a different player is on the trampoline.

Scoring Points

If you hit the ball over the net and your opponent cannot return it, you earn points. Either team may score points, whether or not it is serving. If the ball hits the playing surface on the other side of the net, your team wins points as follows:

Hitting the ball with your hands ("volleyball touch")	• 3 points if the ball hits the trampoline on your opponent's side of the net • 1 point if the ball hits the playing area outside the trampoline
Hitting the ball with another part of your body ("soccer touch")	• 5 points if the ball hits the trampoline on your opponent's side of the net • 3 points if the ball hits the playing area outside the trampoline
If the ball touches the "bossawall" (the ring around the trampoline), no points are scored and play continues.	

Winning the game The first team to score 25 points wins the game. But you must win by 2 points, so if the score is tied at 24–24, the game continues until one team is ahead by 2 points.

C PAIRS Can you explain the scoring system for bossaball?

D Read the model again. Take notes in the chart.

About the game	Players and equipment
- invented in ___ - similar to ___ - to be played with ___	- 2 teams of ___ players - court: ___ surface with ___ high net and ___ with ___ on each side - ball
Object of the game	**Playing the game**
- score points by ___ - hit ball with ___	- ball must go over the net after ___ hits (or fewer) - when team scores, earns ___, get next ___ - players ___ when points are scored
Winning	**Scoring**
- first team to get ___ wins - must win by ___	- "volleyball touch": 3 points on ___, 1 point on ___ - "soccer touch": ___ points on trampoline, 3 points on playing area - ball hits "bossawall": ___, play continues

2 FOCUS ON WRITING

PAIRS Read the Writing Skill. Then reread the model. What techniques does the model employ to be clear to the reader? Work together to make a list.

WRITING SKILL Write like a reader

To make sure that your writing is clear and easy to understand, ask yourself: Would I understand this if I were the reader? Information should be presented in a logical order, and no information should be omitted. Extra wordiness should be avoided, but any technical terms must be explained. Ask a friend to read your writing and tell you if it's clear.

3 PLAN YOUR WRITING

A Think of a sport or a game that you know well. Prepare to write instructions for it. Create a chart like in 1D as a model.

B PAIRS Discuss your ideas.

I don't play sports, but I like board games. I'll write about...

Writing tip

Most writing software includes spelling and grammar checks, but to be extra certain that you have no typos, try reading out loud, backwards. Read one word at a time from the last word back to the first word.

4 WRITE

Write a first draft of a set of instructions. Remember to write like a reader. Use the instructions in 1B as a model.

5 AFTER YOUR FIRST DRAFT

A PEER REVIEW Read your partner's instructions. Answer the questions.

- Do you understand how to play the game or sport after reading the instructions?
- Do subtitles help you see at a glance where the information is?
- Is there an overview of the game or sport at the start of the instructions?
- Do the instructions make it clear how to win the game or sport?
- Do the instructions proceed in a logical way and are all technical terms explained?

B REVISE Write another draft based on the feedback you got from your partner.

C PROOFREAD Check the spelling, grammar, and punctuation in your instructions. Then read it through again for overall sense.

☐ I CAN WRITE A SET OF INSTRUCTIONS.

PUT IT TOGETHER

1 PROBLEM SOLVING

A CONSIDER THE PROBLEM Sports can be a lot of fun to play and a great way to get exercise, but they can also lead to injuries. Some injuries, like bruises, are minor, but others, like concussions, can do long-term damage. Review the picture and circle the correct answers.

1. Elbow injuries are most likely to come from playing **board games / tennis / hockey**.
2. Playing soccer is most likely to result in **finger fractures / shoulder injuries / foot injuries**.
3. The sport most likely to lead to the widest range of injuries is **rugby / swimming / ping pong**.

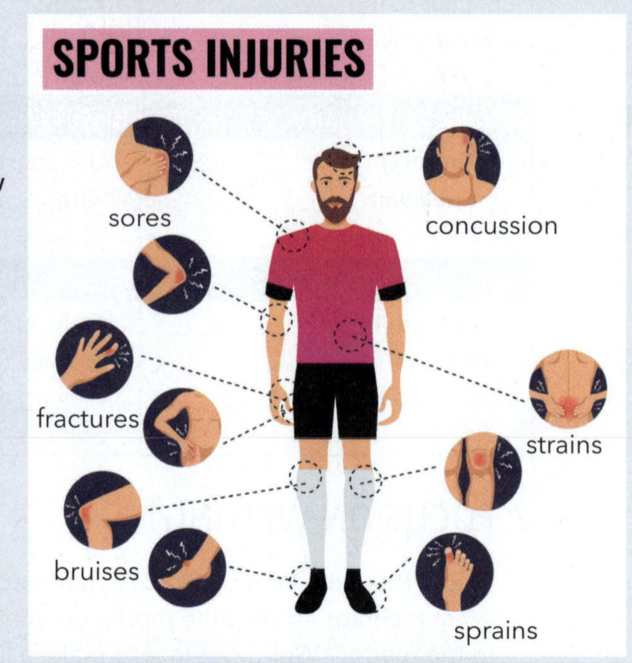

B THINK CRITICALLY Why are some sports more likely to lead to injuries than others? Talk with a partner.

C FIND A SOLUTION Consider the data, the problem, and possible solutions in small groups.

Step 1 **Brainstorm** Think of 3–5 ways that people can continue to enjoy sports and get exercise while limiting the risk of the physical injuries they sometimes cause.

Step 2 **Evaluate** Choose the best solution. Consider things that people can do before, during, and after playing sports.

Step 3 **Present** Explain the best solution to the class. Refer to the data to support your ideas.

2 REFLECT AND PLAN

A Look back through the unit. Check (✓) the things you learned. Highlight the things you need to learn.

Speaking Objectives
- ☐ Talk about athletic competition
- ☐ Talk about esports
- ☐ Talk about what a sport is

Vocabulary
- ☐ Words related to athletic ability

Conversation
- ☐ Build empathy with active listening

Pronunciation
- ☐ Expressions of necessity

Listening
- ☐ Infer the target audience

Note-taking
- ☐ List a series of arguments

Language Choices
- ☐ Modals for speculation and expectation
- ☐ Expressing necessity and obligation
- ☐ Permission, strong advice, and prohibition

Discussion
- ☐ Express strong opinions

Reading
- ☐ Understand referential cohesion

Writing
- ☐ Write like a reader

B What will you do to learn the things you highlighted?

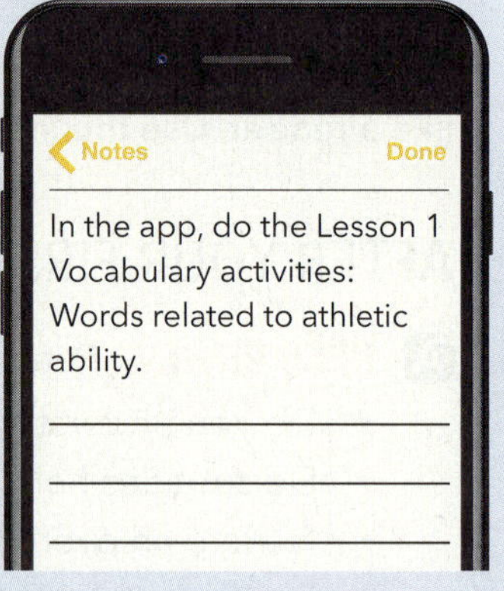

10 REMEMBER WHEN?

LEARNING GOALS

In this unit, you
- talk about a life-changing decision
- talk about a memoir
- discuss life in the past
- read about memories
- write a report

GET STARTED

A Read the unit title and learning goals. People who have experienced the same thing may remember it differently. Why might that be?

B Look at the picture. When you revisit places, you may be struck by how similar or different they are now. Who might be holding the old photo, and why?

C Read Kate's message. What strong memories do you have that are not visual but are based on one of your other senses?

KATE SANDS
@KateS

I've been thinking about memories and how important sounds, smells, and tastes are to me—even the feel of sand between my toes!

1 VOCABULARY Phrasal verbs for talking about life events

A Look at the title. What is meant by "small moments"?

B ▶10-01 Read and listen. Notice the words in bold.

Small Moments That Changed Your Life

SALIM I saw a flyer for a surfing class and decided to **sign up for** it. Now I spend as much time on the waves as I can!

MEI I just kind of **fell into** my career. I **didn't get around to** turning in an application for an office job I wanted, and I **ended up** working for a food truck and eventually getting my own food truck!

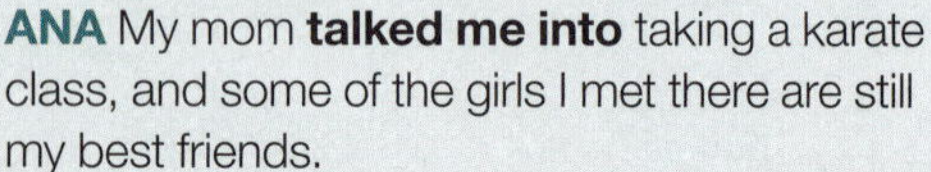
ANA My mom **talked me into** taking a karate class, and some of the girls I met there are still my best friends.

TIM I **met up with** friends for coffee and fell in love with our server!

TONY I **ran into** an old teacher of mine at the market and told him I was looking for work. He gave me the name of a friend who was hiring, I **turned in** an application, and two days later I had a job!

MAHA I started taking guitar lessons because I **came across** my dad's old guitar in the attic. Now I play all the time.

HUGO A friend decided to **pass up** an offer to photograph a wedding. The people needed someone urgently, and I was standing right there, so he recommended me for the job. I've been photographing weddings ever since!

>> FOR PRACTICE, PAGE 152 / DEFINITIONS, PAGE 166

2 LANGUAGE CHOICES Future in the past

When talking about the past, we can refer to a situation that happened after a particular point in the past but before now. To do this, we use expressions for future in the past.

A Read the example sentences. What ideas do these forms express? Check (✓) the correct boxes in the chart. More than one answer may be correct.

Example sentences

1. I **was graduating** soon, so I decided to apply for some jobs.
2. I lost my passport the day before I **was to leave** for Japan.
3. I met Benji on the subway. I never imagined we **would get married** two years later.
4. I thought I **would get** a degree in history, but I ended up studying programming.
5. I always knew you **were going to be** successful.
6. We **were going to stay** in Lima, but I got a great job offer in Dubai.
7. The last time we talked, you **were about to start** a business.

Future in the past

	Prediction	Plan or arrangement	*On the verge of*
would	☐	☐	☐
was / were going to	☐	☐	☐
the past continuous	☐	☐	☐
was / were about to	☐	☐	☐
was / were + infinitive	☐	☐	☐

>> FOR PRACTICE, PAGE 152

B Why does this sentence use *graduated* and *would get*? Did Jon get a job in a big city?

Jon was hoping that when he graduated, he would get a job in a big city.

3 CONVERSATION SKILL

A 10-04 Read the conversation skill. Then listen. Check (✓) the tags you hear.

- ☐ isn't it?
- ☐ aren't they?
- ☐ wouldn't you?
- ☐ right?
- ☐ do you
- ☐ wasn't it?

Maintain interest with question tags

Add question tags to keep your listeners engaged in the conversation and to invite responses. For example:

..., isn't it?

..., would you?

..., right?

B PAIRS Think of a statement to go with each of the tag questions in the conversation skill box. Use one of the statements and its tag question to start a short conversation with your partner.

It's difficult to choose a career, isn't it? I'm interested in so many things.

4 CONVERSATION

A 10-05 Listen. What story does Esra tell?

B 10-05 Listen again. Answer the questions.

1. Why did Kate pick up the key?
2. How did she meet her future husband?
3. What was Esra planning to do after high school?

C 10-06 Listen. Complete the conversation.

Kate: I met up with him to ________________, never knowing that in two years we would be getting married!

Esra: Aww, what a great story! It's incredible how one small decision can change your life, ____________?

Kate: I know! If I hadn't picked up that key, or if I hadn't gotten around to putting up the notice, I probably never would have met him!

Esra: Yeah, it's crazy. I think about that with how I ____________ programming.

5 TRY IT YOURSELF

A THINK Choose a meaningful life event—for example, meeting a friend, finding a job, starting a new hobby, or discovering a favorite place for the first time. Take notes about what led to that event, including small, seemingly insignificant decisions.

Event	
What happened before	
What happened after	

B DISCUSS In small groups, tell your stories. Remember to use question tags to keep your listeners interested. As a group, decide whose story is the most surprising.

☐ I CAN TALK ABOUT A LIFE-CHANGING DECISION.

LESSON 2 TALK ABOUT A MEMOIR

KATE SANDS
@KateS
Some people overcome such difficult circumstances. It's inspiring to read about their lives.

1 BEFORE YOU LISTEN

A PAIRS THINK Would you want to write a memoir—a story about special events in your life? What might inspire others to write their memoirs?

B ▶10-07 VOCABULARY Look at the words and listen to the sentences. Do you know these words?

contemporary	flee	devastating	interweave
an orphanage	harrowing	a passage	grief
an orphan	glittering		

>> FOR PRACTICE, PAGE 153 / DEFINITIONS, PAGE 166

2 LANGUAGE CHOICES Past perfect and past perfect continuous

A Read the example sentences. Then read the rules in the chart. Are they true (*T*) or false (*F*)? Correct the false rules.

Example sentences

1. She **had always dreamed** of becoming a ballerina.
2. They **had never experienced** such a bad storm before.
3. She **had begun** a graduate degree program before she had a stroke.
4. Before moving to New York, she **had been traveling** in South America.
5. Before settling down here, I **had lived** in over a dozen different cities.
6. They **had been vacationing** in Sri Lanka when the tsunami hit.
7. She was exhausted because she **had been dancing** all day.
8. He **had been living** in an orphanage until my aunt adopted him.
9. They **had planned** on fleeing the country, but all the roads were blocked.
10. I **had intended** to read her book but never got around to it.

Past perfect and past perfect continuous

- To form the past perfect, use *have* + past participle. ______
- The past perfect expresses an action that happened after another action in the past. ______
- To form the past perfect continuous, use *had been* + the base form of a verb. ______
- The past perfect continuous shows an activity was in progress before another action in the past. ______
- We can use the past perfect for intentions that were never realized. ______

>> FOR PRACTICE, PAGE 153

B PAIRS What is the difference between these sentences? Discuss your ideas.

Sophie danced for years before she joined the Houston Ballet.
Sophie had danced for years before she joined the Houston Ballet.
Sophie had been dancing for years before she joined the Houston Ballet.

3 PRONUNCIATION

A ▶10-09 Listen. Read the pronunciation note.

B ▶10-10 Listen. Notice how *had* is pronounced. Then listen and repeat.

1. What had he done before he fled the house?
2. When the doctors saw her, they discovered that she'd had a stroke.
3. Christine had been keeping a journal of her struggle to regain her memory.

Auxiliary *had* and stress in past perfect

The auxiliary verb *had* is usually contracted after pronouns and nouns ending in a vowel:

We'd been sitting outside when it started to rain.

After nouns, *had* is often reduced to /əd/:

Matt had finished college before he went to work.

We stress the past participle and present participle. In negatives, *hadn't* is also stressed.

They hadn't moved until the baby was born.

C ▶10-11 Listen and complete the sentences. Add a dot over the stressed verbs. If *had* is reduced to /əd/, cross out the *h* and link (‿) the preceding word with *a* in *had*.

1. When the storm _____________, the cleanup crews came in.
2. Before her traumatic accident, she _____________ a world-class dancer.
3. My friend _____________ the book even though she _____________.

4 LISTENING

A ▶10-12 Listen. What is the purpose of the podcast?

B ▶10-12 Read the Listening Skill. Then listen again and answer the questions.

1. What do the three books have in common?
2. What is different about *Taking Flight*?
3. How is *Tell Me Everything You Don't Remember* different from *Wave*?

LISTENING SKILL Comparisons

Speakers often use words like these to indicate comparisons and contrasts:

in common — *also*
different — *but in this case*
unlike — *on the contrary*

C ▶10-12 Listen again. Take notes in the chart about the events of each memoir.

Taking Flight by Michaela DePrince	
Wave by Sonali Deraniyagala	
Tell Me Everything You Don't Remember by Christine Hyung-Oak Lee	

D PAIRS REACT Which of the three books would you be most interested in reading? Why?

5 TRY IT YOURSELF

A THINK What are three elements that make a memoir interesting to read? Write your ideas.

1. _____________ 2. _____________ 3. _____________

B PAIRS Compare ideas and make a list of the elements of a good memoir. Think of one or two well-known people whose memoir you'd like to read.

C ANALYZE Share your ideas with the class. Decide which three living people might have the most interesting memoir.

☐ I CAN TALK ABOUT A MEMOIR.

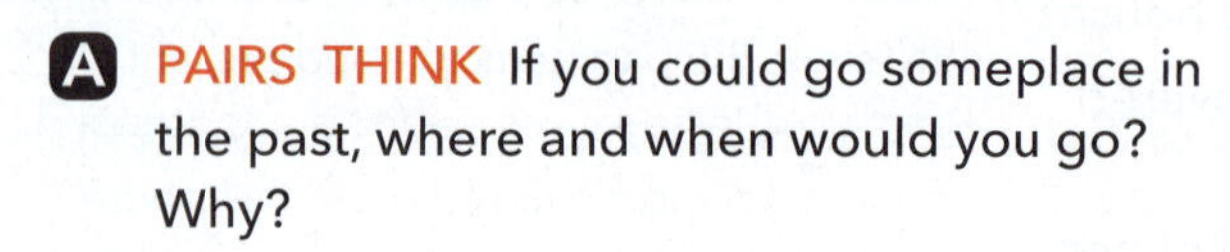

KATE SANDS

@KateS

If I could go back in time, I'd visit western Canada before the Europeans came. I'd love to see what it was like back then!

1 BEFORE YOU LISTEN

A PAIRS THINK If you could go someplace in the past, where and when would you go? Why?

B 10-13 VOCABULARY Look at the words and expressions and listen to the sentences. Do you know what they mean?

nostalgic	an overreliance on	a slab	adequate
a famine	lounge around	upholstery	enticing

>> FOR PRACTICE, PAGE 154 / DEFINITIONS, PAGE 166

2 LANGUAGE CHOICES Expressing the past: Review

A Read the example sentences. Look at the different ways to express the past. Then complete the rules in the chart with the words in the left column.

Form	Example sentences
Simple past	In the nineteenth century, most people **lived** on farms.
Past continuous	In the 1950s, many people **were** still **washing** their clothes by hand.
Present perfect	Technological developments **have changed** the way people live.
Past perfect	By the 1930s, manufacturing jobs **had become** more common.
Past perfect continuous	For centuries before the first airplane, inventors **had been trying** to build a machine that could fly.
Used to	Fruits and vegetables **used to** taste better than they do now.
Would	Before cars were invented, people **would** travel by horse and wagon.

Expressing the past: Review

- Use the ______________ to show an action was in progress at a time in the past.
- Use ______________ or ______________ to show habits or states that were true in the past but are not true now.
- Use the ______________ to show an action occurred at a specific time in the past.
- Use the ______________ to show an action occurred at an indefinite time in the past.
- Use the ______________ to show an action was in progress before another action in the past.
- Use the ______________ to show an action happened before another action in the past.

>> FOR PRACTICE, PAGE 154

B Read this paragraph. Underline each verb and explain why it is used. Pay special attention to *used to* and *would*. What is the difference in meaning between *used to* and *would*?

I've worked at many different places. I used to work at a coffee shop when I was younger. It was my favorite job in college. I used to hang out there all the time, even on days when I wasn't working. I would do my homework or spend time with friends. And by the time I graduated, I'd become a coffee expert.

3 VIDEO TALK

A ▶10-15 Listen or watch. What is the speaker's main idea? Write it in the chart below.

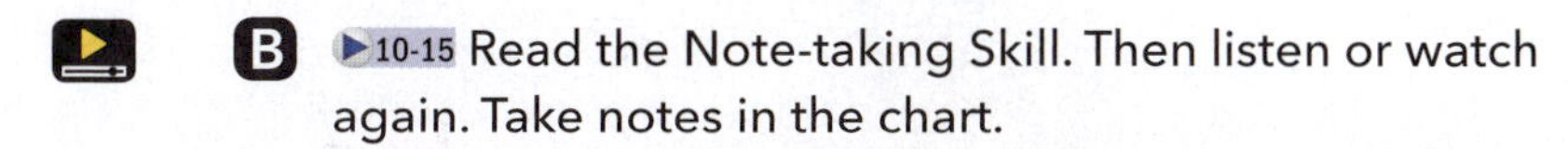

B ▶10-15 Read the Note-taking Skill. Then listen or watch again. Take notes in the chart.

NOTE-TAKING SKILL Listen for reasons

Reasons are facts that explain why something happens. Speakers often give reasons to support a main idea. Listen for the reasons and write them in your notes. Write the reasons under or next to the main idea.

Main idea	Reasons
	1. 2. 3. 4. 5.

C What part of the world does the speaker refer to most? Do you think these problems were the same, worse, or better in other areas?

D PAIRS REACT Were you surprised by any of the speaker's ideas? What are some negative things about living in the past that the speaker didn't mention?

4 DISCUSSION SKILL

Read the discussion skill. Write a rhetorical question that you could use in your discussion about past times.

____

Ask rhetorical questions

You can emphasize a point and engage others by asking a rhetorical question—a question that you want the listener to think about but don't expect him or her to answer. For example:

Don't they look glamorous in their old-fashioned clothes?

Who wouldn't want to be the first person to see this beautiful place?

Why would anyone want to live in a time before the telephone?

5 TRY IT YOURSELF

A THINK Pick a place and time in the past. What do you think would be the best and worst things about living in that time and place? Take notes in the chart.

Place: ______________	Time period: ______________
Best	Worst

B DISCUSS In small groups, discuss your ideas. Choose one of the locations and time periods and add more ideas to the best / worst lists.

C ANALYZE Share your group's ideas with the class. As a class, decide which of the chosen places / time periods would be the best and worst to live in and why.

☐ I CAN DISCUSS LIFE IN THE PAST.

READ ABOUT MEMORIES

KATE SANDS
@KateS
Everyone says college is the best time of your life. But I'm not so sure I agree.

1 BEFORE YOU READ

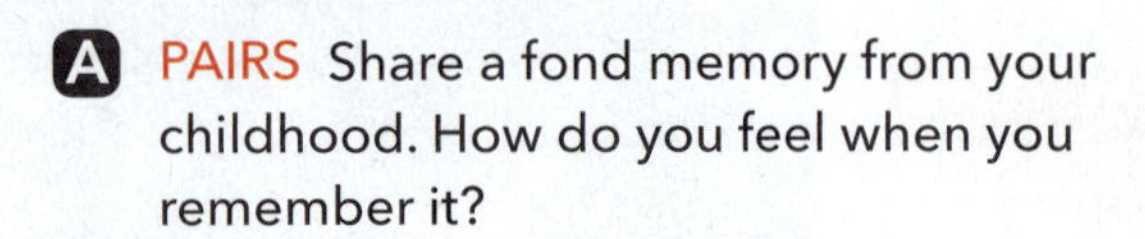

A PAIRS Share a fond memory from your childhood. How do you feel when you remember it?

B ▶10-16 VOCABULARY Read and listen. Do you know these words?

mediocre	rosy	self-esteem	instill	enviable
a recollection	elapse	consequent	a yearning	in retrospect

>> FOR DEFINITIONS, PAGE 166

2 READ

A PREVIEW Read the title, look at the picture, and read the caption. What do you think the article will be about?

B ▶10-17 Read and listen to the article. Was your prediction correct?

Home | Technology | Work | Social Media

DO WE VIEW THE PAST THROUGH ROSE-COLORED GLASSES?

A summer trip with the family to a theme park seems like a wonderful idea. As you load up the car, the kids can hardly contain their excitement. Along the way, you have to deal with a flat tire, and at the park, there are the usual high prices, long lines, occasional rudeness, and mediocre food. It's a relief when you get home, and you tell yourself it's the last time you'll go. But somehow, in the following months, all the negative memories seem to fade, leaving mostly happy recollections and the general sense that you had a good time. Next summer, or the summer after that, you will probably look forward to going again. 5

The memory changes described above are what psychologists call *rosy retrospection,* a cognitive bias that makes past events seem more positive upon later reflection than they were in reality. Several studies have confirmed this bias. For example, bicyclists who were surveyed before, during, and after a three-week tour recalled their trip in a more positive light after some time had elapsed. This provides evidence of a phenomenon known as *fading affect bias*, that is, the way the brain retains positive memories while allowing negative ones to fade. 10

This distorted yet rosy view of the past seems to have a largely positive effect on our well-being as viewing life positively is a coping mechanism that helps fight depression while bolstering an individual's sense of self-esteem and belief in personal control over influences that shape our lives. At work, letting go of negative memories reduces anxiety and enhances productivity. Furthermore, forgetting the pain of past failures eliminates the consequent regrets and fears that could be barriers to healthy risk-taking.

15 However, rosy retrospection has drawbacks. Since we learn from our mistakes, forgetting their negative consequences can prevent us from learning valuable lessons. As a result, we might find ourselves repeatedly in the same bad situation. For example, if you only remember the exciting aspects of a hike climbing a mountain with friends and not how much you regretted having sore legs for a 20 week after, you could easily find yourself making the same mistake again. Rosy retrospection has also been linked to a *declinist* perspective: the belief that a situation is in decline and heading, in the long run, toward collapse. Adopting this perspective instills the idea that our best days are behind us and a yearning for "the good old days." Declinist arguments are often used by politicians, and 25 although historians have shown that they are frequently false, they can effectively appeal to a bias toward a past that looks enviable in retrospect. >>

If you say someone sees the world through rose-colored glasses, you mean they prefer to see everything in a positive light.

So, while researchers have confirmed the benefits of rosy retrospection for our well-being and its value as a coping mechanism, by maintaining an awareness of its effects, we can also improve the accuracy of our judgment and decision-making. This might help us avoid falling into a declinist perspective. In sum, rosy retrospection should have a net positive effect
30 as long as we make sure not to prefer that rosy view of the past to a genuinely bright future.

3 CHECK YOUR UNDERSTANDING

A Answer the questions according to the article.

1. What is the purpose of the story in the first paragraph?
2. What is the relationship between fading affect bias and rosy retrospection?
3. How is a declinist perspective sometimes exploited?
4. How does the writer suggest we deal with the effects of rosy retrospection?

B CLOSE READING Reread the lines. Then circle the correct answers.

1. In the sentence in lines 9–10, why does the author use the phrase *that is?*
   a. to introduce a phrase with the same meaning as *fading affect bias*
   b. to introduce the cause of fading affect bias
   c. to provide an example of fading affect bias
2. Which sentence is closest in meaning to the sentence in lines 24–26?
   a. Because they are often false, declinist arguments have limited appeal in politics.
   b. In politics, declinist arguments, despite often being false, are persuasive.
   c. Declinist arguments by politicians are frequently unconvincing and exposed as false.

READING SKILL Use a cause-and-effect T-chart

Using a T-chart with causes on the left in line with their effects on the right allows you to clearly visualize the effects of phenomena to understand them better.

C Read the Reading Skill. Then complete the chart.

Causes	Effects
1. letting go of negative memories	1. ______________
2. forgetting the pain of past failures	2. ______________
3. forgetting the negative consequences of mistakes	3. ______________
4. a declinist perspective	4. ______________
5. an awareness of the effects of rosy retrospection	5. ______________

D PAIRS Summarize the article in 3–5 sentences.

Search song lyrics or poems for words like *memory*, *remember*, and *recall*. Identify examples that do and don't feature rosy retrospection.

4 MAKE IT PERSONAL

A THINK What did you do yesterday? List three things that you remember fondly and three things you'd rather forget. What are you most likely to remember about yesterday?

B GROUPS Compare yesterday's fond and unpleasant memories and decide which ones are most likely to be remembered over time.

C EVALUATE From the group's findings, write a list of three rules that seem to influence whether a memory will be retained or not.

☐ I CAN READ ABOUT MEMORIES.

KATE SANDS

@KateS

Writing a report on the Jessica Matthews presentation I saw with Carla last week. Luckily, I took great notes! 😉

1 BEFORE YOU WRITE

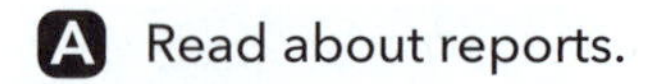

A Read about reports.

In work situations, employees may go to see a lecture or a presentation on a relevant topic. Sometimes the employee is asked to prepare a report to share with other colleagues. The report should summarize the important information and include any "takeaways" or action items: ideas that can be put to use in the employee's workplace.

B Read the report. What takeaways did Kate include?

The Jessica O. Matthews Presentation – Summary Report

Overview

The presentation was about Jessica O. Matthews, the CEO of the company Uncharted Power. This company develops tech / energy products for areas with limited access to stable sources of electricity. The speaker discussed the company's founding, its mission and products, and the personal values Matthews brings to the company.

Summary

Matthews first got the idea for the company when she was a sophomore in college. After attending an aunt's wedding in Nigeria, where the power went out, she came up with the idea for a soccer ball that stores the energy that is generated when it is played with. After one hour of play, this soccer ball (called the Soccket) can light an LED lamp for three hours; it can light the lamp for three days when fully charged.

After college, Matthews went on to found the company Uncharted Play. She added other energy-generating toys to her product line. Then, because she wanted to focus on tech products and not just on toys, Matthews changed the company name to Uncharted Power. The company now designs infrastructure facilities, such as a hydroelectric dam in Nigeria.

The speaker also focused on the personal challenges Matthews faces as a CEO who is a woman of color. Because of her gender and ethnicity, Matthews believes in the importance of having a diverse workforce and working in a diverse community. Uncharted Power is a successful company and an inspiration to others. They have won several awards, and they give back to their community, for example, by supporting the teaching of science, math, and design to students who lack opportunity.

Takeaways

TSW Media seeks to be innovative and to represent many different communities, so we can learn a lot from Jessica O. Matthews. Here are some possible takeaways:

1. *We should think about the "unauthorized use" of objects.* Matthews created the Soccket by taking an ordinary item and using it in a different way than was originally intended. Similarly, we should always be looking at items around us and considering the multiple uses they might have.
2. *We can tap into the diversity of our workforce.* What talents, knowledge, or information might our employees bring to the table? Matthews got her idea by going to an aunt's wedding in Nigeria. Perhaps our employees have knowledge from their personal lives that can inform the company of an unfulfilled need.
3. *We should make sure to create a diverse team.* We can look at our hiring choices, as Matthews did. Which communities can be better represented through these choices?

C PAIRS Do you think the takeaways are useful? Are there other takeaways you can think of?

D Read the model again. Complete Kate's notes.

Key words	Notes
Jessica O. Matthews background	- when sophomore at Harvard, went to ____________ in Nigeria - power went out; used diesel generator – noxious fumes - engineering class assignment: invent something to help people in developing countries → invented ____________ >>

The Soccket	- soccer ball that stores _____________ generated when played with - after one hour of play, can light _____________ for 3 hours! - when _____________, stays lit for 72 hours
Uncharted Play	- after college, founded company _____________ - created kinetic energy toys: jump rope, skateboard
Uncharted Power	- changed name to Uncharted Power – to focus on _____________ - address infrastructure problems → _____________ project in Nigeria - funding from Disney
Diversity	- other challenges: race, gender – rare as CEO - hiring people from _____________ – 30-40% black or Latino - moved headquarters to Harlem – diverse neighborhood
What else?	- _____________ won: *Fortune's* Most Promising Women, *Forbes* 30 under 30, Harvard, *Tech Crunch* - supports teaching math, science, design to students who _____________ - inspires others

2 FOCUS ON WRITING

Read the Writing Skill. Then reread the notes in 1D and the model. Check (✓) the sentences that were included in the final report.

WRITING SKILL Omit unnecessary information

Reports and summaries need to be concise and free of unnecessary information. Ask yourself: *Does the reader need this information to make inferences or draw a conclusion about the topic?* If not, you can probably cut that information.

☐ 1. Jessica O. Matthews got her first idea when she was a sophomore in college.
☐ 2. The diesel generator in Nigeria created noxious fumes.
☐ 3. The Soccket is a soccer ball that stores the energy generated when it is used.
☐ 4. The workforce of Uncharted Power is 30–40% black or Latino.
☐ 5. Matthews won awards from *Forbes*, *Fortune*, Harvard, and *Tech Crunch*.
☐ 6. Uncharted Power supports teaching math, science, and design to students.

3 PLAN YOUR WRITING

A Think of a lecture or presentation that you have recently attended, or choose one of the talks in this book. Review your notes or take new notes, using the chart in 1D as a model.

B PAIRS Discuss your ideas.

I'm going to do a report on the lecture we just heard about life in the past.

4 WRITE

Write a first draft of a report. Remember to omit unnecessary information. Use the report in 1B as a model.

Writing tip

"Sleep on it." After your first draft, or whenever you are feeling stuck, put it aside. Wait until the next day to come back to it. Your brain processes information and makes connections while you sleep. Coming back to the draft with fresh eyes can help you make improvements and continue more easily with the writing.

5 AFTER YOUR FIRST DRAFT

A PEER REVIEW Read your partner's report. Answer the questions.

- Does the report have an overview that summarizes the topic?
- Is all of the information relevant? Can anything be eliminated? Is more information needed?

B REVISE Write another draft based on the feedback you got from your partner.

C PROOFREAD Check the spelling, grammar, and punctuation in your report.

PUT IT TOGETHER

1 PROBLEM SOLVING

A CONSIDER THE PROBLEM The world's estimated 7,000 languages are dying at a rate of about one every two weeks. When a language dies, unique words and expressions are lost. Review the chart and **circle** the correct answers.

International phrases with unique meanings		
Language	Phrase	Meaning
Hawaiian	*pana po'o*	scratching your head to help remember
Inuit	*iktsuarpok*	a feeling of anticipation waiting for someone to arrive
Yaghan	*mamihlapinatapai*	two people wanting to do something but neither does it
Yiddish	*luftmensch*	an impractical dreamer who is bad at business

1. The term *luftmensch* is the opposite of **romantic / entrepreneur / idealist**.
2. You might step outside to check for a guest when you feel ***mamihlapinatapai / iktsuarpok / pana po'o***.
3. The phrase that most relates to memory is ***mamihlapinatapai / iktsuarpok / pana po'o***.

B THINK CRITICALLY Why do you think so many of the world's languages are disappearing? Why might this be considered a problem? Discuss with a partner.

C FIND A SOLUTION Consider the problem *mamihlapinatapai* and possible solutions in small groups.

Step 1 **Brainstorm** Think of 3–5 ways that we can prevent some of the world's languages from disappearing.

Step 2 **Evaluate** Choose the best solution. Consider the impact that the solutions will have on preserving world cultures and diversity.

Step 3 **Present** Explain the best solution to the class. Refer to the chart to support your ideas.

2 REFLECT AND PLAN

A Look back through the unit. Check (✓) the things you learned. Highlight the things you need to learn.

Speaking Objectives
- ☐ Talk about a life-changing decision
- ☐ Talk about a memoir
- ☐ Discuss life in the past

Vocabulary
- ☐ Phrasal verbs for talking about life events

Conversation
- ☐ Maintain interest with question tags

Pronunciation
- ☐ Auxiliary *had* and stress in past perfect

Listening
- ☐ Comparisons

Note-taking
- ☐ Listen for reasons

Language Choices
- ☐ Future in the past
- ☐ Past perfect and past perfect continuous
- ☐ Expressing the past: Review

Discussion
- ☐ Ask rhetorical questions

Reading
- ☐ Use a cause-and-effect T-chart

Writing
- ☐ Omit unnecessary information

B What will you do to learn the things you highlighted?

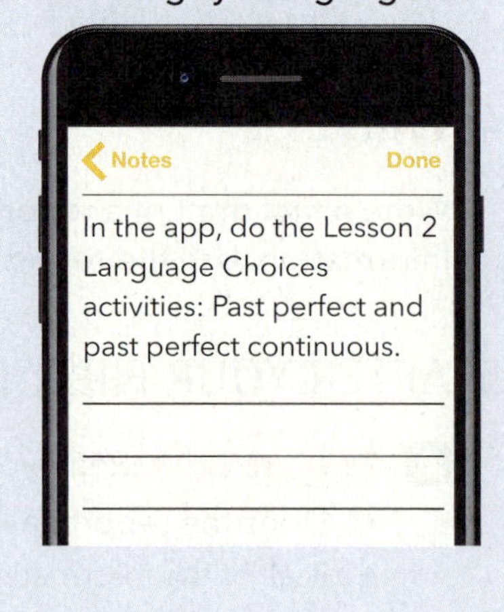

VOCABULARY PRACTICE

▶01-02 Listen. Complete the sentences with the correct form of the words in the box.

high season	low season	plan ahead	an itinerary	plan out	a day trip
play it by ear	open-ended	impromptu	serendipity	take off	

1. They didn't ______________ . They just ______________ on Friday morning. It was a(n) ______________ trip.
2. They don't have a(n) ______________ . They are going to ______________ .
3. They went during ______________ . They took a(n) ______________ to the pyramids.

PRESENT PERFECT VS. SIMPLE PAST

A ▶01-03 Listen. Check (✓) the correct answer.

	Yes	No	Can't say
1. Does he currently live in NYC?	✓	☐	☐
2. Did she lose her wallet a while ago?	☐	☐	☐
3. Are the dancers still performing?	☐	☐	☐
4. Did we return a long time ago?	☐	☐	☐
5. Does Ben still go on a cruise with his family in the summer?	☐	☐	☐
6. Were they on this vacation recently?	☐	☐	☐
7. Does Ping continue to visit her parents in China?	☐	☐	☐
8. Is it past noon now?	☐	☐	☐

B Complete the blog with the correct form of the verb in parentheses. Use contractions when possible.

Home • Blog • News • Logout

To plan or not to plan...?

So, I know a lot of people who __have backpacked__ (1 backpack) through Europe. My brother Zack ______________ (2 go) after college, and he ______________ (3 visit) fourteen countries! He ______________ (4 not have) a plan. Every day he simply ______________ (5 do) something different. Zack always says this was the best experience he ______________ (6 ever have).

That type of spontaneity gives me anxiety. Don't get me wrong, I love to travel. But I ______________ (7 always be) very precise about my planning. ______________ (8 even study) languages before going to a foreign country. How will I know which language I need to know if I don't know where I'm going?

By the way, Zack ______________ (9 not return) to the United States. His last stop ______________ (10 be) Belgium, and he ______________ (11 live) there ever since! He has a good job, a family, and a great life! Maybe there is something to not planning!

VOCABULARY PRACTICE Complete the sentences with the correct form of the words in the box.

a spacecraft	a rover	terraform	colonize	inhospitable
an asteroid	bombard	radiation	a dust storm	toxic

1. ________________ don't usually hit Earth because they burn up in the atmosphere.
2. Last winter we were ________________ by a long series of storms.
3. It takes about 300 days for a(n) ________________ to fly from Earth to Mars.
4. The Arctic is ________________ because of the cold weather and the dark winters.
5. If we ________________ Mars, people will probably have to live under domes.
6. A(n) ________________ can fill the sky until it's so dark that you can't see the sun.
7. The stream water is ________________ now because of pollution from the factory.
8. The ________________ on Mars moves very slowly, but it has taken amazing pictures.
9. The workers at the reactor have to be careful to avoid ________________ poisoning.
10. The movies make it look easy to ________________ a planet, but we don't actually know how to do it yet.

INDEFINITE PRONOUNS

A ▶01-08 **Listen. Circle the sentence similar in meaning.**

1. (a.) All things are possible with space exploration.
   b. Not many things are possible with space exploration.
2. a. Several people are participating.
   b. Not many people are participating.
3. a. Neither item costs a million dollars.
   b. Every item costs a million dollars.
4. a. All parts of the mission were successful
   b. Many parts of the mission were successful, but a few were not.
5. a. Not one and not the other construction is ready.
   b. One of two constructions is ready.
6. a. There is no food left.
   b. There is a little food left.

B **Complete the sentences with the correct form of the verb in parentheses.**

1. Not all applicants ____meet____ (meet) the requirements for the space program.
2. Everything ________________ (need) to be calculated precisely.
3. More time ________________ (be) necessary for research and development.
4. Some stars are bright, and others ________________ (shine) dimly, depending on size and distance from Earth.
5. Nobody that I know ________________ (believe) in extraterrestrial life.
6. Both scientists ________________ (want) their findings to be recognized.

VOCABULARY PRACTICE Complete the sentences with the correct form of the words in the box.

abandon	rust	crumble	peel	rot
collapse	dilapidated	moss-covered	damage	

1. It looks like the walls got wet and now the paint is ________________ .
2. After too much time under water, the wood began to ________________ and fall apart.
3. The old building ________________ in the earthquake.
4. The house was so ________________ that it looked like it was going to fall down.
5. The ancient bricks eventually ________________ into dust.
6. The cool forest was full of ________________ trees.
7. Don't leave your bike out in the rain! It will ________________ .
8. There's no one here. The house was ________________ years ago.
9. The storm did a lot of ________________ . It's going to be expensive to repair it all.

TYPES OF ADVERBS

A ▶01-14 **Listen. Circle the sentence similar in meaning.**

1. (a.) It was fortunate that no people got hurt when the bridge collapsed.
   b. The people were thankful that they didn't get hurt when the bridge collapsed.
2. a. We paint our house very often.
   b. We don't paint our house very often.
3. a. I love historic constructions, but not ruins.
   b. I love historic constructions, including ruins.
4. a. Rob will do one of two things.
   b. Rob will do two things.
5. a. You worked honestly on the contract.
   b. You really did a great job with the contract.
6. a. We are making just enough money.
   b. We are almost not making any money.

B **Rewrite the sentences using the adverb in parentheses. Use correct word order.**

1. (rarely) They don't do repairs often.
   They rarely do repairs.
2. (truthfully) To be honest, your bridge design has many flaws.
   ____
3. (just) I need some rust remover; I don't need anything else.
   ____
4. (mostly) The donations were made by women primarily.
   ____
5. (oddly) It was strange that the door opened by itself.
   ____
6. (hardly) They didn't collect much money.
   ____

VOCABULARY PRACTICE

▶02-02 Listen. Write the superpowers they are talking about.

super strength	telekinesis	teleport	telepathic
X-ray vision	a shape-shifter	invisible	invincible

1. The man is ________________ and the woman has ________________ .
2. He is ________________ .
3. Minerva is ________________ .
4. The woman can ________________ .
5. The man has ________________ .
6. The woman is ________________ .
7. He has the power of ________________ .

PRESENT AND FUTURE UNREAL CONDITIONAL

A ▶02-03 Listen. Check (✓) the correct answer.

		True	False	No information
1.	The speaker doesn't have time to talk.	☑	☐	☐
2.	The speaker is in a position of power.	☐	☐	☐
3.	James works somewhere else now.	☐	☐	☐
4.	The speaker is going to listen to the managers' conversation.	☐	☐	☐
5.	They cannot move the desk by themselves.	☐	☐	☐
6.	The speaker wants to do the project again.	☐	☐	☐

B Rewrite the sentences using the present and future unreal conditional.

Part 1

1. I'm not a superhuman, so I can't do everything.
   If I were a superhuman, I could do everything.
2. I'd like to read minds in order to know what you're thinking.
   ____
3. We can't teleport, so we won't be on time.
   ____
4. Superman is not here, so he won't help us.
   ____
5. Mark can't finish that project in a week because he doesn't have superpowers.
   ____

Part 2

1. I'm meeting you for lunch because I have time.
   I wouldn't meet you for lunch if I didn't have time.
2. We're hiring Claire because she does excellent work.
   We wouldn't ____ .
3. We learn important lessons when we make mistakes.
   We wouldn't ____ .

VOCABULARY PRACTICE Complete the sentences with the correct form of the words in the box.

inspire	optimize	a reflection	persistent
rage	excel	promising	

1. When you finish a task, take some time for _______________ . Consider what went well and what didn't.
2. The speaker's words _______________ me to start my search for a new job.
3. Even if something is difficult at first, you should _______________ . It might pay off in the end!
4. The factory is installing robots to _______________ production.
5. With enough practice and determination, I'm sure you will _______________ .
6. When the child spilled wine on the bride's gown, she shook with _______________ .
7. The new team looks very _______________ . I think they'll have a good season.

FUTURE REAL CONDITIONAL

A ▶02-08 Listen. Circle the correct word.

1. The man **is** / **isn't** ready for his interview.
2. The woman **is** / **isn't** willing to help him practice.
3. The man **will** / **won't** get more nervous if he thinks about the interview questions.
4. The woman thinks practice **will** / **won't** help him.
5. The man **is** / **isn't** sure that he's qualified for the job.
6. The woman thinks he **is** / **isn't** qualified.

B Combine the two sentences to form future real conditionals. Do not change the order of the clauses. Use commas when necessary.

1. He should be more persistent. He might succeed.
   If he is more persistent, he might succeed.
2. We should try this new program. We might achieve optimal results.
   ____
3. Let's use a trial and error approach. We will learn from our mistakes.
   ____
4. You'll excel in the new environment. You should accept the job offer.
   ____
5. I can figure out the problem. I need to reflect on it more.
   ____
6. You need to work on your programming skills. You'll master it soon.
   ____

VOCABULARY PRACTICE Complete the sentences with the correct form of the words in the box.

churn out	innate	self-evident	resemble	intervene
consistently	trauma	avenge	thrust	

1. Don't you know the answer? It seems completely ________________ to me!
2. He has psychological problems because he suffered ________________ at an early age.
3. You should attend class ________________ if you want to improve.
4. The child star was ________________ into the spotlight by her parents.
5. She wrote so many books. She ________________ about three a year.
6. Humans have a(n) ________________ desire to live in communities.
7. We told him not to ________________ in the fight.
8. The speaker's ideas ________________ something I read in an article recently.
9. It's the same old story about a man who wants to ________________ the death of the woman he loved.

PRESENT REAL CONDITIONAL

A ▶02-14 **Listen to the beginning of the sentences. Check (✓) the correct ending.**

1. ☐ if you want to choose your seats.
   ☑ you can choose your seats.
2. ☐ if we aren't busy.
   ☐ if we weren't busy.
3. ☐ it often has a sequel.
   ☐ when it has a sequel.
4. ☐ if the hero wins.
   ☐ the hero usually wins.
5. ☐ if someone is hurt?
   ☐ is someone hurt?
6. ☐ how can the person recover quickly?
   ☐ if they recover.

B **Rewrite the sentences as a general statement of fact using present real conditionals. (Hint: Change the definite article *the* to the indefinite article *a* / *an*.)**

1. I didn't like the movie because the ending was obvious.
   I don't like a movie if the ending is obvious.
2. There was a new superhero movie, so Jackson went to see it.
   ____
3. The audience liked the movie because the character had a great origin story.
   ____
4. Anna cried because the movie was sad.
   ____
5. The book was boring, so I fell asleep.
   ____
6. The story was inspirational because the character overcame a traumatic event.
   ____

VOCABULARY PRACTICE

▶03-02 Listen. Complete the sentences with the correct form of the words in the box.

a prodigy	renowned	a virtuoso	knowledgeable	a genius
talent	insightful	gifted	a legend	

1. Coach Talbert is a(n) ______________ around here.
2. Mara always has ______________ ideas.
3. The kid is a(n) ______________ .
4. Rosa is very ______________ about this place.
5. Tom is ______________ at mathematics, but he has no ______________ for music.
6. Dr. Smith is a(n) ______________ expert.

VERB + GERUND VS. INFINITIVE

go on + *-ing* = to continue
go on + infinitive = to do the next thing
mean + *-ing* = to result in something
mean + infinitive = to intend to do something

A ▶03-03 Listen. Check (✓) the correct answer.

		True	False
1.	The speaker wants to know whether or not you read the article.	☑	☐
2.	They never play soccer any more.	☐	☐
3.	The speaker wanted to take piano lessons but probably didn't.	☐	☐
4.	They wish they had not gone to the ballet.	☐	☐
5.	The speaker did not go to the concert.	☐	☐
6.	Alex continued to play after he was injured.	☐	☐

B Complete the sentences by restating the first sentence or pair of sentences.

1. Julie wants to be healthier, so she no longer eats sugar.
   Julie stopped ______eating sugar______ .
2. The championship game was awesome! Marc scored the winning goal.
   Marc will never forget ______________________ .
3. Kelly lived in New York, but she didn't like it. She moved back to Canada.
   Kelly tried ______________________ .
4. I got my sister a birthday card. I didn't forget this year.
   I remembered ______________________ .
5. Scott joined a book club, but he doesn't like it. Plus, it takes too much of his time.
   Scott regrets ______________________ .
6. Even after the music stopped, Isabel continued to dance.
   Isabel went on ______________________ .
7. Sorry I didn't call you last night. I fell asleep.
   I meant ______________________ .
8. We've been working on this project nonstop for hours. We should eat soon.
   Let's stop ______________________ .

VOCABULARY PRACTICE Complete the sentences with the correct form of the words in the box.

a craft	craft	a map	map	an approach	approach
a detail	detail	a focus	focus on	a comment	comment

1. We've ________________ out our route for next summer's road trip, but it's very general. I'll fill in the ________________ as the time gets closer.
2. The phone keeps ringing and I can't ________________ my work.
3. Did you see that article? There are over 1,000 ________________ about it from readers! I almost ________________ on it myself, but I decided not to say anything.
4. My cousin loves to do ________________, especially sewing and jewelry-making.
5. She always takes a very careful ________________ to solving problems.
6. At the meeting the boss ________________ plans for cutting costs. The company's ________________ is going to be on using more robots and paying less for labor.
7. The politician ________________ a carefully worded statement to avoid getting into trouble.
8. There's a large ________________ of the world on the office wall.
9. You shouldn't ________________ any wild animals; they could be dangerous.

GERUND USAGE

A ▶03-08 Listen. Write the gerund you hear. Then check (✓) how it is used.

Gerund	Subject	Object	Object complement	Object of a preposition	With a possessive
1. *creating*	☐	☐	☐	☑	☐
2.	☐	☐	☐	☐	☐
3.	☐	☐	☐	☐	☐
4.	☐	☐	☐	☐	☐
5.	☐	☐	☐	☐	☐
6.	☐	☐	☐	☐	☐

B Combine the sentences. Change the verb in bold to a gerund.

1. We **watched** that movie last night. We had a great time.
   We had a great time watching that movie last night.
2. He **reads** fantasy books. He enjoys it.
   ____
3. I'm trying to **understand** the plot. I'm having trouble.
   ____
4. He always **comments** on my posts. I'm tired of it.
   ____
5. She's **writing** a novel. It isn't easy.
   ____
6. He worries he **won't succeed**. It is his biggest fear.
   ____

VOCABULARY PRACTICE Complete the sentences with the correct form of the words in the box.

an imagination	a perception	detectable	a combination	visual	associate

1. Reading a review of a movie before you see it can affect your ________________ of it.
2. She has an amazing ________________ . You should see her strange drawings!
3. If you look closely, you can see the spots, but they are barely ________________ .
4. Green with purple is a strange ________________ of colors.
5. Do you ________________ certain songs with certain times in your life?
6. If you close your eyes, can you picture the colors of the rainbow? Some people have a much more ________________ view of the world than others.

VERB + OBJECT + INFINITIVE

A 03-14 Listen. Check (✓) the correct answer.

		True	False
1.	The watch detects my heart rate.	✓	☐
2.	The speaker explored new horizons.	☐	☐
3.	Alyssa's parents suggested that she find a career in music.	☐	☐
4.	Attendance is not required at the meeting.	☐	☐
5.	The speaker thinks Jim probably won't finish the book today.	☐	☐
6.	Daniel left early.	☐	☐

B Report what the person said using the verb in parentheses and an object + infinitive. Use the simple past tense.

1. John said, "You should listen to classical music."
   (advise / me) John advised me to listen to classical music.
2. Ella said, "Don't be late."
   (asked / us) ________________
3. Jack said, "Imagine the possibilities."
   (want / me) ________________
4. Amira said, "Remember to turn off the lights before you leave."
   (remind / us) ________________
5. Chris said, "Could you not sing so loudly?"
   (would like / you) ________________
6. I said, "You shouldn't combine those colors."
   (warn / them) ________________

VOCABULARY PRACTICE

▶04-02 Listen. Circle the word that describes each animal.

1. The woman thinks the frogs are **adorable** / **magnificent**. The man thinks they are **exotic** / **gross**.
2. They think the eagle is **precious** / **magnificent** and **unique** / **cute**.
3. The man thinks the fish is **gross** / **striking**. The woman thinks it is **bizarre** / **astonishing**.
4. The man saw a lot of **exotic** / **adorable** birds. The woman thinks the bird in the picture is **astonishing** / **peculiar**.

ARTICLES FOR GENERAL AND SPECIFIC NOUNS

A ▶04-03 Listen. Is the noun general or specific? Check (✓) the correct answer.

		General	Specific
1.	dog	☑	☐
2.	fish	☐	☐
3.	kangaroo	☐	☐

		General	Specific
4.	elephants	☐	☐
5.	elephants	☐	☐
6.	puppy	☐	☐

B Complete Ava's message to her sister with *a*, *an*, *the*, or Ø (no article).

Hi Zoe,

Seeing how you spend hours and hours watching cute animal videos, I know you really want to get __a__ (1) pet. It's true that __Ø__ (2) pets are great companions and provide meaningful social support for their owners. And, of course, it's fun to walk ______ (3) dog or hold ______ (4) cat. But please think carefully about what's involved.

First, you need to consider ______ (5) time commitment involved in pet ownership. You're so busy. Do you really have enough time to take care of ______ (6) puppy or ______ (7) kitten?

You should also think about ______ (8) expense of owning ______ (9) pet. You'll need to pay for ______ (10) animal's food, vaccinations, medical care, and toys. Depending on ______ (11) pet that you choose, you may also need to get ______ (12) cage or ______ (13) aquarium.

You should also think carefully about what kind of pet is most suitable for you. You have ______ (14) full-time job, so you might consider getting ______ (15) cat instead of ______ (16) dog since ______ (17) cats can generally be left alone for longer stretches of time. Or maybe you should get something smaller and easier to take care of. Have you thought about ______ (18) goldfish or ______ (19) hamster?

Whatever you decide, just remember that once you adopt ______ (20) animal, you're responsible for it for the rest of its life. You can't return your pet to ______ (21) shelter, so please take this decision very seriously. Perhaps this isn't ______ (22) best time to get a pet. And remember, if you're not ready, you can always continue watching ______ (23) animal videos! ☺

Love,

Ava

VOCABULARY PRACTICE Complete the sentences with the correct form of the words in the box.

fearful	pessimistic	a lifespan	a shelter
conduct	extensive	extroverted	excitable

1. African elephants have a long ________________ . They can live about 70 years.
2. My cat is really ________________ . She always hides when people come over.
3. Hearing all the bad news about climate change makes me ________________ about the future.
4. If you're a(n) ________________ person, it's hard for you to spend a lot of time alone.
5. They need to ________________ more research to find out what's causing the fish to die.
6. My dog is super ________________ . He runs around and barks every time someone walks past the house.
7. I used to volunteer at an animal ________________ during the summers.
8. It's a good idea to do ________________ research on a new product before you buy it.

QUANTIFIERS WITH SINGULAR VS. PLURAL VERBS

A ▶04-08 **Listen to the beginning of the sentences. Circle the correct ending.**

1.	does	(do)
2.	is, too	are, too
3.	has a dog	have a dog
4.	is limited to cats	are limited to cats
5.	is very calm	are very calm
6.	is decreasing	are decreasing

B **Rewrite the sentences using the quantifier in parentheses. When necessary, change the verb to agree with the subject.**

1. John's puppies are really excitable.
   (each of) Each of John's puppies is really excitable.
2. Those kittens were adopted.
   (every one of) ________________________________
3. The research is available online.
   (all of) ________________________________
4. That report is incorrect.
   (half of) ________________________________
5. The residents in my apartment complex own cats.
   (Twenty percent of) ________________________________
6. The animals in the shelter never get adopted.
   (some of) ________________________________

VOCABULARY PRACTICE Complete the sentences with the correct form of the words in the box.

grieve	mourn	howl	hold a grudge
dive-bomb	scold	be self-aware	feel guilty

1. Don't make my sister mad. She can ________________ for a long time!
2. I ________________ for hurting his feelings. I really didn't mean to.
3. My dog ________________ whenever I play piano. It sounds like he's trying to sing along.
4. The teacher ________________ the children for talking during the lesson.
5. Now that my daughter is 18 months old, she ________________ . She can recognize herself in the mirror.
6. He's still ________________ for his wife, who died a couple of years ago.
7. Often you see birds ________________ toward the ocean in order to get food.
8. We often ________________ after someone we know dies.

ARTICLES FOR KNOWN AND UNKNOWN INFORMATION

A ▶04-14 Listen. Is the noun known or unknown? Check (✓) the correct answer.

	1. wolf	2. dog	3. dog	4. chimpanzees	5. bird	6. kitten
Known	☐	☐	☐	☐	☐	☐
Unknown	✓	☐	☐	☐	☐	☐

B Complete the sentences with the correct form of the noun in parentheses. You may need to add an article.

1. (elephant) ____Elephants____ are very social creatures. We saw ________________ and its mother at the zoo last week. ________________ at the zoo were wrapping their trunks together to hug and show affection.
2. (crow) I read a story about a lost, abandoned kitten. ________________ suddenly dive-bombed the kitten. Everyone gasped because they thought ________________ would hurt the baby cat. They were shocked to discover ________________ was stuffing worms into the kitten's mouth. I guess ________________ are very caring animals.
3. (octopus) A research team in New Zealand taught ________________ how to take photographs. The team placed a waterproof camera near ________________ in its tank. Whenever ________________ took a picture, the team rewarded it with a snack. It took the team about eight weeks to train ________________ to be a photographer.
4. (wolf) A researcher recently conducted a study on ________________ and found that they communicate with more than just howls. They also whine, bark, growl, and snarl. ________________ that the researcher observed worked together to hunt, raise their young, and protect their territory.

VOCABULARY PRACTICE

▶05-02 Listen. Complete the sentences with the correct form of the words in the box.

a partnership	lease	a supplier	cash flow	cut corners
be in the black	be in the red	break even	profitable	flop

1. His business was ________________ last month.
2. Carol and Maria have formed ________________ .
3. Last year they ________________ .
4. Robert knows about the ________________ of the business.
5. He thinks the ice cream store wasn't a(n) ________________ business in the winter.
6. The man asks a question about a(n) ________________ for the restaurant.
7. She started a cleaning business, but it ________________ .
8. They want to ________________ a place downtown for their restaurant.

REPORTED SPEECH PATTERNS

A ▶05-03 **Listen. Circle the sentence that reports the conversation.**

1. a. She told Andrew to quit his job.
   b. He said that he'd heard the news about Andrew.
2. a. He suggested expanding the business.
   b. He said to make some changes.
3. a. She told her father that he could borrow some money.
   b. She promised to pay the loan back soon.
4. a. He told her to check on Joe.
   b. She said that Joe is doing well.
5. a. She warned him not to cut corners.
   b. She proposed cutting some corners.
6. a. She told him not to order paper.
   b. She asked him to order some paper.

B **Write the quotes as reported speech. Use the simple past of the reporting verb + the pattern in parentheses.**

1. Calvin said, "You should check out the new food truck."
   (*suggest* + gerund) Calvin suggested checking out the new food truck.
2. Mira said, "Business trends change quickly."
   (*explain* + that + clause) ________________
3. Oscar told us, "Set realistic goals."
   (*encourage* + object + infinitive) ________________
4. Lily said, "I'll make some calls."
   (*agree* + infinitive) ________________
5. The supplier told me, "Don't worry."
   (*advise* + object + infinitive) ________________
6. Our investors said, "You shouldn't rush into a partnership."
   (*propose* + gerund) ________________

VOCABULARY PRACTICE Complete the sentences with the correct form of the words in the box.

a sketch	scribble	tinker	go broke	land
an entrepreneur	pitch	publicity	cite	

1. Come in next week and ________________ me your idea.
2. My son likes to ________________ with old machines.
3. At the moment, I work for someone else, but I'd like to be ________________ .
4. He ________________ an amazing job at a major software company.
5. The writers ________________ their sources so you can read more about the topic.
6. The company got a lot of negative ________________ when their phones started exploding.
7. If you keep spending your money like that, you're going to ________________ .
8. The artist sends me a(n) ________________ before she makes the final drawing.
9. He ________________ that note so quickly that I can't even read it.

CHANGES IN REPORTED SPEECH

A ▶05-08 Listen. Circle the sentence that reports the speech.

1. a. She said that Jennifer will be devastated because she didn't land the job.
   b. She said Jennifer was devastated because she hadn't landed the job.
   c. She asked if Jennifer was devastated because she didn't land the job.
2. a. He said his brother was starting a business as soon as he graduates.
   b. He said that his brother would start a business when he graduated.
   c. He said his brother had started a business as soon as he had graduated.
3. a. She said she could scribble some notes.
   b. She asked if you can scribble some notes.
   c. She asked if she could scribble some notes.
4. a. He asked if I saw his sketches.
   b. He asked if I had seen his sketches.
   c. He said that I have seen his sketches.
5. a. She told me to listen to the new podcast she had discovered.
   b. She said listen to the new podcast she discovered.
   c. She said to listen to the new podcast I'd discovered.

B Change the quoted speech to reported speech.

1. The investors asked us, "What is your next plan?"
   The investors asked us what our next plan was.
2. Eva said, "It's important to identify what the market needs."
   ____
3. Zac said, "Stop by my food truck sometime."
   ____
4. I asked, "When will the final decision be made?"
   ____
5. Jacob asked, "Can I pitch my idea at the next meeting?"
   ____
6. Tom asked me, "How long have you been working on your new design?"
   ____

VOCABULARY PRACTICE Complete the sentences with the correct form of the words in the box.

a diesel generator	a hydroelectric dam	an underrepresented community
an infrastructure project	kinetic energy	noxious fumes
a developing country	a diverse background	

1. When the car exploded, a lot of people got sick from the ____________________ .
2. The ____________________ is noisy, but it provides us with electricity when there's a power outage.
3. The company was criticized for having almost no employees from ____________________ .
4. The ____________________ generates a lot of power, but it's bad for the animals that live in the river.
5. Not everyone agrees that that nation is a(n) ____________________ .
6. Something that is huge and moving very fast, like an airplane, generates a lot of ____________________ .
7. We are investing in a large ____________________ that is going to employ a lot of people.
8. Our employees have expertise in engineering, agriculture, education, public relations, and more. They have ____________________ .

COMMON REPORTING VERBS

A ▶05-15 **Listen. Check (✓) the verb that can replace the reporting verb.**

1. ☑ convinced
   ☐ maintained
   ☐ reported
2. ☐ promise
   ☐ warn
   ☐ agree
3. ☐ advised
   ☐ invited
   ☐ requested
4. ☐ reminded
   ☐ suggested
   ☐ agreed
5. ☐ reported
   ☐ warned
   ☐ urged
6. ☐ asks
   ☐ begs
   ☐ maintains

B **Combine the sentences. More than one answer may be possible.**

1. Elena will talk about diversity at our next meeting. She promised.
   Elena promised that she would talk about diversity at our next meeting.
   or: *Elena promised to talk about diversity at our next meeting.*
2. The infrastructure project was completed on time. Dan mentioned this.
   ____
3. I understand how a diesel generator works. You've already explained it.
   ____
4. Luca wants to work on a new project. He requested it.
   ____
5. We shouldn't have rushed the plans. Tim warned us about this.
   ____
6. We'll look for a better solution. Our manager suggested we do so.
   ____

VOCABULARY PRACTICE

▶06-02 Listen. Complete the sentences with the correct form of the words in the box.

personnel	time off	an incentive	a merit raise	a bonus
a commission	a perk	a contribution	flextime	transfer
workload	turnover			

1. She earns a(n) ________________ on her sales.
2. His company has a lot of ________________ .
3. That company has some great ________________ .
4. His company offers ________________ .
5. Her employer makes a 50% ________________ to her retirement account.
6. He applied for a(n) ________________ to the Mexico City office.
7. She gets a(n) ________________ before the holidays.
8. He sees all company ________________ at some point.
9. She is hoping for a(n) ________________ .

SUBJECT-VERB AGREEMENT: REVIEW AND EXPAND

A ▶06-03 Listen. Circle what the speaker would say next.

1. (a.) It was interesting. b. They were surprising.
2. a. It needs further explanation. b. They aren't very clear.
3. a. It is about 70 percent of our staff. b. They are well represented at our company.
4. a. It's too long for a coffee break! b. They're a lot.
5. a. It's a well respected news source. b. They're very popular.
6. a. Who can it be? b. I wonder who they are.

B Rewrite the sentences. Change the verb from the simple past to the simple present.

1. The company offered free childcare to its employees.
   The company offers free childcare to its employees.
2. Three hours gave us more than enough time to finish.
   ____
3. My workload increased during the holidays.
   ____
4. The committee met every other Friday.
   ____
5. The news didn't surprise me.
   ____
6. Did people complain about the new policy?
   ____

VOCABULARY PRACTICE Complete the sentences with the correct form of the words in the box.

a gap	a factor	workforce	equivalent	sanitation
tend to	bring to light	hesitate	turn down	

1. They wanted to ______________ problems about the town at the meeting.
2. New employees ______________ have a lot enthusiasm, but that isn't true for everyone.
3. There are a lot of ______________ to consider before you choose a college.
4. The country needs more immigrants because the ______________ is getting older.
5. Martin ______________ a higher position to spend more time with his family.
6. They say that social media is the ______________ of people gossiping in the town square in the old days.
7. There are lots of job openings for nurses, and not enough nurses applying for them. The hospital is trying to close the ______________ .
8. Gino works in ______________ . It's a dirty job, but he makes good money.
9. Maria ______________ to ask for a raise because she didn't want to seem greedy.

PROBABILITY AND CERTAINTY IN THE FUTURE

A ▶06-08 Listen. How certain is the speaker? Check (✓) the correct answer.

	She is sure.	She thinks so, but she's not 100% sure.	She doesn't think so.
1.	☐	☑	☐
2.	☐	☐	☐
3.	☐	☐	☐
4.	☐	☐	☐
5.	☐	☐	☐
6.	☐	☐	☐

B Rewrite the sentences using the future expression in parentheses.

1. Alice will resign soon.
   (on the verge of) Alice is on the verge of resigning soon.
2. Our company will hire a new CEO.
   (likely to) ______________
3. John probably won't get the position.
   (unlikely to) ______________
4. The company will hire ten new employees this month.
   (expected to) ______________
5. The policy might not change.
   (doubtful) ______________
6. The problem will be brought to light.
   (certain to) ______________

VOCABULARY PRACTICE Complete the sentences with the correct form of the words in the box.

a disparity	by leaps and bounds	economic output	economic downturn
waive	address	level the playing field	take advantage of
crack down on	a haven	redistribute	

1. The company went out of business during the last ________________ .
2. The government is starting to ________________ people who don't pay their taxes.
3. They will ________________ the registration fee for people who can't afford it.
4. Does sexism explain the ________________ between men's and women's incomes?
5. We shouldn't ignore the problem. We should ________________ it right away.
6. Making sure that poor children get a good education is one way to ________________ .
7. Governments use taxes to ________________ wealth from the rich to the poor.
8. Hopefully when the country's ________________ goes up, it will benefit everyone.
9. The town was a(n) ________________ for immigrants who had escaped hardships.
10. I ________________ the free gym and pool as often as I could.
11. The city is growing ________________ . The population has doubled.

EXPRESSING FUTURE TIME

A ▶06-14 Listen. Write the future verb you hear. What does it describe? Then check (✓) the correct answer.

Future verb	Prediction	Scheduled event	Prior plan	Action in progress	First of two future events
1. will be discussing	☐	☐	☐	☑	☐
2.	☐	☐	☐	☐	☐
3.	☐	☐	☐	☐	☐
4.	☐	☐	☐	☐	☐
5.	☐	☐	☐	☐	☐
6.	☐	☐	☐	☐	☐

B Rewrite the sentences to future time.

1. By the end of the day, I had finished my report.
   By the end of the day, I will have finished my report.
2. The tax code changes didn't affect our business.
   ____
3. We were working on the budget all week.
   ____
4. When I got to the office, everyone was attending a meeting.
   ____
5. Did you finish your project before the deadline?
   ____
6. We had been driving for over eight hours by the time we got to New York.
   ____

VOCABULARY PRACTICE

▶07-02 Listen. Complete the sentences with the correct form of the words in the box.

a campaign	raise awareness	a cause	a fundraiser	a sponsor
kick in	cynical	back on track	make a difference	

1. He has a(n) ________________ attitude.
2. She thinks protecting wildlife is an important ________________, so she is trying to ________________.
3. They are raising money for research as part of ________________ to fight cancer.
4. They haven't decided what kind of ________________ to do.
5. The theater puts the names of ________________ in the program.
6. The organization has gotten ________________ lately.
7. He thinks that people can ________________.
8. She wants people to ________________ a little money.

PASSIVE VOICE: FORM AND USE

A ▶07-03 **Listen. Write the passive verb you hear. Circle the agent.**

1. passive verb: was sponsored
   agent: a. fundraiser (b.) university c. not known
2. passive verb: ________________
   agent: a. land b. school c. not known
3. passive verb: ________________
   agent: a. campaign b. college students c. not known
4. passive verb: ________________
   agent: a. our programs b. your donations c. not known
5. passive verb: ________________
   agent: a. wilderness b. pollution c. not known
6. passive verb: ________________
   agent: a. community leaders b. fundraising event c. not known

B **Rewrite the sentences in the passive voice. Do not change the verb tense. Do not include the agent.**

1. The company prints the sponsors' names in the program.
   Sponsors' names are printed in the program.
2. People recognize that man for his generosity.
   ____
3. We raised a lot of money for a great cause.
   ____
4. Someone is donating a building for a new hospital.
   ____
5. Our organization has kicked off our annual fundraiser.
   ____
6. We have already sold more than a thousand tickets.
   ____

VOCABULARY PRACTICE Complete the sentences with the correct form of the words in the box.

feed	breaking	footage	a bystander	break down	accompany
consume	a fraud	agitate	clickbait	biased	a perspective

1. I get a notification whenever there's ________________ news.
2. They thought he was a real lawyer, but he was actually a(n) ________________ .
3. The documentary showed some amazing ________________ from deep in the jungle.
4. Wait a few days before you make a decision. Time will give you a new ________________ .
5. Lena wasn't involved in the accident. She was just a(n) ________________ .
6. I'm getting very annoyed at all of these ________________ posts I'm seeing lately. They never say anything interesting.
7. It's my job to check the social media ________________ and respond to comments as necessary.
8. Franco knew the situation could be dangerous, so he asked the police to ________________ him.
9. It's obvious that this site is ________________ against the mayor. It never says anything nice about him.
10. A lot of the news we ________________ comes from social media sharing.
11. Esme is very upset. Try not to ________________ her even more.
12. Can you help ________________ these instructions for me? They're really complicated.

PASSIVE VOICE: REPORTING STRUCTURES

A ▶07-08 Listen. Circle the correct word.

1. The **president** / **CEO** is said to be retiring soon.
2. The organization is reported to **be losing** / **have lost** over ten million dollars.
3. The **politician** / **journalist** is rumored to have accepted money.
4. **Media-sharing sites are** / **Citizen journalism is** thought to have become more accessible.
5. The top journalist is reported to **be covering** / **have covered** the story.
6. The news site **has not been proven** / **is proven** to be a reliable source.

B Rewrite the sentences using the passive form of the underlined reporting verbs.

1. People believe that the story is true.
   It is believed that the story is true. or: The story is believed to be true.
2. Everyone knows citizen journalists are biased.
   ________________ or: ________________
3. Bystanders reported that the suspect had escaped.
   ________________ or: ________________
4. The police believe the suspect is hiding in the city.
   ________________ or: ________________
5. They say the documents were destroyed in a fire.
   ________________ or: ________________
6. We assume that this generation is getting all of their news on their phones.
   ________________ or: ________________

VOCABULARY PRACTICE Complete the sentences with the correct form of the words in the box.

a fad	a phenomenon	provoke	empathy	convey
self-expression	spread like wildfire	a positive force	at (the very) least	

1. Vinod has been a very ________________ at this company, and they're sorry to see him go.
2. Have you seen the phosphorescence? It's a beautiful natural ________________ that makes the water light up at night.
3. Meng is not a professional artist; for her, painting is a kind of ________________ .
4. Please visit your sister tomorrow. Or, ________________ , give her a call.
5. Matt is already in a bad mood, so don't ________________ him by complaining right now.
6. It seems like every year there's a new ________________ in kids' toys, I can't keep up!
7. Kim is shy, but she can ________________ her ideas in writing brilliantly.
8. We need to have ________________ for people who are suffering.
9. The news ________________ through the school. Within an hour, everyone was talking about it.

PASSIVE INFINITIVES AND CAUSATIVES

A ▶07-14 Listen. Circle the correct answer.

1. Who got a promotion? (a.) Julie b. someone else
2. Who needs to approve the photos? a. David b. someone else
3. Who repaired the laptop? a. Alex b. someone else
4. Who has to finish the report? a. Leah b. someone else
5. Who gave someone a last-minute assignment? a. Tim b. his manager
6. Who cut Sherri's hair? a. She did it herself. b. someone else

B Complete the sentences using passive infinitives or causatives.

1. I would have preferred it if someone had notified me about the problem sooner.
   I would have preferred *to have been notified about the problem sooner.*
2. Our manager doesn't want anyone to call her on weekends.
   Our manager doesn't want ________________________________ .
3. The blog contains several errors. We need to correct it as soon as possible.
   The blog needs ________________________________ .
4. It looks like someone has modified the original story.
   The original story appears ________________________________ .
5. You should ask someone to review your account.
   You should get ________________________________ .
6. Rob wants someone to clean his house.
   Rob wants to have ________________________________ .

VOCABULARY PRACTICE

▶08-02 Listen. Complete each sentence with the correct form of the words in the box.

a strategy	a social media presence	a brand	a product launch
promotional materials	customer interaction	damage control	stand out

1. They are having a(n) ________________ in November.
2. She didn't see the building at first because it doesn't ________________ .
3. They need to figure out a(n) ________________ for attracting more customers.
4. She remembers what the toothpaste looked like, but she can't remember the ________________ name.
5. Their social media intern handles ________________ online.
6. They want to increase their ________________ .
7. The city is trying to do ________________ .
8. They have several different kinds of ________________ .

MODIFYING RELATIVE CLAUSES

A ▶08-03 Listen. Circle the correct word.

1. We got useful feedback from two / **more than a dozen** surveys.
2. **One** / **Two** project managers will present at the next meeting.
3. **One** / **More than one** company designed our logo, website, and promotional materials.
4. We haven't met the needs of **many** / **any** of our overseas clients.
5. **Our marketing team is** / **Consumers are** loyal to familiar brands.
6. **Michael** / **I** had never heard anything similar to those ideas.

B Combine the two sentences. Use the second one to make a modifying relative clause.

1. We're currently developing five new products. Only one of them is ready to launch.
   We're currently developing five new products, only one of which is ready to launch.
2. We have two new interns. Both of them are really talented.
   ____
3. I have to meet with several clients. A few of them are difficult.
   ____
4. I've reviewed the new promotional materials. All of them look great.
   ____
5. We're launching an ad campaign in Asia. It's a market we'd like to expand in.
   ____
6. They've spent many years developing their brand. It is a name that most people have respect for.
   ____

VOCABULARY PRACTICE Complete the sentences with the correct form of the words in the box.

vouch for	plug	computer-generated	get in on	authenticity
word of mouth	an endorsement	engage	put off	turn into

1. You should try to ________________ this deal. You'll save a lot of money!
2. We don't need to advertise. Everyone hears about us by ________________ .
3. That scene doesn't look very realistic. You can tell it's ________________ .
4. I'm not sure if I should believe Zoe. Can you ________________ her honesty?
5. Have you thought about what you'll do to ________________ the customers' interest?
6. The shoe company got an important ________________ from the soccer star.
7. Gaby is hoping the lessons will ________________ her ________________ a great chef.
8. The customers were ________________ by the unfriendly man at the front counter.
9. Oscar doesn't dress in expensive clothes, but people like his ________________ .
10. Ali brought the company T-shirts to the party so that he could ________________ the business.

PARTICIPLE CLAUSES

A ▶08-08 Listen. Circle the sentence similar in meaning.

1. (a.) Being unprepared, Tony wasn't confident.
   b. Feeling confident, Tony delivered his presentation.
2. a. Having brought her lunch to work, Christine didn't want to go out.
   b. Being really busy, Christine couldn't go out with her friends.
3. a. Injured in an accident, Jim couldn't come to work.
   b. Driving to work, Jim got in an accident.
4. a. Not having seen Elena in a long time, her friends called her.
   b. Having started a new business, Elena hasn't spent much time with her friends.
5. a. Not having the technical skills to shoot a video, they hired someone to help them.
   b. Lacking the funds to hire someone, they decided to shoot the video themselves.
6. a. Feeling uncertain about the contractor's skills, they decided not to hire him.
   b. Having worked with the contractor before, the man could vouch for him.

B Rewrite the sentences. Change the adverb clause to a participle clause.

1. After she explained the problem, our manager asked us to solve it.
   Having explained the problem, our manager asked us to solve it.
2. When I look at their social media feed, I want to learn more about that company.
   ____
3. While I was listening to a podcast, I learned about some new promotional strategies.
   ____
4. After we tried the usual strategies without success, we decided to do something different.
   ____
5. Since it is full of mistakes, that ad isn't ready yet.
   ____
6. Because we were all exhausted, we took a break from the project.
   ____

VOCABULARY PRACTICE Complete the sentences with the correct form of the words in the box.

stumble upon	expertise	a peer	dream up	iconic
designate	hit it big	the premises	a stretch	captivating

1. I don't know how Edgar can ________________ all these crazy ideas.
2. I'm pretty sure the band is going to ________________ with this next song. It's really good.
3. The movie tells the ________________ story of a girl who lived in ancient Greece.
4. Tarek says he can finish building the cabinet in two hours, but I think that's a(n) ________________ . I'm pretty sure it's going to take longer.
5. Sometimes you ________________ a great idea when you aren't even looking for one.
6. We work with dangerous chemicals, so only employees are allowed on the company ________________ .
7. Elly is the first one of her ________________ to get a promotion to management.
8. Please ________________ someone to take over your work while you're out of town.
9. Jules has studied for years. You won't find anyone with more ________________ .
10. Whenever we visit a country, we take a selfie in front of one of the ________________ landmarks, like the Eiffel Tower in France or Mt. Fuji in Japan.

INFINITIVE CLAUSES

A 08-15 Listen. Check (✓) the correct answer.

	True	False
1. She needed something to write with.	☑	☐
2. They expected Bill to accept the job in China.	☐	☐
3. He watched a video to learn some design tricks.	☐	☐
4. It's not necessary for Diane to come to the office.	☐	☐
5. He's going to call the hotel to make a reservation.	☐	☐
6. Ethan decided not to start a new business with his brother.	☐	☐

B Rewrite the sentences. Change the words in bold to infinitive phrases.

1. Please remind me **that I should call Max tomorrow.**
   Please remind me to call Max tomorrow.
2. We were happy **because we finished our project on time.**
   ____
3. I expect everyone **will make their best effort.**
   ____
4. She rented a car **so that she could travel around the country.**
   ____
5. We decided **that we shouldn't hire another manager.**
   ____
6. It's important **that we not forget our history.**
   ____

VOCABULARY PRACTICE

▶09-02 Listen. Complete the sentences with the correct form of the words in box.

athletic ability	hand-eye coordination	uncoordinated	score a run
competitive spirit	play your heart out	demolish an opponent	win fair and square

1. She thinks she is ________________ .
2. He thinks the most important thing is to ________________ .
3. Ameen has a lot of ________________ .
4. Matt has good ________________ .
5. She beat him ________________ .
6. His team didn't ________________ any ________________ .
7. Stacey has a lot of ________________ .
8. Her team ________________ the ________________ .

MODALS FOR SPECULATION AND EXPECTATION

A ▶09-03 **Listen. Circle what the speaker would say next.**

1. a. He must be excited. b. That can't be right.
2. a. She must be a natural athlete. b. She might be a good player.
3. a. He should be here any second. b. He might not be feeling well.
4. a. It should fit you fine. b. It might not be the right fit.
5. a. You should win the next match. b. That must have been tough.
6. a. She might exercise. b. She could be exercising.

B **Read each situation. Rewrite the second sentence using the modal in parentheses.**

1. I fell while I was playing tennis. It's possible I sprained my ankle.
   (might) I might have sprained my ankle.
2. Our team is by far the best in the league. I think we'll win the competition.
   (should) ________________________________
3. I can't believe that the team lost the tournament. Their fans were probably shocked.
   (must) ________________________________
4. It's almost midnight. I don't think John is playing basketball right now.
   (can't) ________________________________
5. Did our manager really use to be a professional ice skater? I think you're joking.
   (must) ________________________________
6. Mark's softball team is terrible, but they seem very happy today. Maybe they finally won a game.
   (could) ________________________________

VOCABULARY PRACTICE Complete the sentences with the correct form of the words in the box.

get a paying gig	keep in mind	make big money
kick back	keep up with	have fast reaction times
go pro	take a calculated risk	make a split-second decision
keep a cool head	have a good sense of humor	have a backup plan

1. I know I'm going fast, but please try to ________________ me.
2. Sun-hee has been playing golf since age 5. She's hoping to ________________ after college.
3. It hard to make a living as an actor. You should probably ________________ .
4. Brian ____________________ when he invested all that money in one place.
5. Erin had to ____________________ about whether to jump off the train.
6. Rick wants to play guitar at the cafe; he hopes to ________________ .
7. Young people may ____________________ , but older people are more careful drivers.
8. Cindy ____________________ . She laughs at all my jokes.
9. They'll pay you a decent wage at that job, but you're not going to ________________ .
10. I think I'm going to just ________________ on the sofa for a while and watch TV.
11. I know dealing with the boss is frustrating, but you need to ____________________ .
12. You can go out. Just ________________ that you need to be home by midnight.

EXPRESSING NECESSITY AND OBLIGATION

A ▶09-08 Listen. Check (✓) the correct answer.

	True	False
1. Jackson brought some extra snacks.	☑	☐
2. They don't have to buy tickets ahead of time.	☐	☐
3. Daniel parked in the company parking lot.	☐	☐
4. The speaker registered for the class online.	☐	☐
5. Omar will probably join his friends and play video games.	☐	☐
6. The speaker was required to take digital photography class.	☐	☐

B Rewrite the sentences in past time. Do not change the meaning of the sentences.

1. We must fill out the entire application.
   We had to fill out the entire application.
2. Employees are required to work one weekend every month.
   ____
3. You needn't bring anything with you to the game.
   ____
4. I wear contact lenses, so I needn't wear glasses.
   ____
5. I've got to find a paying gig.
   ____
6. She doesn't have to go to practice.
   ____

VOCABULARY PRACTICE Complete the sentences with the correct form of the words in the box.

call for	as opposed to	play catch	fetch
a tournament	regard as	eliminate	enlightening

1. We use a large ball to ________________ with the younger children.
2. I was confused before, but Dr. Singh's lecture was very ________________ .
3. Who do you ________________ the best musician alive today?
4. Being a nurse ________________ a lot of patience.
5. No matter how many times you throw the ball, my dog will happily ________________ it.
6. Our software will help you finish the job in a few minutes ________________ a few hours.
7. There are just too many choices here. We need to ________________ one of them.
8. My nephew is participating in a martial arts ________________ next week.

PERMISSION, STRONG ADVICE, AND PROHIBITION

A ▶09-14 Listen. What does the speaker express? Check (✓) the the correct answer.

	Permission	Strong advice	Prohibition
1.	☐	☐	☑
2.	☐	☐	☐
3.	☐	☐	☐
4.	☐	☐	☐
5.	☐	☐	☐
6.	☐	☐	☐

B For each situation, write a sentence with the subject *you* and a word or phrase in the box.

had better	~~supposed to~~	not allowed to	may

1. The coach said to bring a towel and water bottle to practice.
   You're supposed to bring a towel and water bottle to practice.
2. Don't forget to take your medicine tonight. It's very important.
   ____
3. Our manager said it's OK if you leave early today.
   ____
4. Don't park next to the building. Those are all reserved spaces.
   ____

ought to	can	can't

5. Do not use your phone during the game. It's against the rules.
   ____
6. It's a good idea to arrive at least an hour before the game begins.
   ____
7. It's OK to take breaks between games.
   ____

VOCABULARY PRACTICE

▶10-02 Listen. Complete the sentences with the correct form of the words in the box.

sign up for	fall into	get around to	end up	talk (someone) into
meet up with	run into	turn in	come across	pass up

1. He ________________ someone at the gym.
2. She's going to ________________ her friends after the movie.
3. He hasn't ________________ doing the shopping.
4. She wants to ________________ a yoga class.
5. He ________________ a career in construction.
6. She doesn't think you should ________________ the offer.
7. His brother ________________ going to the party.
8. She ________________ some old photos.

FUTURE IN THE PAST

A ▶10-03 Listen. Check (✓) the correct answer.

	True	False
1. You showed me your vacation pictures.	☐	☑
2. Michelle moved to Alaska.	☐	☐
3. Vanessa went to medical school.	☐	☐
4. Jane competed in the tennis tournament.	☐	☐
5. Chris became a famous actor.	☐	☐
6. Jim and Megan got married.	☐	☐

B Rewrite the first sentence to express the future in the past. Look at the second sentence for context.

1. I think Maya will get a promotion.
   I thought Maya would get a promotion.
   We were all shocked when she was laid off.
2. Oscar is going to do some volunteer work.
   ____.
   But he never got around to it.
3. I know you will be successful.
   ____.
   I'm not surprised you've been promoted to vice president of marketing.
4. Martin is about to quit his job.
   ____.
   He changed his mind when he got a huge raise.
5. John wants to sell his car because he is moving overseas soon.
   ____.
   But now he's dating someone new, and suddenly he isn't so sure about moving.

VOCABULARY PRACTICE Complete the sentences with the correct form of the words in the box.

contemporary	an orphanage	an orphan	flee	harrowing
glittering	devastating	a passage	interweave	grief

1. The teacher asked them to memorize their favorite ________________ from the book.
2. There were children of all different ages living at the ________________ .
3. She didn't cry at the funeral, but her ________________ was easy to see.
4. The streets were crowded with people trying to ________________ from the fire.
5. The journey was long and ________________ , but we all survived it.
6. The hotel was old-fashioned but they redecorated in a more ________________ style.
7. The ice on the trees was ________________ in the bright morning sun.
8. A lot of children became ________________ during the war.
9. The loss of their coach was ________________ for the team's performance.
10. The movie ________________ the stories of two young girls, one who grows up in a wealthy family in the city, and another who lives her entire life on a farm.

PAST PERFECT AND PAST PERFECT CONTINUOUS

A ▶10-08 **Listen. Write *1* next to the event that happened first and *2* next to the event that happened second.**

1. They got out of the city. __1__
   They got a flat tire. __2__
2. Ren turned 12. ______
   Ren experienced traumatic events. ______
3. Sara told people about the problem. ______
   Sara suffered from headaches. ______
4. Paula cried. ______
   Paula got home. ______
5. Helen finished medical school. ______
   Helen wrote a memoir. ______
6. The sun set. ______
   John walked for hours. ______

B **Combine the two sentences using the words in parentheses. Use the past perfect or the past perfect continuous for the action that occurred first in the sequence of events.**

1. I read the book three times. Then I saw the movie.
   (by the time) I had read the book three times by the time I saw the movie.
   or: By the time I saw the movie, I had read the book three times.
2. She fled the country. Then the war broke out.
   (before) ________________________________
3. She became a famous dancer. Then I saw her again.
   (by the time) ________________________________
4. He was working outside. Then we arrived.
   (when) ________________________________
5. He recovered from his accident. Then he wrote a book about it.
   (after) ________________________________
6. She was running. Then she injured her foot.
   (until) ________________________________

VOCABULARY PRACTICE Complete the sentences with the correct form of the words in the box.

nostalgic	a famine	an overreliance on	lounge around
a slab	upholstery	adequate	enticing

1. They covered the hole in the ground with a large ________________ of rock.
2. There's a terrible ________________ in that country, people have nothing to eat.
3. We need to make sure the company doesn't have ________________ just one supplier.
4. Sometimes I'm ________________ for my younger days when I didn't have any worries.
5. The sofa and the armchairs have matching ________________ .
6. The hotel isn't great, but it's ________________ for our needs.
7. We've been working so hard. I think we need a weekend just to ________________ .

EXPRESSING THE PAST: REVIEW

A ▶10-14 Listen. Circle the correct word.

1. My grandfather started a business (**before**) / **when** he turned 24.
2. Jackie went skiing **before** / **after** she moved to Switzerland.
3. I started texting you **before** / **when** you called.
4. Alex left for work **before** / **after** it stopped raining.
5. Gabi **still** / **no longer** grows her own vegetables.
6. Marco **still** / **no longer** works for a security company.

B Complete the sentences with the correct form of the verb in parentheses. More than one answer may be possible.

Centenarians are people who live to be 100 years or older. As life expectancy increases, we see a growing number of centenarians. According to United Nations estimates, there _____were_____ **1 (be)** about 100,000 centenarians worldwide in 1990, but by 2015 that number ________________ **2 (grow)** more than four times. Just imagine the technological advances that centenarians ________________ **3 (witness)** over the past 100 years! Today we expect to have our phone at arm's length at all times, but 100 years ago the idea of instantly chatting with someone anywhere in the world probably ________________ **4 (seem)** impossible. In the early 1900s, cars ________________ **5 (just, start)** to replace the horse and buggy. People ________________ **6 (question)** the safety of those new electric vehicles. We can compare those concerns to the ones we have today as self-driving cars begin to replace those with human drivers. Color television first ________________ **7 (come)** around in the 1950s. The first color TV ________________ **8 (have)** a 15-inch screen contained in a large wooden box. It ________________ **9 (look)** nothing like the large 4K flat screens that are so common today. Even in just the past half century, we ________________ **10 (see)** incredible changes in technology. The Sony Walkman first ________________ **11 (go)** on sale in 1980. It had a cassette tape deck and was considered the first portable stereo. Listeners ________________ **12 (change)** the cassette each time they ________________ **13 (want)** to hear a different artist. Over the past decade, we ________________ **14 (become)** accustomed to streaming whatever music we want to hear quickly and easily on our mobile devices. Of course, there are thousands of other changes. If you're fortunate enough to know a centenarian, ask him or her what new technology has been the most surprising.

GLOSSARY

UNIT 1, LESSON 1, page 6

high season: the time of year when businesses make a lot of money and prices are high
low season: the time of year when businesses have fewer visitors and prices are cheaper
plan ahead: to make all arrangements in advance of something happening
an itinerary: a list of the places you will visit on a trip
plan out: to make thorough and detailed arrangements for the future
a day trip: a journey made to and from within a day
play it by ear: to decide what to do according to how a situation develops, without making plans
open-ended: without a definite ending
impromptu: done or said without any preparation or planning
serendipity: the process of accidently discovering something that is interesting or valuable
take off: to leave somewhere

UNIT 1, LESSON 2, page 8

a spacecraft: a vehicle that can travel in space
a rover: a vehicle that travels on the surface of a planet
terraform: to transform a planet to support human life and look like Earth
colonize: to control an area and send your own people to live there
inhospitable: difficult to live or stay in because of severe weather conditions
an asteroid: one of many small planets
bombard: to attack a place
radiation: a form of energy that comes from nuclear reactions, that is harmful
massive: very large and powerful
a dust storm: wind mixed with small pieces of dirt that looks like powder
toxic: poisonous or containing poison

UNIT 1, LESSON 3, page 10

rust: reddish, brown substance that forms on iron, steel, etc., when it gets wet
abandon: to leave someone or something you are responsible for
damage: a bad effect on something
crumble: to break apart in small pieces
peel: to come off in layers from the surface of an object
dilapidated: old, broken, and in very bad condition
moss-covered: having a layer of thick furry plant usually growing on soil, trees, or rocks
rot: to decay by a gradual, natural process
collapse: to fall down or inward suddenly

UNIT 1, LESSON 4, page 12

malfunction: to not work properly
illuminate: to make light shine on something
nutrients: chemicals or food that help plants, animals, or people to live and grow
be accustomed to: to be used to something
transmit: to send or pass something from one place, person, etc., to another
an artifact: a small object that was used a long time ago, especially one that is studied by scientists
a wealth of: a large amount of money or things
a spire: a structure shaped like a cone or pyramid
bacteria: very small living things, some of which can cause disease
dissolved: mixed with liquid so as to have become part of it

UNIT 2, LESSON 1, page 18

super strength: a great amount of physical power and energy
X-ray vision: the ability to see through objects
invisible: not able to be seen
invincible: too strong to be defeated or destroyed
a shape-shifter: the supposed ability to change their physical form at will
teleport: to transport or be transported across space instantly
telekinesis: the supposed ability to move objects in space by mental power
telepathic: supposedly capable of communicating thoughts directly to someone else's mind without speaking, writing, or using signs

UNIT 2, LESSON 2, page 20

excel: to do something very well or much better than most people
optimize: to make the best out of something
a reflection: careful thought, or an idea or opinion based on this
inspire: to encourage someone to do or produce something good
persistent: the act or state of doing something, even though it is difficult or other people do not like it
rage: a strong feeling of uncontrollable anger
promising: showing signs of being successful or good in the future

UNIT 2, LESSON 3, page 22

churn out: to produce large quantities of something
innate: a quality that has been part of your character since you were born
self-evident: clearly true and needing no proof
resemble: to look like or be similar to someone or something
intervene: to do something to try to stop an argument, problem, or war
consistently: always happening in the same way
trauma: a state of extreme shock that is caused by a very frightening experience
avenge: to hurt or punish someone because he or she has harmed or offended you
thrust: to push something somewhere with sudden or violent movement

UNIT 2, LESSON 4, page 24

pioneering: introducing new and better methods or ideas
microscopic: extremely small and very difficult to see
adhere: to stick firmly to something
scale: to climb to the top of something that is high
sheer: extremely steep
state-of-the-art: using the newest methods, materials, or knowledge
bulky: big and heavy
limbs: arms and / or legs
render: to cause something to be in a particular state
imperative: extremely important and urgent

UNIT 3, LESSON 1, page 30

a prodigy: a young person who is extremely good at doing something
a virtuoso: a very skillful performer, especially in music
talent: a natural ability to do something well
gifted: having a natural ability to do something well
renowned: famous for a special skill or for something that you have done
knowledgeable: knowing a lot
insightful: having a deep understanding of something
a genius: someone who has much more intelligence, ability, or skill than is usual
a legend: an old well-known story, often about brave people or adventures

UNIT 3, LESSON 2 , page 32

to craft: to make something using a special skill, especially with your hands
a craft: a job or activity that you need to have a lot of skill to do, especially one in which you make things
to map: to plan something carefully
a map: a drawing of an area, or country, showing roads, rivers, cities, etc.
to approach: to move toward or closer to someone or something
an approach: a way of doing something or dealing with a problem
to detail: to list things or give all the facts or information about something
a detail: a small fact or piece of information about something
to focus on: to pay special attention to a particular person or thing instead of others
a focus: a thing, person, situation, etc., that people pay attention to
to comment: to express an opinion about someone or something
a comment: an opinion that you give about someone or something

UNIT 3, LESSON 3, page 34

an imagination: pictures or ideas in your mind
perceive: to notice or understand something
detectable: able to be noticed or discovered, especially with something that is not easy to see, hear, etc.
visual: related to seeing or to your sight
a combination: two or more different things, substances, etc., that are used or put together
associate: to make a connection in your mind between one thing or person and another

GLOSSARY

UNIT 3, LESSON 4, page 36

writer's block: a problem that a writer sometimes has of not being able to think of ideas to write
be purported to: *formal* to claim that something is true, especially when it is possible that it is not true
jump-start: to help a process or activity start working better or more quickly
clearheaded: to think in a clear and sensible way
amplify: *formal* to make something stronger
inconsequential: not important; insignificant
a pose: the position in which someone deliberately stands or sits
a blindfold: a piece of cloth you use to cover someone's eyes so that he or she can't see
on the threshold of: at the beginning of a new event or development
doze: to sleep for a short time

UNIT 4, LESSON 1, page 42

exotic: something that is unusual and exciting because it is foreign
unique: not like anything or anyone else
striking: unusual or interesting enough to be noticed
cute: attractive to look at
precious: very important or special to you
adorable: very pretty and easy to love
weird: unusual and strange
peculiar: strange, out of the ordinary
bizarre: very unusual and strange
gross: very unpleasant
magnificent: very good or beautiful, and very impressive
astonishing: very surprising

UNIT 4, LESSON 2, page 44

conduct: to do something in an organized way
extensive: containing a lot of something, especially information
extroverted: a person who is confident and likes being with people
excitable: becoming happy, eager, or interested very easily
fearful: afraid
pessimistic: believing that bad things will happen, not good things
a lifespan: the length of time a person or animal lives
a shelter: a place where people or pet animals can go if they have no home or are being treated badly

UNIT 4, LESSON 3, page 46

scold: to tell someone in an angry way that he or she has done something wrong
feel guilty: to feel unhappy and ashamed because you have done something that you know is wrong
dive-bomb: to fly steeply downward to attack something
hold a grudge: to keep an unfriendly feeling toward someone because he or she did something bad to you in the past
be self-aware: to have a conscious knowledge of one's own character and feelings
howl: to make a long loud sound like a dog crying
grieve: to feel very sad because someone you love has died
mourn: to feel very sad because someone has died

GLOSSARY

UNIT 4, LESSON 4, page 48

mimic: to copy the way someone speaks
primitive: belonging to an early stage of development
in the wild: in natural and free conditions, not kept or controlled by people
captivity: kept in a cage or enclosure and not allowed to go free
deprived of: kept from having something important or desired
befriend: to behave in a friendly way toward someone
be suited to: to have the right qualities to do something
albeit: used to add information that reduces the force or importance of what you have just said
nasal: related to the nose
a cavity: *formal* a hole or space inside something
ungrammatical: incorrect according to the rules of grammar
intelligible: if speech, writing, or an idea is intelligible, it can be easily understood

UNIT 5, LESSON 1, page 54

a partnership: a relationship in which two or more people, organizations, etc., work together
lease: to use or let someone use buildings, property, etc., when he or she pays rent
a supplier: a company that provides a particular product to another company or a consumer
cash flow: the movement of money into and out of a company
cut corners: to do something in a way that is not as good as it should be, to save time, effort, or money
be in the black: to have more money than you owe
be in the red: to owe more money than you have
break even: to reach a point when profits are equal to costs
profitable: producing money or a useful result
flop: to be unsuccessful because people do not like it

UNIT 5, LESSON 2, page 56

a sketch: a quick drawing that does not have a lot of details
scribble: to write something quickly in a messy way
tinker: to try to improve something by making small changes to it, without a careful plan
go broke: for a company or business to no longer operate because it has no money
land: to finally succeed in getting a particular job, contract, or deal
an entrepreneur: someone who starts a company and arranges business deals to make money
pitch: to try to persuade someone to buy or do something
publicity: attention that someone or something gets from newspapers, television, etc.
cite: to mention something as an example or proof of something else

GLOSSARY

UNIT 5, LESSON 3, page 58

a diesel generator: a combination of a fuel-powered engine and an electric engine
a hydroelectric dam: a human-made structure used to control a river and generate electricity for power
an underrepresented community: a smaller percentage of a larger population that often does not have power or influence
an infrastructure project: a plan related to the basic systems and structures that a country needs, for example, roads, hospitals, and telephone systems
kinetic energy: a type of power that is caused by movement, or relating to movement
noxious fumes: a strong-smelling gas or smoke that is harmful or poisonous
a developing country: a country without much money or industry, but that is working to improve life for its people
a diverse background: variety in family, education, previous work, and other experiences

UNIT 5, LESSON 4, page 60

an ecological footprint: the impact a business has on the environment expressed as the amount of land it needs to sustain its use of natural resources.
culture: *technical* to grow bacteria or cells for medical or scientific use
culinary: *formal* related to cooking
a stem cell: *technical* a special type of cell that can divide to form other types of cells that have particular qualities or purposes
a biopsy: the surgical removal of cells or tissue from a human or animal body
incubate: to keep something warm so it can develop and grow
a serum: a protein-rich liquid that is part of blood
proliferate: to grow by the rapid production of new cells
a hurdle: a problem or difficulty that you must deal with before you can achieve something
recoup: to get back an amount of money you have lost or spent

UNIT 6, LESSON 1, page 66

personnel: people who work for an organization
time off: time when you do not do your usual work
an incentive: an award given for increased productivity
a merit raise: a performance-related pay increase
a bonus: extra money that someone is paid, separately from his or her regular pay
a commission: an amount of money, in addition to the salary, that is paid to an employee for selling a product as part of his or her job
a perk: money, goods, or other advantages that you get from your job in addition to your salary
a contribution: some money that you give to help pay for something
flextime: a system in which people work a particular number of hours each week or month, but can change the times at which they start and finish working each week
transfer: to move someone or something from one place to another
workload: the amount of work that you must do
turnover: the rate at which employees leave a company and then are replaced

UNIT 6, LESSON 2, page 68

a gap: a big difference between two situations, amounts, groups of people, etc.
a factor: one of many things that affects a situation
workforce: all the people who work in a country or company
equivalent: something that is equal in amount, value, or importance to something else
sanitation: the process of keeping places clean and healthy
tend to: to be likely to do something, or to usually do something
bring to light: to make widely known
hesitate: to wait before you do or say something, because you are thinking about it
turn down: to decline or reject something

UNIT 6, LESSON 3, page 70

a disparity: a great difference
by leaps and bounds: with surprisingly rapid progress
economic output: the total value of all goods and services produced in a country
economic downturn: a part of a business cycle that refers to very little or no growth
waive: to state officially that a right or a rule can be ignored
address (a problem): *formal* to start trying to solve a problem
level the playing field: to make something fair so that everyone has the same advantages
take advantage of: to make use of for an opportunity or gain
crack down on: to become stricter when dealing with bad behavior or an illegal activity
a haven: a place that people go to be safe
redistribute: to give something out differently or again, often to achieve social equality

UNIT 6, LESSON 4, page 72

disciplined: obeying rules and controlling your behavior
the advent of: *written* the time when something first begins to be widely used
an advocate: someone who publicly supports someone or something
sweeping: affecting many things or making an important difference to something
sidestep: to evade (a problem, issue, question, etc.)
the lion's share of: the largest part of something
streamlined: made to work more simply and effectively (such as a business, organization, etc.)
indispensable: so important or useful that it is impossible to manage without
size up: to consider a situation and make a judgment about it
a prerequisite: something needed for a particular purpose

UNIT 7, LESSON 1, page 78

a campaign: a series of actions intended to achieve a particular result relating to politics, business, or a social improvement

raise awareness: to make people think more seriously about a particular subject or situation

a cause: an organization or an idea that a group of people support or do things for

a fundraiser: an event that is held to collect money for a charity or a political party

a sponsor: a person or company that provides money to help pay for a team, an event, or an activity, usually on an ongoing basis

cynical: unwilling to believe that people have good, honest, or sincere reasons

back on track: to progress in a successful way after a misstep or misfortune

make a difference: to have a significant effect on a situation or person

kick in: *informal* to join with others in giving money or help

UNIT 7, LESSON 2, page 80

feed: frequently updated data that is provided to users on the internet

breaking: making the news about an important event known to everyone

footage: film or video that shows a particular event

a bystander: someone who is in a place when something happens

break down: *informal* to separate something into parts in order to understand it

accompany: *formal* to go somewhere with someone

consume: to use as a customer

a fraud: someone who deceives people in order to get something they want

agitate: to make someone feel anxious, upset, and nervous

clickbait: something designed to make users want to access content with questionable value

biased: thinking that a person, group, or idea is better than another, and treating them differently

a perspective: a way of thinking about something

UNIT 7, LESSON 3, page 82

a fad: something that is popular for a short time

a phenomenon: a notable event that happens in society or in nature

provoke: to deliberately make someone angry

empathy: the ability to understand someone's feelings and problems, because you have been in the same situation yourself

convey: to express feelings or ideas to someone

self-expression: the expression of your feelings, thoughts, ideas etc., especially through the arts

spread like wildfire: to put forth with great speed

a positive force: a good and useful effect on someone

at (the very) least: not less than, at the very minimum

GLOSSARY

UNIT 7, LESSON 4, page 84

strewn with: having things scattered around a large area
a lifeguard: someone whose job at a beach or swimming pool is to help swimmers who are in danger
haul in: to pull in something heavy with a continuous steady movement
daunting: frightening in a way that makes you feel less confident
bear: *formal* to have or show a sign or a mark
settle on: to decide or agree about something
gender-neutral: suitable for both males and females
custom: specially designed and made for a particular person
novel: not like anything known before and unusual or interesting
rest on your laurels: to be satisfied with what you have done so that you do not make any further effort

UNIT 8, LESSON 1, page 90

a strategy: a planned way of achieving something
a social media presence: how frequently someone posts on shared websites
a brand: a type of product made by a company, that has a particular name or design
a product launch: to start or introduce something that people make in order to sell it
promotional materials: things given out to advertise something to make people want to buy it
customer interaction: the activity of communicating between a buyer and a store
damage control: an attempt to limit the bad effects of something
stand out: to be very easy to see or notice

UNIT 8, LESSON 2, page 92

vouch for: to say that you firmly believe that something is true or good because of your knowledge
plug: *informal* to advertise a book, movie, idea, etc., by talking about it publicly
computer-generated: designed or created by a computer program
get in on: *informal* to become involved in something that other people are doing or planning
authenticity: the quality of being real or true and not a copy
word of mouth: information or news that someone tells you instead of you reading about it or seeing an advertisement
an endorsement: a statement in which you officially say that you support or approve of someone or something
engage: to attract someone and keep his or her interest
put off: to arrange to do something at a later time or date, especially because there is a problem
turn into: to become something different

UNIT 8, LESSON 3, page 94

stumble upon: to discover something or meet someone when you do not expect to
expertise: special skills or knowledge
a peer: a person who is the same age as you
dream up: to think of a plan or idea, especially an unusual one
iconic: relating to a famous person who is admired by many people and is thought to represent an important idea
designate: to choose someone or something for a particular job or purpose
hit it big: *informal* to suddenly become very famous, successful, and rich
the premises: the buildings and land that a store, restaurant, company etc. uses
a stretch: *informal* something that is not completely true or is made to seem more important than it actually is
captivating: very attractive or interesting

UNIT 8, LESSON 4, page 96

wrongdoing: *formal* illegal or immoral behavior
deceptive: appearing to be one thing while in fact being something different
mislead: to make someone believe something is not true by giving information that is false or incomplete
abhorrent: completely unacceptable because of seeming morally wrong
biodegradable: materials that are changed naturally by bacteria into substances that do not harm the environment
reassuring: making you feel less worried or frightened
a municipality: a town, city, or other small area that has its own government to make decisions about local affairs
detrimental: causing harm or damage
disintegrate: to break apart into small pieces or particles
suggestive: causing mental associations

UNIT 9, LESSON 1, page 102

athletic ability: strength, coordination, speed of reflexes, and other qualities that are required for a person to do well in sports
hand-eye coordination: the way in which your hands and eyes work together to make you able to do things well
uncoordinated: not good at physical activities, because of an inability to control their movement effectively
score a run: to earn a point in baseball or softball by running around all of the bases
competitive spirit: a drive to win and to do your best and succeed
play your heart out: to exert maximum effort while playing a sport, game, or instrument
demolish an opponent: to overwhelmingly defeat someone you are playing against
win fair and square: to be successful in a competition without cheating

UNIT 9, LESSON 2, page 104

get a paying gig: *informal* to get a job, usually a temporary one, that will pay money
keep in mind: to be aware or reminded of something
make big money: to earn a lot of money
kick back: *informal* to relax and not worry about your problems
keep up with: to maintain the same level of engagement as somebody and not fall behind
have fast reaction times: to respond to something
go pro: to go from amateur status to professional
take a calculated risk: to do something potentially dangerous after thinking carefully about what might happen
make a split-second decision: to make a choice in an extremely short amount of time
keep a cool head: to remain calm in a difficult or stressful situation
have a good sense of humor: to be able to appreciate a joke or perceive humor
have a backup plan: to have a second plan in case the first one doesn't work out

UNIT 9, LESSON 3, page 106

call for: to need or deserve a particularly type of behavior or treatment
as opposed to: expression used to compare two things and show that they are different from each other
play catch: to take turns throwing and catching a ball back and forth
fetch: to go and get something and bring it back
a tournament: a competition in which many players or teams compete against each other until there is a winner
regard as: to consider to be
eliminate: to get rid of something completely
enlightening: making someone learn or understand something better

UNIT 9, LESSON 4, page 108

strut: to walk in a very proud and confident way, with your head up and your chest forward
eye-catching: unusual or attractive in a way that makes you notice it
prioritize: to decide what is most important, so that you can do it first
disproportionate: too much or too little in relation to something else
ostracize: to stop accepting someone as a member of the group
manifest: *formal* to clearly show a feeling, attitude, disease, etc., so that it is easy to see
eccentric: behaving in a way that is unusual and different from most people
contradictory: statements or facts that are different and cannot both be true
monotonous: boring and always being the same
take its toll: to have a damaging effect

GLOSSARY

UNIT 10, LESSON 1, page 114

sign up for: to put your name on a list because you want to take a class, belong to a group, etc.
fall into: to begin to do something by chance
get around to: to do something you have been intending to do for a long time
end up: to come to be in a place, situation, or condition that you did not expect or intend
talk (someone) into: to persuade someone to do something
meet up with: to meet someone informally in order to do something together
run into: *informal* to meet someone by chance
turn in: to deliver something that is due to someone else
come across: to discover something, usually by chance
pass up: to not use a chance to do something

UNIT 10, LESSON 2, page 116

contemporary: contemporary art, music, dance, or literature belongs to the present time
an orphanage: a home for children whose parents are dead
an orphan: a child whose parents are dead
flee: to leave a place very quickly in order to escape from danger
harrowing: a harrowing sight or experience is one that frightens, shocks, or upsets you very much
glittering: shining with shimmering light
devastating: causing tremendous damage or suffering to someone or something
a passage: a short piece of writing or music, that is taken from a longer piece
interweave: to combine two or more ideas or things so that they cannot be easily separated
grief: great sadness

UNIT 10, LESSON 3, page 118

nostalgic: feeling slightly sad about a happy time you remember from the past that you wish had not changed
a famine: a very bad situation when a lot of people do not have enough food to eat
an overreliance on: an unhealthy dependence on something, leaving you open to risk if it runs out or goes away
lounge around: to sit or lie in a place in a very relaxed way without doing much
a slab: a thick, flat piece of something
upholstery: material that has been used for covering a chair or seat
adequate: enough or good enough
enticing: something that is attractive because of the advantages it offers

UNIT 10, LESSON 4, page 120

mediocre: not very good, but not very bad
a recollection: something from the past that you remember
rosy: seeming to be successful or happy
elapse: *formal* if a particular period of time elapses, it passes
self-esteem: the feeling that you deserve to be liked and respected
consequent: *formal* happening as a result of a particular event or situation
instill: to teach someone to think, behave, or feel in a particular way over a period of time
a yearning: a strong desire for something
enviable: respected and desired by others
in retrospect: thinking back to a time in the past, especially with the advantage of knowing more now than you did then

Photo Credits

Cover

Guvendemir/Getty Images; Tovovan/Shutterstock.

To the Teacher

Page viii: Marco Bottigelli/Moment/Getty Images; ix (p. 6, top right): Daniel M Ernst/Shutterstock; ix (p. 6, plane): StudioByTheSea/Shutterstock; ix (p. 2, beach): Anton Gvozdikov/Shutterstock; ix (p. 7): Kyrien/Shutterstock; ix (p. 5, main photo): Marco Bottigelli/Moment/Getty Images; ix (p. 5, bottom right): Daniel M Ernst/Shutterstock; ix (p. 82, top right): Daniel M Ernst/Shutterstock; ix (p. 83): Sjstudio6/Shutterstock; ix (bottom): G-Stockstudio/Shutterstock.

Welcome Unit

Page 2: Shutterstock; 3 (StartUp Level 7 cover): Guvendemir/E+/Getty Images; 3 (image on cell phone): Marco Bottigelli/Moment/Getty Images; 4 (Tae-Ho Kang): AJR_photo/Shutterstock; 4 (Esra Kara): Daniel M Ernst/Shutterstock; 4 (Carla Lugo): TierneyMJ/Shuttertsock; 4 (Hiro Matsuda): Metamorworks/Shutterstock; 4 (Mateo Romero): Pressmaster/Shutterstock; 4 (Kate Sands): Mangostar/Shutterstock; 4 (Adriana Lopez): Pearson Education Inc; 4 (Kendrick Scott): Pearson Education Inc; 4 (David Cruz): Pearson Education Inc.

Unit 1

Page 5 (main photo): Marco Bottigelli/Moment/Getty Images; 5 (Esra Kara): Daniel M Ernst/Shutterstock; 6 (Esra Kara): Daniel M Ernst/Shutterstock; 6 (plane): StudioByTheSea/Shutterstock; 6 (beach): Anton Gvozdikov/Shutterstock; 7: Kyrien/Shutterstock; 8 (Esra Kara): Daniel M Ernst/Shutterstock; 8 (Mars robotic rover): Marc Ward/Shutterstock; 8 (Mars dust storm): Jan Kaliciak/Shutterstock; 10 (Esra Kara): Daniel M Ernst/Shutterstock; 10 (empty warehouse): Szantai Istvan/Shutterstock; 10 (falling down buildings): MBoe/Shutterstock; 10 (burned out room): Laborant/Shutterstock; 10 (old bicycle): Estherca/Shutterstock; 11: KEG-KEG/Shutterstock; 12 (Esra Kara): Daniel M Ernst/Shutterstock; 12 (undersea robot): S.Bachstroem/Shutterstock; 14 (Esra Kara): Daniel M Ernst/Shutterstock; 14 (desert background): IrinaK/Shutterstock; 16 (Great Wall of China): Teinstud/Shutterstock; 16 (Colosseum, Italy): Teinstud/Shutterstock; 16 (Machu Picchu): Teinstud/Shutterstock.

Unit 2

17 (main image): Aslysun/Shutterstock; 17 (Tae-Ho Kang): AJR_photo/Shutterstock; 18: AJR_photo/Shutterstock; 19: Tatiana Shepeleva/Shutterstock; 20: AJR_photo/Shutterstock; 22 (Tae-Ho Kang): AJR_photo/Shutterstock; 22(superheroes): LightField Studios/Shutterstock; 23: Malchev/Shutterstock; 24 (Tae-Ho Kang): AJR_photo/Shutterstock; 24 (gecko leg): Ketpachara Yoosuk/Shutterstock; 24 (gecko): Anant Kasetsinsombut/Shutterstock; 26 (Tae-Ho Kang): AJR_photo/Shutterstock; 26 (woman): Imtmphoto/Shutterstock; 28: Iconspro/Shutterstock.

Unit 3

Page 29 (main photo): Carlos Amarillo/Shutterstock; 29 (Kate Sands): Mangostar/Shutterstock; 30 (Kate Sands): Mangostar/Shutterstock; 30 (girl at piano): Vitalii Petrushenko/Shutterstock; 31: Anastasia Petrova/Shutterstock; 32 (Kate Sands): Mangostar/Shutterstock; 32 (old map): Tribalium/Shutterstock; 33: Hbo/Kobal/Shutterstock; 34: Mangostar/Shutterstock; 35: SpeedKingz/Shutterstock; 36 (Kate Sands): Mangostar/Shutterstock; 36 (Brad Meltzer): Johnny Louis/Getty Images; 38 (Kate Sands): Mangostar/Shutterstock; 38 (idea lightbulb): Peshkova/Shutterstock.

Unit 4

Page 41 (main photo): Vicki Jauron/Babylon/ Beyond Photography/Moment/Getty Images; 41 (Hiro Matsuda): Metamorworks/Shutterstock; 42 (Hiro Matsuda): Metamorworks/Shutterstock; 42 (bird): Apiguide/Shutterstock; 42 (panda): SJ Travel Photo and Video/Shutterstock; 42 (fish): Ian Ratcliffe/Shutterstock; 42 (tiger): Jack Bell Photography/Shutterstock; 43: Benedikt K/Shutterstock; 44: Metamorworks/Shutterstock; 45: Javier Brosch/Shutterstock; 46 (Hiro Matsuda): Metamorworks/Shutterstock; 46 (two girls arguing): Antonio Guillem/Shutterstock; 46 (bird diving): Paul Reeves Photography/Shutterstock; 46 (angry couple): Antonio Guillem/Shutterstock; 46 (baby): Matrix images/Shutterstock; 46 (wolf): Takiev Alexander/Shutterstock; 46 (burial): Kzenon/Shutterstock; 47: Scarabea/Shutterstock; 48 (Hiro Matsuda): Metamorworks/Shutterstock; 48 (Dr Patterson & Koko): Keystone Pictures USA/ZUMA Press, Inc./Alamy Stock Photo; 50 (Hiro Matsuda): Metamorworks/Shutterstock; 50 (elephant): Bilgeari/Shutterstock.

Unit 5

Page 53 (main photo): Rana Dias/Caiaimage/Getty Images; 53 (Carla Lugo): TierneyMJ/Shuttertsock; 54: TierneyMJ/Shuttertsock; 55: Antoniodiaz/Shutterstock; 56 (Carla Lugo): TierneyMJ/Shuttertsock; 56 (smart home): Zhu Difeng/Shutterstock; 57: Forgem/Shutterstock; 58: TierneyMJ/Shuttertsock; 59: Brad Barket/Getty Images; 60 (Carla Lugo): TierneyMJ/Shuttertsock; 60 (science lab): New Africa/Shutterstock; 62: TierneyMJ/Shuttertsock; 63: Aslysun/Shutterstock.

Unit 6

Page 65 (main photo): Hero Images/Getty Images; 65 (Mateo Romero): Pressmaster/Shutterstock; 66 (Mateo Romero): Pressmaster/Shutterstock; 66 (happy office workers): Nd3000/Shutterstock; 67: Tero Vesalainen/Shutterstock; 68 (Mateo Romero): Pressmaster/Shutterstock; 68 (man standing at bins): Andrey_Popov/Shutterstock; 68 (woman and child): Shutterstock; 70: Pressmaster/Shutterstock; 72 (Mateo Romero): Pressmaster/Shutterstock; 72 (rideshare app): Tero Vesalainen/Shutterstock; 74 (Mateo Romero): Pressmaster/Shutterstock; 74 (dream job): Dirk Ercken/Shutterstock.

Unit 7

Page 77 (main photo): Piranka/E+/Getty Images; 77 (Esra Kara): Daniel M Ernst/Shutterstock; 78 (Esra Kara): Daniel M Ernst/Shutterstock; 78 (volunteer): Wavebreakmedia/Shutterstock; 79: Rawpixel/123RF; 80 (Esra Kara): Daniel M Ernst/Shutterstock; 80 (taking photo on smartphone): Think4photop/Shutterstock; 82: Daniel M Ernst/Shutterstock; 83: Sjstudio6/Shutterstock; 84 (Esra Kara): Daniel M Ernst/Shutterstock; 84 (fish & pollution): Rich Carey/Shutterstock; 86 (Esra Kara): Daniel M Ernst/Shutterstock; 86 (bicyclists): ID-VIDEO/Shutterstock.

Unit 8

Page 89 (main photo): Filadendron/E+/Getty Images; 89 (Carla Lugo): TierneyMJ/Shuttertsock; 90 (Carla Lugo): TierneyMJ/Shuttertsock; 90 (team meeting): Rawpixel.com/Shutterstock; 91: Den Rise/Shutterstock; 92 (Carla Lugo): TierneyMJ/Shuttertsock; 92 (woman with camera): Art_Photo/Shutterstock; 94: TierneyMJ/Shuttertsock; 95: Alita Xander/Shutterstock; 96: TierneyMJ/Shuttertsock; 97: Studio Barcelona/Shutterstock; 98 (Carla Lugo): TierneyMJ/Shuttertsock; 98 (man thinking): GaudiLab/Shutterstock.

Unit 9

Page 101 (main photo): Stefan Holm/Shutterstock; 101 (Tae-Ho Kang): AJR_photo/Shutterstock; 102 (Tae-Ho Kang): AJR_photo/Shutterstock; 102 (tennis lesson): Rawpixel.com/Shutterstock; 103: Adwisual/Alamy Stock Photo; 104: AJR_photo/Shutterstock; 105: Gorodenkoff/Shutterstock; 106 (Tae-Ho Kang): AJR_photo/Shutterstock; 106 (capoeira): Vladimir Gappov/Shutterstock; 107 (balls): Chones/Shutterstock; 107 (boat race): Muratart/Shutterstock; 108 (Tae-Ho Kang): AJR_photo/Shutterstock; 108 (sports fans): ESB Professional/Shutterstock; 110 (Tae-Ho Kang): AJR_photo/Shutterstock; 110 (bossaball): Ju1978/Shutterstock; 112: Macrovector/Shutterstock.

Unit 10

Page113 (main photo): Georgy Dorofeev/EyeEm Premium/Getty Images; 113 (Kate Sands): Mangostar/Shutterstock; 114 (Kate Sands): Mangostar/Shutterstock; 114 (Ali): StevenK/Shutterstock; 114 (Mei): Metamorworks/Shutterstock; 114 (Ana): Marcos Mesa Sam Wordley/Shutterstock; 114 (Tim): Stockfotografie/Shutterstock; 114 (Tony): Stockfour/Shutterstock; 114 (Maha): Michaeljung/Shutterstock; 114 (Hugo): Andy Dean Photography/Shutterstock; 115: Tab62/Shutterstock; 116 (Kate Sands): Mangostar/Shutterstock; 116 (woman thinking): GaudiLab/Shutterstock; 116 (graduation thought): Nirat.pix/Shutterstock; 117: Yulia Grigoryeva/Shutterstock; 118: Mangostar/Shutterstock; 119: Kirn Vintage Stock/Corbis Historical/Getty Images; 120 (top right): Mangostar/Shutterstock; 120 (glasses): Iryna Kuznetsova/Shutterstock; 122: Mangostar/Shutterstock.

Illustration Credits

John Goodwin (Eye Candy Illustration)

PRONUNCIATION TABLE

Vowels

Symbol	Key Words
i	b**ea**t, happ**y**
ɪ	b**i**t
eɪ	d**a**te, p**ai**d
ɛ	b**e**t
æ	b**a**t
ɑ	b**o**x, f**a**ther
ɔ	d**o**g, b**ough**t
oʊ	b**oa**t, g**o**
ʊ	b**oo**k, p**u**t
u	b**oo**t, n**ew**
ʌ	c**u**p, m**o**ther
ə	ban**a**na, **a**bout
ɚ	sh**ir**t, m**ur**d**er**
aɪ	b**i**te, b**uy**, **eye**
aʊ	ab**ou**t, h**ow**
ɔɪ	v**oi**ce, b**oy**
ɪr	d**eer**, n**ear**
ɛr	h**air**, b**are**
ɑr	b**ar**, h**ear**t
ɔr	d**oor**, m**ore**
ʊr	t**our**, p**oor**

Consonants

Symbol	Key Words
p	**p**ack, ha**pp**y
b	**b**ack, ru**bb**er
t	**t**ime, da**t**e
d	**d**o, mi**dd**le
k	**c**ome, **qu**ick, **k**ey
g	**g**ame, **gu**est
tʃ	**ch**ur**ch**, na**t**ure
dʒ	**j**u**dge**, **g**eneral
f	**f**an, **ph**otogra**ph**
v	**v**an, co**v**er
θ	**th**ing, brea**th**
ð	**th**en, brea**the**
s	**s**it, **c**ity
z	**z**oo, plea**se**, goe**s**
ʃ	**sh**ip, ma**ch**ine, ac**ti**on
ʒ	mea**s**ure, vi**s**ion
h	**h**ot, **wh**o
m	**m**an, so**me**
n	su**n**, **kn**ow
ŋ	si**ng**
w	**w**et, **wh**ite
l	**l**ong, si**ll**y
r	**r**ight, **wr**ong
y	**y**es, **u**se, m**u**sic
t̬	li**tt**le, bu**tt**er